M000308442

Feminist Spirituality

Feminist Spirituality

The Next Generation

EDITED BY
CHRIS KLASSEN

LEXINGTON BOOKS

A division of
ROWMAN & LITTLEFIELD PUBLISHERS, INC.
Lanham • Boulder • New York • Toronto • Plymouth, UK

LEXINGTON BOOKS

A division of Rowman & Littlefield Publishers, Inc.
A wholly owned subsidiary of The Rowman & Littlefield Publishing Group, Inc.
4501 Forbes Boulevard, Suite 200
Lanham, MD 20706

Estover Road
Plymouth PL6 7PY
United Kingdom

Copyright © 2009 by Lexington Books

All rights reserved. No part of this publication may be reproduced,
stored in a retrieval system, or transmitted in any form or by any
means, electronic, mechanical, photocopying, recording, or otherwise,
without the prior permission of the publisher.

British Library Cataloguing in Publication Information Available

Library of Congress Cataloging-in-Publication Data

Feminist spirituality : the next generation / edited by Chris Klassen.
    p. cm.
Includes bibliographical references and index.
ISBN 978-0-7391-2794-0 (cloth : alk. paper)
ISBN 978-0-7391-3917-2 (electronic)
1. Goddess religion. 2. Feminism—Religious aspects. I. Klassen, Chris (Chris A.)
BL325.F4F47 2009
204.082—dc22   2009009892

Printed in the United States of America

♾™ The paper used in this publication meets the minimum requirements of American
National Standard for Information Sciences—Permanence of Paper for Printed Library
Materials, ANSI/NISO Z39.48–1992.

Contents

Part II

Introduction:
Feminist Spirituality and Third-Wave Feminism

Chris Klassen

In 2000, just in time for a new century and a new millennium, Jennifer Baumgardner and Amy Richards published *Manifesta: Young Women, Feminism, and the Future*. Though the term "third-wave feminism" had officially been coined earlier in the 1990s,[1] Baumgardner and Richards brought to the fore the activities, thoughts and politics of young American women of the third-wave. In response to the popular media claim that feminism was dead, and the laments by some second-wave feminists that young women were uninvolved, *Manifesta* revealed a world of young women passionately concerned and involved in feminist practice, albeit in places and ways often unrecognized by their feminist foremothers or the mainstream media.

Third-wave feminism, for Baumgardner and Richards, as well as others who explore this movement[2] is a multifaceted, complex movement. For example, today's young feminists come from a very different place than previous generations. They have benefited from the struggles of second- (and first-) wave feminists and take for granted an expectation of opportunity and equality. As Baumgardner and Richards write, "For our generation, feminism is like fluoride. We scarcely notice that we have it—its simply in the water."[3]

That third-wave feminists have benefited from the work of feminists before them does not mean they do not recognize the need for continued struggle. In fact, as some of the papers in this volume highlight, some third-wave feminists have been involved in that second-wave work. This challenges the notion that the 'next generation' of feminism is solely the purview of 'young' feminists. However, many of the questions and methods of those engaged in third-wave feminism are different from that of the second wave—as should be expected of

1

a different social and political era. Third-wave feminists are embedded in a technological society which is often as familiar to them as feminism. They are embedded in a multicultural society which fosters multiple identities and politics of *diversity* rather than difference.

A discouraging, though by no means surprising, absence in *Manifesta* and other accounts of third-wave feminism is a discussion of the engagement of third-wave feminists with religion and spirituality. Though Baumgardner and Richards point to the popularization of Wicca among young women in America, by referencing their own dabbling, ultimately they "ditched" the Wicca and concentrated on, what one could presume is, the "real" work of intellectual and personal support of one another in the process of political, social and cultural activism.

Within the sphere of religious studies, third-wave feminists have not fared much better. In the discourse of feminist spirituality there has been little discussion of what young feminists are doing and/or little consideration of the impact third-wave feminism may have on shaping spiritual or religious lives.

This book is a response to this glaring absence of discussion of third-wave feminism and spirituality. It comes out of a particular frustration with being unable to find adequate academic resources to use in the classroom when discussing spirituality, Goddess religion, feminist theology and women's religious lives in general as expressed and experienced by young women who were raised with a feminist understanding of the sacred. These feminists are not content to just accept what is handed to them by their feminist mothers but are invested in further engagements, further challenges and further questioning.

Development of Feminist Spirituality

In 1993, Cynthia Eller published *Living in the Lap of the Goddess*, her study of feminist spirituality. She describes feminist spirituality as an eclectic and extremely varied movement which is located primarily outside of traditional religion in the English speaking Western world. Though feminist spirituality overlaps with contemporary Paganism and Feminist Goddess Worship, it is not identical to these new religious movements. In particular, Eller points out, there are Christian and Jewish versions of feminist spirituality. Similarly there are non-feminist versions of contemporary Paganism. As such, feminist spirituality is a movement rather than a coherent tradition. It is characterized by a focus on women's spiritual needs drawing on a feminist consciousness; as Eller writes, feminist spirituality involves "believing that either women's condition or the general state of gender roles in society as we now find them are unsatisfactory and need to be changed."[4]

The feminist spirituality Eller outlines is largely that of second-wave feminists. These feminists were addressing a concern with patriarchal religious structures which gave little to no place for women to speak with any degree of authority. For these women, it was revolutionary to think of God as She or shift to Goddess imagery and language. It was also revolutionary to incorporate women's lived experiences in ritual processes. Though there certainly was a critique of traditional religion in first-wave feminism, much of that work had been forgotten and second-wavers need to recreate the wheel, so to speak.

Second-wave feminism did not start out with much of a consideration of religion, although this soon changed. In 1971 Mary Daly, a Catholic theologian, was asked to give a sermon at the Harvard Memorial Church—this was historic as it was the first instance of a woman preaching there. She entitled her sermon "The Women's Movement: An Exodus Community" and ended it with an exodus of her own. She argued that the Church held no place for women and asked everyone who felt the same way to join her as she walked down the aisle and out of the church. Mary Daly continues to be a strong advocate of women leaving the Church arguing that Christianity and other organized religions are inherently patriarchal and irredeemable.[5] In the same year, Z. Budapest, a Hungarian woman living in California, formed the Susan B. Anthony coven No. 1 thus beginning Dianic Witchcraft (although other, less feminist versions of Wicca were already in existence in North America) and the larger feminist spirituality movement. Both these women inspired many others to look at religion as significant to the women's movement.

Some feminists chose to work from within existing religious traditions to combat sexist oppression and patriarchy. Often these feminists tried to find the root of their belief system, beyond the imposed patriarchal structures and ideologies. However, the implications for these traditional religions are complex. In her 1979 text, *Changing of the Gods*, Naomi Goldenberg argues that transcendent and patriarchal religion (meaning for the most part Judaism and Christianity) is at its end. With feminists trying to reform biblical traditions, or creating their own spiritualities outside of traditional religion, Yahweh and Christ will inevitably die off—or be so transformed as to no longer be Yahweh and Christ. Goldenberg sees the future of religion in psychology—looking into oneself for the mythology and mysticism which will satisfy one's spiritual needs rather than looking to an external deity. Goldenberg comes to her conclusions about the end of traditional religions through an analysis of symbols and images. She writes,

> When feminist succeed in changing the position of women in Christianity and Judaism, they will shake these religions at their roots. The nature of a religion lies in the nature of the symbols and images it exalts in ritual and doctrine. It is the psychic picture of Christ and Yahweh that inspires the loves, the hates and the behavior patterns of Christian and Jews. The psychology of the Jewish and Christian religions depends on the masculine image that these religions have of their God. Feminist change the major psychological impact of Judaism and

Christianity when they recognize women as religious leaders and as images of divinity.[6]

Many feminists chose to step out of the religion of their upbringing. They often thought traditional, established religions were essentially patriarchal. They created new rituals and new ways of worshipping to fit their lives and their feminist perspectives. This included a search in history or pre-history for more woman-friendly religious practices and mythology. In 1979, as part of this search, Starhawk published *The Spiral Dance* which launched the great popularity of feminist Witchcraft. Another influential writer was Carol Christ who began her academic career as a Christian theologian and eventually left the church and participated in developing a specifically feminist Goddess religion. Her 1997 text, *Rebirth of the Goddess*, provides a systematic theology for this new religion. These two major traditions, Feminist Goddess Worship and Feminist Witchcraft, became the core (though not the entirety) of feminist spirituality.

Feminist Goddess Worship began as a North American movement in the 1960s and early 70s in consciousness raising groups of the feminist movement, where mostly white and middle-class women who began sharing their frustration with the sexism in churches and synagogues, particularly with the idea of God the Father, began to look for and find alternative religious options. They were not willing, as some feminists were, to discard religion all together, even though all the 'major' religions seemed hopelessly patriarchal to them. They began to research ancient goddesses and meet together for ritual circles. This was happening in different places across North America and the resulting groups and movements are eclectic and autonomous—that is they do not follow a standard organizational pattern or have a unified belief system. This is why the term spirituality is used more often than religion, although some, like Carol Christ, have begun to use the term religion to gain a sense of validity for Feminist Goddess Worship. Some Feminist Goddess Worshippers focus on ancient European mythology, some focus on Native Spirituality, some African-based traditions, some look to Buddhism, Hinduism and Shinto. Basically what ever tradition has goddesses feminist Goddess worshippers have investigated.

Contemporary Paganism incorporates a number of nature religions (religions which focus on honouring the earth and which structure their religious calendar around seasonal cycles) the largest of which is Witchcraft or Wicca. Wicca began in the 1940s-50s in Britain when Gerald Gardner started his coven, claiming to be carrying into the 'new age' an ancient tradition. This continuity is debatable, but in any case, what Gardner did was new and most Wiccans would agree that what we know today as Wicca began with Gardner. Gardner was no feminist. His focus on the Goddess had more to do with an androcentric concept of woman as Muse (that is, only significant as inspiration to men) than with uncovering female images to empower women. Wicca was brought to North America by Raymond Buckland where it developed in a variety of ways and eventually met the feminists. Two women are key to the construction of feminist witchcraft. Z. Budapest began what is now known as Dianic Witchcraft, which is separatist—no men allowed. Starhawk encountered Witchcraft as a young woman in the early 70s and blended it with feminist, environmental and peace activism. Along with a number of others in the area, she formed the Reclaiming Collective in 1980, which has since developed into a full-fledged feminist witchcraft tradition. Reclaiming is not separatist and has many men involved as well as those of less definable gender. Unlike Dianic Witchcraft which is primarily concerned with sexism, Reclaiming Witchcraft is concerned with power relations—including but not limited to sexism. Thus members are involved in all manner of activism protesting sexism, racism, heterosexism, environmental abuses, poverty, etc.

Feminist Goddess Worship and feminist Witchcraft, as well as reforming traditional religions, are not the only outlets for feminist spirituality, however. Many women refused to reconstruct or recreate religion and chose to develop a more self-reflective non-collective spirituality. One example of this is Emily Culpepper. Drawing on her experiences in the civil rights movement, anti-war protests and women's liberation, Emily Culpepper shares the stories of her journey from organized religion (Protestant Christianity) to freethinking. She explains, "A freethinker, according to the Oxford English Dictionary, is 'One who refuses to submit his reason to the control of authority in matters of religious belief.' Feminist freethinkers add to this definition our exuberant biophilia, with its iconoclastic, pluralistic openness to inner guides wherever we may find them."[7] While she is trying to show the importance of spirituality, Culpepper is suspicious of and distances herself from religion as any sort of organized movement of thought, belief or action. As such she draws on many sources including goddesses, but not Feminist Goddess Worship which she views as too monotheistic to be revolutionary. She also draws on witchcraft (as a way of being a strong woman not as a religion), and even to a degree Christianity (as the compost feeding her growing spirituality). Instead of trying to change traditional religion to be less patriarchal, or try to move back to a pre- or non-patriarchal core of these traditions, Culpepper creates for herself a "crazy quilt of spiritual paradoxes."[8] She eclectically uses what works for her, what she finds meaningful, to develop her sense of connection with the natural world and all upon it and nourish her own spirit.

The impetus to reform traditional religions, create new religions and/or shape a more individually satisfactory spirituality outside the confines of religious organization were revolutionary for second-wave feminists. However, these activities were also present in the first-wave of feminism. First-wave feminism gained its momentum through two important political and social movements of the nineteenth century: the suffrage movement and the abolition movement. In both these movements women took leadership in speaking out against injustice and working for political and social change—largely a liberal movement—focusing on the principles of liberal democracy: rationality, equality and utilitarianism. First-wave feminists had a close tie to religion in that many were Christian and some were Jewish, and their religion motivated their politics just as much as their politics challenged their religion. Their concern with religion was often in showing how religion actually supported their causes—either of abolition or suffrage. A good example of this is Sojourner Truth who uses the story of Jesus's birth from Mary and God to show the importance of women within the Christian story.[9] Some first-wave feminists, such as Elizabeth Cady Stanton, were concerned with revising Christian understandings of the Bible. Stanton compiled "the Women's Bible" which was a commentary on all the passages in the Bible which dealt with women. She argued that the Bible had portions in it which were sexist because it was written by men in a patriarchal era. Her argument was not that different from many second-wave writers. Though Stanton did not dismiss the reality of God (and never moved to Goddess imagery or language) she proclaimed that Christianity was patriarchal and the Bible promoted sexism and women's subordination and needed to be abolished or radically changed.[10]

Other first-wave feminists became involved in new religious movements which flourished in the nineteenth century. One example of these movements was the Theosophical Society founded by Madame Helena Blavatsky and Colonel Henry Olcott. The Theosophical Society was based on a philosophy which searches for divine wisdom in the religious and mystical traditions of the world. This group provided a new model of women as occult leaders (mediums, prophets, priestesses and adepts) without the appeal to the 'cult of womanhood' which was so popular in the nineteenth century (that is, the idea that women are morally and spiritually superior to men because they are pure and good). Blavatsky was not a feminine, demure, morally blameless woman. She was an aggressive, sometimes conniving, always confrontational cross-dresser who shocked many. Her successor, Annie Besant, was previous to her conversion to Theosophy, an outspoken atheist and political activist who argued that the institution of marriage was inherently oppressive to women.[11] These first-wave feminists challenged gender norms and pushed for women's involvement in shaping religious values, beliefs and practices.

In the early 1900s feminist fervour died down somewhat. Women achieved the vote. Slavery was abolished. The "big" issues were solved, many thought. Many of the writings of first-wave feminists were forgotten in archives and dusty libraries. Thus when, in the 1950s and 1960s, many women began to see that not all problems were solved and some new issues were becoming important, such as access to education, employment opportunities, etc., it took a while before these earlier feminists' work was remembered.

The lack of continuity between first-wavers and second-wavers was due to a time lapse between the two movements. This is not the case between second-wavers and third-wavers. However, there is little information gathered as of yet, on how third-wavers are adapting and/or rejecting the feminist spirituality of the 1970s and 1980s. Many third-wavers have been raised to at least recognize if not adopt female deity imagery and language. Others have participated in the creation of this imagery and language. They all expect their experience to shape their ritual worldview. The essays in this volume explore what has not been fully explored: what does feminist spirituality look like in the twenty-first century? How have young women taken the work of their mothers, aunts, grandmothers and other forerunners and shaped it into something they could own for themselves? How have some second-wave feminists morphed into third-wavers?

This volume is divided into two sections. Part I consists of third-wave, predominantly young, feminists engaging in the development of spiritual discourse. It begins with Sarah Marie Gallants comparison of the imaginative process in Carol P. Christ's formation of the Goddess to the construction of medieval Christian hagiography. Drawing on Paul Ricoeur, Gallant argues that imaginative constructions are in danger of sliding into the ideological and/or utopian. However, if these imaginings are understood as provisional, they can be continually re-evaluated and re-formulated to remain relevant. This is the task of third-wave feminists today. Catherine Telford-Keogh engages in this reformulating from the context of feminist Witchcraft. Using postmodern and queer theories, she calls for a fluidity of identity categories and the construction of transformative spaces which can be welcoming to all who choose to identify as Witch, whether female, feminine, male, masculine, transgender, or other. Anna Mercedes and Jennifer Thweatt-Bates take the imaginative process of embodied spirituality into the realm of the technological. Meditating on their own differing experience of childbirth, they declare the spiritual and feminist significance of the cyborg and/or the posthuman. This engagement with the theories of Donna Haraway and transhumanism shows a commitment to a non-essential, yet fully embodied understanding of twenty-first-century women's lives. Gena Meldazy moves us into another realm of the technological: that of popular culture. She argues for a (re)definition of the term *Fandemonium* as a way to include the non-religious, non-theistic into the discourse of feminist spirituality. Fandemonium expands the relationship with the 'other'—including the celebrity—into a spiritual relation, while continually deconstructing the performative personae. Kate McCarthy's essay continues the discussion of third-wave feminist spirituality's interaction/utilization of popular culture, particularly the genre of women's rock music and the disruption of gendered/sexed bodies in the performances of such artists as Ani DiFranco, Courtney Love and Tori Amos. Glenda Bonifacia's chapter brings the third-wave engagement with spirituality into the classroom. Based on her experiences of teaching a course on the Goddess in the heart of Canadian conservatism, Southern Alberta, Bonifacia shares the multiple intentions that her students hold in choosing this course. Ultimately she claims that goddess imagery remains an empowering tool for many young women, and men, today.

Some scholars, such as Astrid Henry and Lisa Maria Hogeland, argue that the use of generational language between second- and third-wave feminists is problematic. Talking of generations assumes second-wavers are the mothers and third-wavers are the rebellious daughters. This structure can build up an atmosphere of antagonism between the two groups (though to name either "wave" as one group misses the multiplicity of voices in both). Hogeland is particularly concerned that generational language creates a "rupture" which works "to prevent us from seeing the powerful persistence of political beliefs, of specific women's issues, and of strategies for change."[12] Part II of this volume includes three essays which not only highlight some of the various spiritual activities of third-wave feminists (such as festival attendance, protest activism and reading), they also engage with the generational assumptions of third-wave feminism. Giselle Vincett draws on interviews with Goddess Feminists in Boomer, X and Y generations to show how changes in Goddess Feminism seem to parallel changes in approaches to religiosity and politics in the broader generational categories. However, she maintains that these shifts should not be perceived as radical breakages as much as "continuations and intensifications of societal trends." Laurel Zwissler focuses on "young manifestations of spirituality" observed in feminist Catholic, feminist Protestant and feminist Pagan participation in political activism. Though not all her informants are "young," their ritualizing in protest spaces challenges their respective religious traditions and the larger activist communities with which they are associated in ways very much congruent with third-wave feminism. Finally, Dawn Llewellyn's interviews with women in their 50s-80s provides a context to further the expansion of third-wave feminism beyond age-based categories. Where Zwissler focuses on participation in protest activist, Llewellyn explores the reading experiences of her participants, showing how many have shifted from a second-wave gynocritical approach to reading to one which moves beyond essentialist notions of identity in reader and author.

Though there is sometimes animosity between second-wave and third-wave feminist discourses, the essays in this book are not about dissing the second-wave but rather are about giving third-wave voices space to speak their issues, their concerns, and their ideas. This does not require second-wave feminists to step aside. We do have challenges for those who have paved the way for our scholarship. But these challenges demand dialogue, not replacement.

Notes

1. See Rebecca Walker, "Becoming the Third Wave," *Ms.* January/February 1992. 39-41 and Naomi Wolf, *The Beauty Myth: How Images of Beauty Are Used Against Women.* New York: William Morrow, 1991.

2. Henry, Astrid, *Not My Mother's Sister: Generational Conflict and Third-Wave*

Feminism, Bloomington: Indiana University Press, 2004; Dicker, Rory and Alison Peip-meier, eds., *Catching a Waver: Reclaiming Feminism for the 21st Century*, Boston: Northeastern University Press, 2003; Heywood, Leslie and Jennifer Drake, *Third Wave Agenda: Being Feminist, Doing Feminism*, Minneapolis: University of Minnesota Press, 1997.

3. Baumgardner, Jennifer and Amy Richards, *Manifesta: Young Women, Feminism, and the Future*, New York: Farrar, Straus and Giroux, 2000, 17.

4. Eller, Cynthia, *Living in the Lap of the Goddess: The Feminist Spirituality movement in America*, Boston: Beacon Press, 1993, 7.

5. See Mary Daly, *Beyond God the Father: Toward a Philosophy of Women's Liberation*, Boston: Beacon Press, 1985.

6. Goldenberg, Naomi, *Changing of the Gods: Feminism and the End of Traditional Religion*. Boston: Beacon Press, 1979, 5.

7. Culpepper, Emily, "The Spiritual, Political Journey of a Feminist Freethinker," in *After Patriarchy: Feminist Transformations of the Word Religions*, eds, P. Cooey, W. Eakin and J. McDaniel, Maryknoll, NY: Orbis, 1991, 147.

8. Culpepper, "Feminist Freethinker," 150.

9. For more on Sojourner Truth see Nell Irvin Painter, "Representing Truth: Sojourner Truth's Knowing and Becoming Known," *Journal of American History*, 81, no. 2 (1994): 461-492.

10. For more on Elizabeth Cady Stanton see Lisa S. Strange, "Elizabeth Cady Stanton's *Woman's Bible* and the Roots of Feminist Theology," *Gender Issues*, 17, no. 4 (1999): 15-36.

11. For more on Theosophy see Joy Dixon, *Divine Feminine: Theosophy and Feminism in England*, Baltimore: The Johns Hopkins University Press, 2001.

12. Hogeland, Lisa Marie, "Against Generational Thinking, or, Some Things that 'Third Wave' Feminism Isn't," *Women's Studies in Communication*. 24, no. 1 (2001): 107-121, 117.

Bibliography

Baumgardner, Jennifer and Amy Richards. 2000. *Manifesta: Young Women, Feminism, and the Future*. New York: Farrar, Straus and Giroux.

Christ, Carol P. 1997. *Rebirth of the Goddess: Finding Meaning in Feminist Spirituality*. New York: Routledge.

Culpepper, Emily. 1991. "The Spiritual, Political Journey of a Feminist Freethinker." In *After Patriarchy: Feminist Transformations of the World Religions*. Eds, Paula Cooey, William Eakin and Jay McDaniel. Maryknoll, NY: Orbis.

Daly, Mary. 1985. *Beyond God the Father: Toward a Philosophy of Women's Liberation*. Boston: Beacon Press.

Dicker, Rory and Alison Peipmeier, eds. 2003. *Catching a Wave: Reclaiming Feminism for the 21st Century*. Boston: Northeastern University Press.

Dixon, Joy. 2001. *Divine Feminine: Theosophy and Feminism in England*. Baltimore: The Johns Hopkins University Press.

Eller, Cynthia. 1993. *Living in the Lap of the Goddess: The Feminist Spirituality Movement in America*. Boston: Beacon Press.

Goldenberg, Naomi. 1979. *Changing of the Gods: Feminism and the End of Traditional Religion*. Boston: Beacon Press.

Henry, Astrid. 2004. *Not My Mother's Sister: Generational Conflict and Third-Wave Feminism*. Bloomington: Indiana University Press.

Heywood, Leslie and Jennifer Drake. 1997. *Third Wave Agenda: Being Feminist, Doing Feminism*. Minneapolis: University of Minnesota Press.

Hogeland, Lisa Marie. 2001. "Against Generational Thinking, or, Some Things that 'Third Wave' Feminism Isn't." *Women's Studies in Communication*. 24(1) 107-121.

Painter, Nell Irvin. 1994. "Representing Truth: Sojourner Truth's Knowing and Becoming Known." *Journal of American History*. 81(2) 461-492.

Strange, Lisa S. 1999. "Elizabeth Cady Stanton's *Woman's Bible* and the Roots of Feminist Theology." *Gender Issues* 17(4) 15-36.

Starhawk. 1979. *The Spiral Dance: A Rebirth of the Ancient Religion of the Great Goddess*. San Francisco: Harper & Row.

Walker, Rebecca. 1992. "Becoming the Third Wave." *Ms*. January/February. 39-41.

Wolf, Naomi. 1991. *The Beauty Myth: How Images of Beauty Are Used Against Women*. New York: William Morrow.

Part I

Chapter One:
Imagination, Empowerment, and Imaginary Figures

Sarah Marie Gallant

Feminist scholars such as Carol P. Christ and Starhawk have insisted upon the importance of reimagining images of female strength and power. Both Christ and Starhawk have undertaken the task of imagining and presenting a goddess figure in order to inspire and empower modern women. This imaginative recuperation of an ancient goddess figure and ancient goddess traditions has not gone unchallenged. Various critiques of this endeavor have come from not only archaeologists and classicists but also from within the feminist movement itself. In light of the strong criticism that has been evoked in response to this Goddess movement, it is evident that a closer examination of the imaginative endeavor employed in the creation of such purposefully constructed figures, especially figures that present images of perceived "feminine" ideals, must be undertaken. It is also necessary to evaluate this goddess figure as she has been presented in order to discern whether or not goddess imagery is still potent and powerful for the next generation of spiritual feminists.

This study will explore the imaginative endeavor taken up by Carol Christ, Starhawk and Marija Gimbutas. Each of whom have been criticized for presenting utopian constructions of prehistoric societies or simply recycling traditional images and roles for women, i.e., as nurturer and child bearer. The comparison will be made between the imaginative process employed by Christ in the construction of the Goddess and a similar process employed by medieval Christian hagiographers in the construction of saintly figures. I will show that in the construction of such figures an imaginative process is vital. However, imaginative constructions, while potentially inspirational and empowering, are provisional and temporary. As Christ has argued, previously imagined female figures are no

longer relevant nor are they empowering images for modern women and therefore new figures like the Goddess must be imagined. Alternatively, as Christ's
critics have pointed out, such inspiring images can run the risk of being unbelievable and therefore uninspiring if they are taken to their extreme. This study
will therefore conclude with a discussion of the extremes identified by Paul Ricoeur in order to shed some light on the territory that young spiritual feminists
must navigate when attempting to imagine their own inspiring figures.

The Goddess Imagined by Carol Christ

Carol Christ was among the first to draw attention to the Goddess movement as
part of a contemporary feminist expression of women's spirituality. A scholar,
writer, and spiritual feminist, Christ has been interested in women's religious
experience and expression throughout her scholarly career but is best known for
her work involving the reimagining of an ancient goddess figure for contemporary purposes. She remains a vocal advocate of the Goddess and has spent a
great deal of time articulating what the Goddess is and what she can offer modern women.

The Goddess movement uses a variety of images when invoking, celebrating, and imagining the Goddess although her advocates insist that there is an
important unity underlying the plurality of images. Christ asserts that multiple
images are needed in order to avoid getting stuck imagining God *only* as an old
man with a white beard. The Goddess is therefore a response to the fact that
western conceptions of God use primarily male images or male language to refer
to the divine. Christ believes that this is problematic for western women because
it means that women are not able to see themselves in these "masculine" images
and thus perceive themselves to be different or distant from the "godly" or the
divine. She argues that equating God with maleness denies a woman from "having her full sexual identity affirmed as being in the image and likeness of God."[1]
As a result, women's selves, bodies, and actions become separated from the perceived sacred. She thus discerns the need for a Goddess figure to reconcile this
problem and has undertaken the task of reimagining prehistoric goddess images
so that she can imagine a fully female, fully powerful goddess for western wom-
en.[2]

The Goddess, according to Christ, is an ancient figure that embodies female
strength, power and creativity. She is sympathetic and strong; suffering with
those who have broken hearts, bodies, and spirits. Christ's Goddess is present in
the world, not ruling over it from afar. She is aligned with the celebration of
women's bodies and women's experiences. In this manner, Christ proposes the
Goddess figure as a way of radically rethinking the way we conceptualize power,
particularly female power. She believes that it is not enough to simply use the
titles "Lady" and "Queen" to refer to the divine because "these images, like the

more common Lord and King of the Bible and traditional liturgies, reflect the model of power *over*."[3] To borrow a phrase from Cynthia Eller, the Goddess is "not just God in a skirt."[4] She does not dominate or coerce. "She must work in and through finite and limited individuals who may resist her power."[5] This does not mean, however, that the Goddess is not a great source of power and strength.

Since the publication of her influential article "Why Women Need the Goddess" (1979) Christ has maintained that reimagining symbols is important psychologically for women in western traditions. She insists that "psychic damage is done to the sexual identity of those who never find the experience of their own sex reflected in text or tradition, and who must always appropriate text and traditions through the experience of the opposite sex."[6] Furthermore, Christ insists, "religions centered on the worship of a male God create 'moods' and 'motivations' that keep women in a state of psychological dependence on men and male authority."[7] For Christ the Goddess is the acknowledgment of the legitimacy of female power as an independent power.[8] This is of the utmost importance for women in western cultures where not only are images of female power severely lacking, says Christ, but the ways in which women can attain and hold power are also limited. In western cultures, she argues, women are "considered powerful when they are young and beautiful, but they are said to lose this power as they age."[9] This is not really power at all according to Christ. She has been granted power because she is perceived as beautiful by male beauty standards and this power has an extremely short time limit. In contrast, the Goddess gives women "real" power, according to Christ. She is its source and because she is "celebrated in the triple aspect of youth, maturity, and age"[10] this power is readily accessible to women of all ages. The Goddess also celebrates women's relationships with other women, which means that women not only have access to the power of the Goddess within themselves, but they can also access it through being in relation with other women.

By presenting the Goddess as a source of female strength and power Christ is responding to a lack of female images of the divine in western traditions. She is also responding to a lack of the female as powerful in her own right and she is employing an imaginative process in order to fill this gap. As novel and innovative as Christ's Goddess figure is, it is important to note that the imaginative process she employs is not new. In the construction and presentation of female saintly figures medieval hagiographers similarly employed an imaginative process. Medieval hagiographers composed and recorded the lives of the saints and in doing so they also responded to perceived gaps and inadequacies in their existing models of the "feminine." In contrast to medieval hagiographers, however, Christ is consciously trying to imagine empowered female figures to inspire contemporary women and is therefore promoting very different "feminine" ideals. She is radically reimagining the "feminine" outside of the old hierarchies and ideals. She has therefore chosen not to build upon previous saintly models but rather on alleged prehistoric images of goddesses and goddess myths from ancient Greece. For these ancient images she relies on the version of prehistory presented in the work of archaeologist Marija Gimbutas, a move that would bring a great deal of criticism which will be discussed in more detail later.

Christ has drawn upon Elisabeth Schüssler Fiorenza's work on reconstructing the history of early Christian women to support her reimagining of prehistoric symbols. Schüssler Fiorenza has created an interpretive model and methodological theory for analyzing biblical history which Christ insists can be used by feminist scholars of prehistory. In *Laughter of Aphrodite* (1987), Christ cites Schüssler Fiorenza when she says that "the feminist critical method could be likened to the work of a detective in that it does not rely solely on historical 'facts' nor invents [sic] its evidences but it engages in an imaginative reconstruction of reality."[11] Christ adds that "feminist critical reconstruction as method does not oppose itself to other forms of history that are based solely on the 'facts,' but rather points out that all history is told within the framework of a 'unifying vision' that involves all scholars in an imaginative selection and reconstruction of the past."[12] Therefore, it is possible, and extremely important according to Christ, to reimagine the past in the gaps and silences in order to include the presence of female figures because "the gaps and silences in the androcentric tradition deny women a potentially empowering knowledge of history."[13] Christ uses ancient Goddess traditions as a source of inspiration for imagining a Goddess figure that reflects what she believes are ideals for women today, fashioned from this past. She says, "I believe that Goddess images arose in cultures where women were not subordinate. Certainly Goddesses were also worshiped in cultures that were patriarchal. I sort through the evidence that remains—reminding myself that so much has been lost, so much has been destroyed—seeking a glimpse of Goddess who is source and reflection of the strength and creativity of women."[14] Thus, Christ is very much aware that she employs the imagination in her selective and creative reconstruction of the ancient past. It is because of this creative reimagining and reinterpreting of the past and ancient figures of the past that Christ is able to present alternative models and images for women to celebrate and emulate. However, this imaginative endeavor and the goddess figure Christ has created through it requires further investigation.

"Feminine" Ideals Presented by the Goddess

In presenting this Goddess and the power she offers western women, Christ proposes specific "feminine" ideals. These can be detected by various images she presents of the Goddess. As it has been pointed out, there are many images of the Goddess. There are, however, certain images that are mentioned repeatedly. The most commonly referred to is the Goddess as nurturing mother. In drawing attention to her life-giving and creative powers, Christ refers to the Goddess as the Goddess of birth, death, and regeneration. This means that she primarily invokes the Goddess as a birth-giving, nurturing mother that continually draws everything from herself and eventually back to herself again. This repeated image of the Goddess as nurturing mother reveals specific "feminine" ideals that Christ wishes to stress, precisely because she believes these ideals have been undervalued or ignored entirely in western contexts.

By presenting the Goddess as a nurturing mother, Christ is invoking certain "feminine" ideals, specifically those of woman as care-giver and creative force. It may seem that Christ is presenting precisely the same image of a maternal figure that patriarchal traditions have long promoted in order to negate women's authority outside of the domestic sphere and deny them actual power. Christ does not believe this to be the case. Such a simplistic interpretation does not acknowledge the complexity or plurality which Christ insists is vital to her goddess figure. For Christ, the Goddess is thus the ideal mother. She is not a 'helicopter parent' that hovers over her children to the point of suffocation. Instead, she first nurtures (gives birth) and then severs the tie (allows the connection to die) in order for further growth to happen (regeneration). Christ claims to draw these ideals from ancient Goddess traditions that precede Roman and Greek civilizations. She believes that "the Goddess of Old Europe and Ancient Crete represented the unity of life in nature, delight in the diversity of form, the powers of birth, death and regeneration."[15] The Goddess is, according to Christ, an older figure; one that influences and oversees vital relationships and vital life processes. She has undertaken the task of reimagining this ancient Goddess in a deliberate attempt to empower women. Through the rediscovering and/or wholesale reimagining of "feminine" ideals Christ presents the Goddess which she hopes will provide inspiring models for women and also reaffirm female experience. She has drawn upon various sources when she imagines the Goddess, including selective source material on prehistoric societies. To better understand Christ's Goddess and the imaginative process she employs two important influences on Christ's work must be examined: Starhawk, a social activist writer and archaeologist Marija Gimbutas.

Starhawk and Psychological Empowerment through the Goddess

Starhawk, a self-proclaimed social activist, ritual educator, and witch, has had a profound impact on Christ's work as writer.[16] Starhawk and Christ are both advocates of the Goddess although they are situated within different communities; Starhawk in the Wiccan or Pagan community and Christ in the Goddess movement associated with the spiritual feminist community. Despite the differences in affiliation, Starhawk and Christ agree on the specific ideals the Goddess embodies and what she can offer women today. They have often drawn inspiration from each other's work and have collaborated on various anthologies and film projects.

Starhawk sees Witchcraft as a form of Goddess religion because "to Witches, the cosmos is the living body of the Goddess."[17] Like Christ, she stresses the psychological importance of the Goddess and her symbols for women today. In *The Spiral Dance* (1979), Starhawk outlines some of reasons she began to look to the Goddess.

> The concept of a religion that worshiped a Goddess was amazing and empowering. Raised Jewish, I had been very religious as a child and had pursued my Jewish education to an advanced level. But as I reached young womanhood in the late sixties, something seemed lacking. . . I had never heard the word *patriarchy*, but I sensed that the tradition as it stood then was somehow lacking in models for me as a woman and in avenues for the development of female spiritual power.[18]

For Starhawk the Goddess tradition opened up new possibilities.[19] It confirmed for her that her body, "in all its femaleness, its breasts, vulva, womb, and menstrual flow, was sacred."[20] The Goddess became a psychological symbol with the power to redeem the spiritual value of her body.

According to Starhawk, the many symbols of the Goddess engage us both emotionally and spiritually.[21] Meditating on the symbols of the Goddess is an exercise given to initiates in some Pagan traditions. "As part of an initiate's training, she is taught to visualize symbols, to meditate on them and *play with them in her imagination* until they reveal their meaning directly."[22] The psychological significance of these symbols is extremely important for they open up joyful possibilities of imagining female strength and power. For Starhawk, the Goddess opened up avenues for rejoicing in her female body and femininity, something she did not find possible within the Jewish tradition. Starhawk, therefore, is indicating an important imaginative process that she herself initiated. She believes that women can engage with these Goddess symbols imaginatively in order to fulfill their psychological needs that have often been ignored entirely by western religious traditions, in her case Judaism. "Witchcraft" says Starhawk "recognizes that when material needs are satisfied deeper needs and longings may remain."[23] She continues by insisting that these needs "can only be satisfied by connection with the nurturing, life-giving forces within, which we call *Goddess*."[24]

Women must first recognize that they have these needs and not be afraid to ask the Goddess to fulfill them, says Starhawk. Women need to recognize that their whole selves are sacred and that they are not separated or alienated from the divine because they are female. Thus, in Starhawk's view, they need to see their femaleness or "femininity" reflected in images of the divine in order to reconcile the perceived separation between themselves and what is sacred. Only then can they approach the divine with their needs without hesitation. Starhawk insists that only with the Goddess does this become possible. "We are already one with the Goddess—She has been with us from the beginning. So fulfillment becomes, not a matter of self-indulgence, but of self-*awareness*."[25]

Goddess Symbols

Starhawk talks about the Goddess and the various symbols of the Goddess mainly in terms of their psychological importance. "The symbolism of the Goddess has taken on an electrifying power for modern women,"[26] insists Starhawk. The Goddess presents a model of female strength that asserts the sacredness of female bodies and female creativity. She thus opens up possibilities for women. She does not present a one size fits all model to follow. For example, the nurturing aspect of the Goddess does not exclusively pertain to nurturing children. A woman meditating on the Goddess can focus on her nurturing or motherly aspects in other ways. "A woman may choose to mother children or nurture a career, a project, or a cause."[27] She is still a reflection of the Goddess by pouring herself and her energy into cherished projects. "The Goddess," therefore, "does not limit women to the body; She awakens the mind and spirit and emotions."[28]

In Starhawk's understanding, the Goddess is a rich source for imagining a mythical ideal feminine. Above all else, however, she is a tool that women can use in order to empower themselves. This is why Starhawk cautions that the possibilities presented by the Goddess should not limit our own imaginative quest for ideals that empower us as women. She says that "while I have found images of the Goddess empowering to me as a woman, I no longer look at Goddesses and Gods to define for me what woman or man should be."[29] She continues by saying "the Goddess and the Old Gods can open doorways for us into new dimensions of our own possibilities, for they are not just symbols but channels of power."[30] The Goddess is meant to empower, not to limit. Starhawk believes that "the Goddesses and Gods are not figures for us to copy—they are more like broomsticks: grab hold, and they will take us away somewhere beyond the boundaries of our ordinary lives."[31] The various images of the Goddess are options, or 'broomsticks' as Starhawk puts it, more than they are prescriptive models. She acknowledges the fact that "women have lacked religious models and spiritual systems that speak to female needs and experience"[32] in the west, but believes that this is a symptom of a larger problem. The problem is "women are not encouraged to explore their own strength and realization; they are taught to submit to male authority to identify masculine perceptions as their spiritual ideals, to deny their bodies and sexuality, to fit their insights into a male mold."[33]

In Starhawk's work, the Goddess as symbol presents alternative images of female strength and creativity. She shows the depth to which women (and men) can find "mothering" and "nurturing" qualities within themselves. Most impor-

tantly, however, for Starhawk this symbol becomes a tool for imagining different kinds of female power. The Goddess is simply a way of finding such power
within one's self. This is what Starhawk calls "power-from-within, or empowerment."[34] Through the Goddess, says Starhawk, "we can move beyond narrow, constricting roles and become whole."[35]

Starhawk's Appeal to Myth

Starhawk is primarily concerned with the psychological aspect of the Goddess
because she is a social activist and is interested in empowering women. She believes that "true social change can only come about when the myths and symbols of our culture are themselves changed."[36] She has therefore undertaken the
task of changing primary myths and symbols of power so that, as an activist, she
can potentially bring about social change. This is why Starhawk stresses the
psychological symbols of the Goddess. For her they are potent images that can
be used to reimagine female strength and power which can in turn empower
women. Christ is in agreement with Starhawk though Christ also insists upon the
historical existence of matriarchal societies and the worship of the Goddess in
these ancient societies. This aspect of Christ's presentation of the Goddess relies
heavily on the work of archaeologist Marija Gimbutas.

Marija Gimbutas' Appeal to Archaeology

Marija Gimbutas (1921-1994) examined the remnants of prehistoric societies
from what she refers to as "Old Europe" and insisted that in the distant past
there were societies that highly valued women's roles as child bearer and food
gatherer. From the great number of small figurines excavated from various sites
all over Europe, she concluded that not only did these societies live a relatively
peaceful and prosperous existence but they also had a complex system of symbols and images which surrounded the worship of a Goddess figure. Her presentation of a Goddess of birth, death, and regeneration, and her reconstruction of
prehistoric matriarchal societies has attracted the attention of many feminist
writers including Christ.
      Gimbutas examined a large number of the figurines dating from the Paleo-
lithic and Neolithic periods in various parts of Europe.[37] She noted that they
appear to be remarkably similar in style; all possessing large breasts, large but-
tocks, and thick thighs. The similarities among these figurines seem to suggest a
common religious tradition throughout Europe at this time. However, the main
purpose of these figurines remains unclear. While some archaeologists have
suggested that they are crude objects used in funerary or fertility rituals, Gimbutas suggested that they represent pregnancy and are representations of a goddess

giving birth. She believes that the presence of these figurines, as well as the vast number of them found, is indicative of an intricate symbolic system centered around the worship of a goddess figure. As her critics are quick to point out, there are plenty of variations among these figurines as well. Many of them include animals or appear to be part female, part animal. Some are marked with intricate spirals or chevrons while others are smooth and plain. Gimbutas insists that these variations indicate a complex system of symbols and images that represent a complex goddess. More than just a mother goddess, she is the "Great Goddess of Life, Death and Regeneration" and a variety of symbols and images are necessary to communicate the many aspects of her power. She has spent a great deal of time reconstructing this seemingly forgotten civilization that worshiped this great goddess.

In Gimbutas' Old Europe, the power was with women as it was with the Goddess. She asserts that "the worship of female deities is connected to a mother-kinship system and ancestor worship in which the sexual identity of the head of the family and kin formulated the sexual identity of the supreme deity."[38] She has also drawn upon burial and settlement remains to support her conclusion. She has found that "the graves of older women were honored with symbolic items, often with richly decorated vases"[39] which indicates that these older women had revered status. Gimbutas' work on prehistoric societies in Old Europe has convinced her that the Goddess was not only an important figure but was widely worshiped in many forms throughout prehistoric Europe. Images of her appear on pottery, cave walls, and in small figurines. From these images Gimbutas has concluded that prehistoric societies valued women as mothers and as community leaders. Her presentation of an ancient Goddess figure and peaceful matriarchal societies has had profound impact on the work of many feminist writers. Carol Christ is no exception. Christ has often made reference to the ancient Goddess worshipers and their way of life and has identified them as a source of inspiration in her work. This version of prehistory is a crucial element in the Goddess figure presented by Christ, though it is not without its critics.

Christ's endeavor to imagine an empowering Goddess figure involves an intertwining of Gimbutas and Starhawk's ideas. She has combined Starhawk's appeal to the mythical or psychological with Gimbutas' archaeological evidence for the existence of a prehistoric Goddess figure. Thus, Christ's Goddess figure has both historical and mythical elements as well as real and imagined ones. Her goal, like Starhawk's, is to psychologically empower women and give them images of the "feminine" to celebrate and hold sacred. The emphasis on psychological empowerment through meditation on mythical symbols of the Goddess is influenced by Starhawk ideas. The idea of a Goddess figure that encompasses birth, death and regeneration comes directly from the goddess figure as described by archaeologist Marija Gimbutas. Christ is relying heavily upon Gimbutas for her prehistoric context in which an ancient goddess figure was worshiped in many peaceful pre-patriarchal societies. She holds Gimbutas in high regard, referring to her as not only an archaeologist, but also a "mythographer, and historian of religion."[40] She has thus come to rely heavily on Gimbutas not only as a source for prehistory, but also as a source of women's myth and religion as she believes it was practiced in ancient societies. Christ's presentation of the Goddess can be appreciated as a product of her own spiritual experiences imaginatively woven together with the prehistoric setting provided by Gimbutas' archaeological work.

By combining the work of Starhawk and Gimbutas, Christ can be understood to be engaging in an imaginative process. She is gathering elements from both myth and history (the psychological unconscious and the prehistoric) in order to present her version of the Goddess. Christ is very much aware that she is employing an imaginative process because she sees her task as one that necessarily involves remembering *and* inventing.[41] She has also said that "all history is told within the framework of a 'unifying vision' that involves all scholars in an *imaginative selection* and reconstruction of the past."[42] She therefore recognizes that her own prehistory with its prehistoric goddess figure is no different. However, one cannot ignore that fact that her imaginative endeavor has come under heavy fire.

The Goddess Controversy

This imaginative recuperation of a prehistoric goddess worshiping society has been challenged by scholars in the fields of archeology and classics as well as scholars within the feminist movement itself. Classicist Helene P. Foley has pointed out several problematic areas in the attempt to reimagine the Goddess and ancient goddess cults. By presenting the Goddess as a nurturing mother, feminists are actually presenting a very narrow view of woman. "The insistence on celebrating through the Goddess both the female body and the female life cycle runs the risk of representing a naively unitary view of the female and of reflecting and reproducing dominant cultural assumptions about women."[43] This description essentially reinforces mistaken assumptions about women being closer to nature (and further from culture) than men. She also points out that the "pagan religions of Greco-Roman antiquity were primarily based on cult."[44] Thus, they borrowed and collected various practices from the other cults around them in the Mediterranean area but they did not have anything like a theology, or "thea-logy," that Christ is proposing. Therefore the goddess movement is a new cult, not necessarily a re-emergence of an old one.[45] Also, according to Foley, the cults of Greek and Roman civilizations that Christ uses as inspiration for her myth and ritual in Goddess traditions were not actually a celebration of female powers. Foley views them as merely consolation prizes of a period when female deities were demoted or given less authority.[46] Therefore the ancient Greek and Roman goddess cults were not as free from patriarchal influences as modern goddess worshipers would like to believe, according to Foley's assessment.

Archaeologist Margaret Ehrenberg has criticized the work of Gimbutas and by extension the assumption of prehistoric matriarchal societies that Christ has relied upon. In *Women in Prehistory* (1989) Ehrenberg has pointed out that the figurines that Gimbutas labels as goddesses could have been made for any number of purposes. Rather than images of a great goddess, as Gimbutas assumed, they could have been used as a substitute for human sacrifice, part of a funerary ritual, or buried with women who had died in childbirth.[47] It cannot be assumed that every human figurine made during this period in question had the same function. "The likelihood of a significant continent-wide cult of a Mother Goddess has been greatly exaggerated,"[48] says Ehrenberg. She also argues that it is dangerous to assume that these Goddess images indicate that women held revered positions within that society. They may, like the image of the Virgin Mary, point to one particular revered woman but do not necessarily reflect the status of ordinary women in that society.[49] More recently Ruth Tringham and Margaret Conkey have criticized Gimbutas for not providing the context for the figurines she refers to. They point out that Gimbutas downplays the diversity among the figurines and her assumption that the figurines' large breasts and large stomachs indicate fertility is not demonstrated or considered critically. It is more likely, they say, that these figurines indicate "womanhood" not "motherhood" and it is uncertain at best what "motherhood" may have meant 20,000 years ago.[50]

Other critics like Cynthia Eller insist that it is problematic to present a wishful matriarchal narrative as historical fact. The myth "reaches well beyond the inner circle of its devotees"[51] and therefore, in Eller's estimation, spiritual feminists that present these constructions are opening themselves up (and the rest of the feminist camp as well) to easy criticism. For Eller, the solution is to "embrace the myth of matriarchal prehistory as myth." She says that "if feminist matriachalists abandon their ambitions to historical veracity, then accusations of sloppy or wishful thinking will not tarnish their myth."[52] From Eller's perspective, they cannot have claim to both women's history and myth. They can either construct imaginative matriarchal myths for their own spiritual purposes or engage in the scholarly pursuits of history and archaeology.

In Defense of the Goddess

In response to Foley's critique that she presents only traditional types and roles for women, Christ insists that she does not want to confine women to traditional roles.[53] Her attempt at reimagining those roles and images in an empowering Goddess figure is her way of reclaiming those roles and images which have been equated with the "feminine" but deemed as less than or secondary to those perceived as "masculine." She also believes, like Starhawk, that "the life-giving powers of the Goddess in her creative aspect are not limited to physical birth, for the Goddess is also seen as the creator of all the arts of civilization, including healing, writing, and the giving of just law. Women in the middle of life who are not physical mothers may give birth to poems, songs, and books, or nurture other women, men, and children."[54]

Christ also argues that powerful symbols are influencing both groups and individuals to act in extremely harmful ways towards each other and the environment here and now. She argues that

> Symbols of God as a dominant male other are inspiring both acts of terrorism and preparations for wars of revenge as I write. Symbols of God as a dominant male other and notions of infallible revelation are fueling campaigns to control female sexuality around the world. In America, Africa, Asia, Europe, Australia, New Zealand, and the Pacific islands, women and girls submit to male violence every minute of every day because religions have taught them to believe that if God is male, then male is God.[55]

Thus Christ believes that "the process of re-imagining symbols is itself a social, political, and profoundly ethical act. It is one of the ways we transform the world."[56] Christ continues with her defense of reimagining prehistoric symbols by saying that, "the process of reimagining symbols is on-going. Though we will discover and create new symbols that can work for ourselves and in communities over periods of time, we should not imagine that we will ever get our symbols 'right' once and for all, for this would be to stop the process of creative re-imagining."[57] It is clear that spiritual feminists like Christ are fully aware that they are employing a creative process of reimagining history and ancient goddesses.[58] They are actively constructing such images because they "see their task as a process of discovery *and* recreation, of remembering *and* inventing"[59] in order to address the imbalance of power symbols and combat the symbols and images that are presently being employed to do harm. Christ has shown that the imagining and reimagining of "feminine" images, figures and models is on-going. Nevertheless one must take into account the criticisms raised against imaginative endeavors undertaken by the previous generation of spiritual feminists like Christ as the next generations of spiritual feminists begin to undertake their own imaginative endeavors.

Something Old, Something New, Something Borrowed

Having acknowledged the controversy surrounding the use of prehistoric goddess images and symbols, it is important to point out that this imaginative endeavor that Christ has engaged in is not something entirely new. The imaginative process employed in the construction of saintly figures shares many similarities with that employed by spiritual feminists like Christ. Therefore, to shed some light on this imaginative process a brief examination of other imagined figures such as saint is in order.

Saints and Goddesses: Imagining Ideal "Feminine" Figures

Hagiographical texts deal with the "lives" of the saints. The lives of female saints are similar presentations of "feminine" ideals for the particular Christian community that venerated that figure.[60] The life of a female saint is "intended as an *exemplum* for others."[61] According to Gail Ashton, hagiography "tells of a holy subject worthy of veneration, offers witness to it, and becomes approved by the community as a source of wisdom. It is part of a sacred tradition which implicates writer, text, audience, and a larger community such as the Church."[62] It is the constructed ideal or example which connects the writer to their intended audience and to the larger religious community. The imagination is employed by the medieval hagiographer when they write about such ideal figures.

Like Christ's Goddess, the saint is created with a specific purpose in mind. In this case to convey a particular model of saintliness intended to inspire other Christians. Saints' stories appear to fill the gap between theory and practice that must be addressed and the saint functions as a role model on which to pattern one's own spiritual devotion. The kinds of model-saints that are put forth or imagined by hagiographers are in response to what the hagiographer perceives as an inadequacy in his or her time. Therefore, the creation of saints stems from a perceived need to refocus the world in a particular direction. Hagiographies or accounts of saints' lives are written in response to a need, and the story that is created reveals the desires of the hagiographer much more than the historical circumstances of the saint's life. When there appears to be a lack of spiritual dedication or moral grounding the hagiographer then draws upon the story of an extraordinary person to put forth an example of the ideals they wish to stress. For example, in the *Life of Saint Mary of Egypt*, Mary, a fourth century Egyptian harlot turned desert ascetic, is presented as a model of humility and repentance.[63] The "feminine" ideals promoted by this text are those of humility and obedience and it encourages one to reject worldly pleasures and the sinful sexual body.[64]

Stories about these saintly figures are meant to be heard by others. They are intended to inspire and encourage other believers, as well as to provide avenues for imagining the possibility of living a dedicated Christian life. In order to create these inspiring models the hagiographer must creatively weave elements of myth, history and scripture, thus encoding a moral or scriptural ideal. The imagination will be employed not only in the construction of the text, but also by the listener to process the various images, references, and subtle messages that are intentionally planted in the text. This appears to be the same process undertaken by Christ and others presenting the Goddess to inspire and empower modern women. Both employ the imagination and attempt to engage the imaginations of others for the purpose of focusing on a gap or need previously ignored by existing models.

Hagiographical texts present specific "feminine" ideals for a prescriptive purpose. However, they are more than just guidelines or commands. While there are many occasions where scripture deals with such prescriptions, they seem to leave unanswered practical questions. In other words, they leave the "how" up to the imagination. Saints provide an example rather than a simple direction or command.[65] The lives of these religious figures are meant to complement the scripture prescribed to women. They take up the imaginative endeavor precisely where scripture leaves off because they show *how* to live the exemplary life outlined in sacred text.

Christ's writing on the Goddess does not belong to the hagiographical genre but it certainly contains descriptive/prescriptive elements in her presentation of "feminine" ideals. The "feminine" ideals that she presents in the Goddess are very different, however, from those presented by many hagiographers. Whereas the figure of St. Mary of Egypt presents the ideal female figure as one that denies her own "sinful" body, seeks out seclusion from the world and submits herself entirely to God, Christ's Goddess figure presents a nurturing mother that is at peace in her own body, part of the world and submits her creative powers to no one. Contrasting views of the ideal "feminine" are presented by these two figures. Nevertheless, it is evident that both saintly figures and the Goddess figure have been created for the same purpose: to engage the imagination and to inspire these "feminine" qualities in members of these religious communities.

Imagination and Inspiration

It is evident that the imagination plays a necessary role in the creation and presentation of such ideal figures. It is the means by which various elements or sources (often both mythical and historical elements) are selected and woven together. It is also the means by which the ideals are transmitted as it inspires and stimulates the imaginations of those that receive the image or story of the ideal figure. Christ's Goddess is meant to inspire and encourage the expression of female creativity and reassure women that being female and powerful is not only okay, it is an aspect of the sacred. Thus, in the creation of such exemplary or ideal figures one engages in an imaginative process in order to appeal to both historical and mythical aspects and create an exemplary model. These exemplary models appeal to the inspiring aspect of myth while at the same time appealing also to aspects of history as it is in their grounding in historical realities that give these figures weight or make them inspiringly possible. However, the balance between the mythical and the historical elements in these purposefully constructed figures matters greatly because there are extremes that can occur in such imaginative endeavors. Indeed, one should not accept such imagined figures, medieval or modern, at face value or at least not without critical assessment.

As the next generation of spiritual feminists begin to sift through the previously imagined figures for appropriate ideals and models for themselves, a carefully evaluation must take place. They must ask themselves whether or not the Goddess that spiritual feminists like Christ have imagined address current concerns and ideals. If none of the preexisting figures seem to fit or if they create more ambiguities than certainties, then the re-imagination process must be taken up again and a new figure, goddess or saint or something else entirely, must be imagined. This is certainly no easy task. What kinds of criteria should be applied when evaluating previously imagined figures? How can one tell when an imaginative endeavor has gone too far on the side of myth into the realm of the unbelievable or too far on the side of history so that it becomes chained to the factual and redundant? I submit that Paul Ricoeur's work on imagination might provide a way to begin evaluating these imagined figures. Ricoeur proposes that any imaginative endeavor is in danger of falling into extremes, what he identifies as "ideology" and "utopia."[66] These extremes may also serve as the boundaries for future imaginative endeavors.

Paul Ricoeur (1913-2006), the French-born philosopher and phenomenologist, insists that products of imaginative construction must be approached critically because there is always the possibility of a perversion or distortion. He thus provides a "hermeneutics of suspicion" as a means by which the imagination and these imaginative endeavors can be critically evaluated. Ricoeur's theory can help to understand the problematic areas in the presentation of purposefully imagined figures. For example, older saintly figures have the potential to stray into the realm of ideology. Once a saint's life has enjoyed a measure of popularity for some time, their exemplary life begins to enjoy almost the same authority as scripture. It can then cease to be an inspiring model of the possible and become simply a direction or command. In that case the imaginative and inspirational aspect dies and it becomes like a puzzling passage of scripture, no longer inspiring and positive but repressive and enforcing narrow definitions of the ideal Christian life. In many cases, female saints narrow the definition of the ideal "feminine" and enforce one particular type of "feminine" on all women. At the other end of the spectrum, Christ's presentation of a matriarchal prehistory and ancient Goddess figure has the potential to be seen as the utopian extreme. If not grounded firmly in the realm of historical reality, Christ's presentation could be dismissed outright as fanciful and unfounded, as it has been by some critics. Therefore her meticulously imagined Goddess figure lacks the driving power to change and inspire because some have found her work strays too far into the mythical, the romantic. Thus, for Christ's critics, the Goddess lacks the connection to the worldly and is not convincing in its presentation of the possible.[67]

Ricoeur has stated that "the imagination is always working on the basis of already established laws and it is its task to make them function creatively, either by applying them in an original way or by subverting them; or indeed both."[68] Therefore when the imaginative endeavor responsible for creating such ideal feminine figures is original and innovative it takes already established images and ideas and makes them seem fresh and new. It illuminates possibilities and inspires new ways of thinking and being. However, one must always be cautious of imaginative endeavors that stray into the extremes.[69]

To conclude this examination of imagined figures it will simply be noted that imaginative endeavors can certainly be innovative, creative, and intuitive and can illuminate new possibilities that had not previously been considered. Feminist scholars have long acknowledged the imagination as a powerful and all too underutilized tool.[70] One must remember, however, that imagined figures are provisional. Eventually a figure is no longer creative and informative for present contexts. It can become either a narrow and one-sided worldview or an otherworldly fantasy. These are the ideological and utopian extremes that Ricoeur has cautioned against. Spiritual feminist Carol Christ has openly acknowledged that she employs the imagination in her construction of a goddess figure and has presented the Goddess as a way of celebrating the "feminine" qualities that she feels have been undervalued in western societies; qualities such as female creativity, female friendship, and female expression of sexuality. The hope is to engage the imaginations of others—to inspire and empower them by showing alternative models and images of the "feminine." Figures like the Goddess are potent and powerful when they make the assumed impossibilities seemingly possible or dare to explore what was previously unexplored. They do not, however, retain their potency indefinitely. Thus, the Goddess figure that inspired Christ, Starhawk and many others from the previous generation of spiritual feminists must be reevaluated as to how well she addresses the concerns of the next generation of spiritual feminists. If it is found that new figures must be imagined, then these would have to be checked against new findings from the fields of archaeology and history so that they do not stray too far into the realm of utopian fantasy as some believe the Goddess has.

Notes

1. Carol P. Christ, "Why Women Need the Goddess: Phenomenological, Psychological, and Political Reflections," in *Womanspirit Rising*, ed. C. Christ and J. Plaskow (New York: Harper & Row, 1979), 275.

2. Luce Irigaray has made a similar claim. She insists that a creative reimagining of the divine as woman will empower women and aid them in becoming "woman." See Luce Irigaray, "Divine Women," in *Sexes and Genealogies*, trans. Gillian C. Gill (New York: Columbia University Press, 1993), 57-72.

3. Carol P. Christ, *She Who Changes: Re-Imagining the Divine in the World* (New York: Palgrave Macmillan, 2003), 230 [emphasis mine].

4. Title of chapter seven in Cynthia Eller, *Living in the Lap of the Goddess: The Feminist Spirituality Movement in America* (New York : Crossroad, 1993).

5. Carol P. Christ, *Rebirth of the Goddess: Finding Meaning in Feminist Spirituality*, (New York: Addison-Wesley Publishing, 1997), 106.

6. Carol P. Christ, "Feminist Studies in Religion and Literature," *Journal of the American Academy of Religion* 44, no. 2 (1976): 318.

7. Christ, "Why Women Need the Goddess," 275.

8. Christ, "Why Women Need the Goddess," 277.

9. Christ, "Why Women Need the Goddess," 281.

10. Christ, "Why Women Need the Goddess," 281.

11. Elizabeth Schüssler Fiorenza, *Bread Not Stone: The Challenge of Feminist Biblical Interpretation*, (Boston: Beacon Press, 1984) quoted in Carol P. Christ, *Laughter of Aphrodite: Reflections on a Journey to the Goddess* (San Francisco: Harper and Row, 1987), 162.

12. Christ, *Laughter of Aphrodite*, 162.

13. Christ, *Laughter of Aphrodite*, 165.

14. Christ, *Laughter of Aphrodite*, xi.

15. Christ, "Words about the Goddess," *Ariadne Institute for the Study of Myth and Ritual*, http://www.goddessariadne.org/carolwords.htm.

16. Christ, *She Who Changes*, 21.

17. Starhawk, *Truth or Dare: Encounters with Power, Authority, and Mystery* (New York: HarperCollins, 1987), 7.

18. Starhawk, *The Spiral Dance: A Rebirth of the Ancient Religion of the Great Goddess* (San Francisco: Harper and Row 1979, 1989), 2.

19. Starhawk, *The Spiral Dance*, 2.

20. Starhawk, *The Spiral Dance*, 2.

21. Starhawk, *The Spiral Dance*, 95.

22. Starhawk, *The Spiral Dance*, 95. [emphasis mine].

23. Starhawk, *The Spiral Dance*, 96.

24. Starhawk, *The Spiral Dance*, 96.

25. Starhawk, *The Spiral Dance*, 99 [emphasis hers].

26. Starhawk, *The Spiral Dance*, 91.

27. Starhawk, *The Spiral Dance*, 94.

28. Starhawk, *The Spiral Dance*, 99.

29. Starhawk, *The Spiral Dance*, 8.

30. Starhawk, *The Spiral Dance*, 8.

31. Starhawk, *The Spiral Dance*, 9.

32. Starhawk, *The Spiral Dance*, 23.

33. Starhawk, *The Spiral Dance*, 23.

34. Starhawk, *Truth or Dare*, 10.

35. Starhawk, *The Spiral Dance*, 24.

36. Starhawk, *The Spiral Dance*, 25.

37. There have been a few male figurines found but the majority of figurines dating from the Paleolithic period in Europe are female. Margaret Ehrenberg, *Women in Prehistory* (Norman: University of Oklahoma Press, 1989), 37.

38. Marija Gimbutas, *The Civilization of the Goddess: the World of Old Europe*, ed. Joan Marler (New York: HarperCollins, 1991), 342.

39. Gimbutas, *The Civilization of the Goddess*, 334.

40. Christ, *Rebirth of the Goddess*, 54.

41. Christ, "Why Women Need the Goddess," 277.

42. Christ, *Laughter of Aphrodite*, 162 [emphasis mine].

43. Helene P. Foley, "A Question of Origins: Goddess Cults Greek and Modern," in *Women, Gender, Religion: A Reader*, edited by Elizabeth A. Castelli (New York: Palgrave, 2001), 221.

44. Foley, "A Question of Origins," 221.

45. Foley, "A Question of Origins," 221.

46. Foley, "A Question of Origins," 222-3.

47. Ehrenberg, *Women in Prehistory*, 72.

48. Ehrenberg, *Women in Prehistory*, 73.

49. Ehrenberg, *Women in Prehistory*, 37.

50. Ruth Tringham and Margaret Conkey, "Rethinking Figurines: A Critical View from Archaeology of Gimbutas, the 'Goddess' and Popular Culture," in *Ancient Goddesses: The Myths and the Evidence*, edited by Lucy Goodison and Christine Morris (London: British Museum Press, 1998), 25.

51. Cynthia Eller, *The Myth of Matriarchal Prehistory: Why an Invented Past Won't Give Women a Future* (Boston: Beacon Press, 2000), 11.

52. Eller, *The Myth of Matriarchal Prehistory*, 182.

53. Christ, *Rebirth of the Goddess*, 92.

54. Christ, "Why Women Need the Goddess," 281.

55. Christ, *She Who Changes*, 228.

56. Christ, *She Who Changes*, 228.

57. Christ, *She Who Changes*, 244.

58. Christ, "Why Women Need the Goddess," 277.

59. Kathryn Rountree, "The Past is a Foreigners' Country," *Journal of Contemporary Religion* 16 (2001): 9-10. See also Foley, "A Question of Origins," 217.

60. Gail Ashton, *The Generation of Identity in Late Medieval Hagiography: Speaking the Saint*, Routledge Research in Medieval Studies (New York: Routledge, 2000), 3.

61. Ashton, *The Generation of Identity*, 11 [emphasis hers].

62. Ashton, *The Generation of Identity*, 11.

63. See Benedicta Ward, *Harlots of the Desert: A Study of Repentance in Early Monastic Sources* (Kalamazoo, MI: Cistercian Publications, 1987) for a translation of the story of Mary of Egypt as well as the stories of other harlot saints.

64. See Lynda L. Coon, *Sacred Fictions: Holy Women and Hagiography in Late Antiquity* (Philadelphia: University of Pennsylvania Press, 1997), 84-94.

65. Edith Wyschogrod, *Saints and Postmodernism: Revisioning Moral Philosophy* (Chicago: University of Chicago Press, 1990), 3.

66. See Paul Ricoeur, *Lectures on Ideology and Utopia*, ed. George H. Taylor (New York: Columbia University Press, 1986).

67. It is also important to note that the Goddess could also become an ideological extreme if she becomes a narrow definition of the ideal "feminine."

68. Paul Ricoeur, "The Creativity of Language," in *Dialogues with Contemporary Continental Thinkers*, ed. Richard Kearney (Oxford: Manchester University Press, 1984), 25.

69. Ricoeur is not alone in asserting that potentially harmful extremes can and do occur in imaginative endeavors. Christian theologian, Sallie McFague, has also alluded to such extremes in religious language and metaphor. McFague identifies these as "idolatry" and "irrelevance." See Sallie McFague, *Metaphorical Theology: Models of God in Religious Language* (Philadelphia: Fortress Press, 1982), 4-10.

70. Juanita Weaver, "Images and Models – in Process," in *The Politics of Women's Spirituality: Essays on the Rise of Spiritual Power within the Feminist Movement*, edited by Charlene Spretnak (New York: Doubleday, 1982), 249.

Bibliography

Ashton, Gail. *The Generation of Identity in Late Medieval Hagiography: Speaking the Saint*, Routledge Research in Medieval Studies. New York: Routledge, 2000.

Christ, Carol P. "Words about the Goddess." *Ariadne Institute for the Study of Myth and Ritual*. http://www.goddessariadne.org/carolwords.htm.

———. "Why Women Need the Goddess: Phenomenological, Psychological, and Political Reflections," in *Womanspirit Rising*, edited by C. Christ and J. Plaskow (New York: Harper & Row, 1979), 275.

———. *She Who Changes: Re-Imagining the Divine in the World*. New York: Palgrave Macmillan, 2003.

———. *Rebirth of the Goddess: Finding Meaning in Feminist Spirituality*. New York: Addison-Wesley Publishing,1997.

———. "Feminist Studies in Religion and Literature," *Journal of the American Academy of Religion* 44, no. 2 (1976): 318.

———. *Laughter of Aphrodite: Reflections on a Journey to the Goddess*. San Francisco: Harper and Row, 1987.

Coon, Lynda L. *Sacred Fictions: Holy Women and Hagiography in Late Antiquity*. Philadelphia: University of Pennsylvania Press, 1997.

Ehrenberg, Margaret. *Women in Prehistory*. Norman: University of Oklahoma Press, 1989.

Eller, Cynthia. *The Myth of Matriarchal Prehistory: Why an Invented Past Won't Give Women a Future*. Boston: Beacon Press, 2000.

Foley, Helene P. "A Question of Origins: Goddess Cults Greek and Modern." In *Women, Gender, Religion: A Reader*, edited by Elizabeth A. Castelli, 216-236. New York: Palgrave, 2001.

Gimbutas, Marija. *The Civilization of the Goddess: the World of Old Europe*, edited by Joan Marler. New York: HarperCollins, 1991.

Irigaray, Luce. "Divine Women." In *Sexes and Genealogies, translated by Gillian C. Gill*, 57-72. New York: Columbia University Press, 1993.

McFague, Sallie. *Metaphorical Theology: Models of God in Religious Language*. Philadelphia: Fortress Press, 1982.

Ricoeur, Paul. *Lectures on Ideology and Utopia*. New York: Columbia University Press, 1986.

————. "Myth as Bearer of Possible Worlds." In *Dialogues with Contemporary Conti-nental Thinkers,* edited by Richard Kearney, 36-45. Manchester: Manchester University Press, 1984.

————. "The Creativity of Language." In *Dialogues with Contemporary Continental Thinkers,* edited by Richard Kearney, 17-36. Oxford: Manchester University Press, 1984.

Kathryn Rountree, "The Past is a Foreigners' Country," *Journal of Contemporary Religion* 16 (2001): 9-10.

Schüssler Fiorenza, Elizabeth. *Bread Not Stone: The Challenge of Feminist Biblical Interpretation.* Boston: Beacon Press, 1984.

Starhawk. *Truth or Dare: Encounters with Power, Authority, and Mystery.* New York: HarperCollins, 1987.

————. *The Spiral Dance: A Rebirth of the Ancient Religion of the Great Goddess.* San Francisco: Harper and Row, 1979,1989.

Tringham, Ruth and Margaret Conkey. "Rethinking Figurines: A Critical View from Archaeology of Gimbutas, the 'Goddess' and Popular Culture." In *Ancient Goddesses: The Myths and the Evidence,* edited by Lucy Goodison and Christine Morris, 22-45. London: British Museum Press, 1998.

Ward, Benedicta. *Harlots of the Desert: A Study of Repentance in Early Monastic Sources.* Kalamazoo, MI: Cistercian Publications, 1987.

Weaver, Juanita. "Images and Models – in Process." In *The Politics of Women's Spirituality: Essays on the Rise of Spiritual Power within the Feminist Movement,* edited by Charlene Spretnak, 249-257. New York: Doubleday, 1982.

Wyschogrod, Edith. *Saints and Postmodernism: Revisioning Moral Philosophy.* Chicago: University of Chicago Press, 1990.

Chapter Two:
Queering Feminist Witchcraft

Catherine Telford-Keogh

Introduction

In the era of postmodernism, the critique of identity has become a prominent topic within feminist and queer theory and theology.[1] "Feminist Witch" has thus become an identity which I have recently begun to deconstruct. The widely available literature regarding Feminist Witchcraft has largely been written by second-wave feminists, consequently I have found identifying as a Feminist Witch has become problematic in light of postmodern theory. This paper attempts to delve into the treatment of identity and identity categories within Goddess Centered Feminist Witchcraft and what could be considered "postmodern" Reclaiming and Faerie Witchcraft in order to aid in the understanding of what it means to be a Feminist Witch in postmodernity.

The domains of representation set out criterion by which identity is formed. Thus, representation is only given to identities that can be understood within that specific domain.[2] In the construction of gender, specifically women as a category, dominant patriarchal, heterosexist order has set out specific criterion defining what it means to be a woman, exercising power over and thus subordinating that domain of representation. These mechanisms of power that form the idea of "woman" are perpetuated when a subject acts out the criterion set out by the "woman" category through what Foucault terms "techniques of the self." According to Foucault one becomes a subject of power when one either is controlled by power or is regulated by one's own identity. He terms "techniques of the self" as operations that someone, by their own means, imposes upon their body, thoughts and behavior to modify or transform themselves to achieve an identity category, for example.[3] Resisting and transgressing these mechanisms of power that control to whom representation is extended can be accomplished by

challenging the rigidity of categories, such as "woman"—as defined by patriarchy—through enacting new forms of "techniques of the self", revealing
gender as a performance, rather than a natural abiding identity. The concept of
gender as something performative has largely been theorized by feminist philosopher Judith Butler. Generally this theory poses gender as something that is
performed by a number of *repeated* acts and gestures which create the appearance of an abiding gender identity. She affirms that due to gender's performative
nature it is possible to trouble one's gender identity revealing it's naturalness as
a falsity through resisting or troubling the acts that constitute the authenticity of
that identity.[4]

Resistance, in the Foucaultian sense, is described as a counterattack enacted
by the body, as it is the body that is disciplined, that "threatens power, hence it
stands against power as an adversary."[5] Transgression is an act that "forces the
limit to recognize and acknowledge what it excludes, and hence 'the world is
forced to question itself.'"[6] Playing with or troubling gender categories or modes
of representation can also dismantle power mechanisms that seek to regulate
individuals. What becomes problematic is that this action may deny someone
representation within the dominant domain, as they do not follow appropriate
criterion.

What first interested me in Witchcraft was this challenging of the patriarchal heterosexist construction of what it means to be a woman. As a young feminist I became disinterested in my religious tradition—which was the United
Church of Canada—as I felt it did not speak to my experiences as a woman
questioning her identity and sexuality. I enrolled in a class at my university entitled "Women and the Great Religions" and became acquainted with Goddess
Centered Feminist Witchcraft. I found this tradition fascinating as it addressed
and centrally focused on the rejection of patriarchal constructions of womanhood. Goddess Centered Feminist Witchcraft emerged as part of the Feminist
Spirituality Movement in the 1970s, during the second wave feminist movement. Western Feminists disillusioned by patriarchy, sexism and heterosexism
within their religious tradition, especially Christianity and Judaism, began to
reject imagining the divine as male identified and masculine, which I had also
recently found problematic in the church in which I was raised.[7] Goddess Centered Feminist Witchcraft constructs the divine as female identified, drawing on
elements of goddess worship across cultures and religious traditions and places
women's experiences, such as menstruation and childbirth, at the center of spiritual practice. I found that constructing the divine as female identified allowed
me to establish a physical and direct connection, something I had never experienced before. It also affirms that goddess-worshiping cultures existed at the
advent of civilization and were eventually overtaken by the global shift towards
patriarchy revealing the naturalness of patriarchy as a falsity. I began researching Goddess Centered Witchcraft first reading Rosemary Radford Ruether's *The
Divine Feminine,* Starhawk's *Spiral Dance* and later the *Holy Book of Women's
Mysteries* by Zsuzsanna Budapest. Budapest is the founder of Dianic Feminist
Witchcraft a type of Goddess Centered Feminist Witchcraft. In her early stages

of practice, Starhawk, contributed greatly to the creation of ideology, rituals and spells though she later moved away from Goddess Centered Feminist Witchcraft to participate in the formation of the Reclaiming tradition.[8]

I informally attended a few open circle meetings held by a loosely structured Goddess Centered Feminist coven in Toronto. I was very enthusiastic about my new found spirituality and started to "come out" as a Witch to close friends. A year after practicing as a solitary Witch I started to question the focus on the Goddess and ideologies regarding womanhood after reading Judith Butler's book *Gender Trouble*. I began to think that constructing the divine as female and feminine and performing rituals as well as rites that reinstituted patriarchal ideologies of "woman" as nurturing, menstruating and life-giving was not liberating but restrictive. The Goddess Centered Feminist Witchcraft tradition, from my experience, did not extend representation to others that did not fit into this rigid category of what it meant to be a woman. Though I found that lesbian and sometimes queer-identified people participated in coven meetings and rituals, they were only merely tolerated and their bodies where unrecognizable within the discourse of the Goddess and rituals, for example, those centered on menstruation. Upon recommendation from a Witchen friend, I began reading about Radical Faerie and Reclaiming Feminist Witchcraft. I learned that the Radical Faeries identify as a part social, part "counter-hegemonic" and part spiritual movement which began in the late 1970s, inspired by the thinking of several leaders in the lesbian and gay consciousness movement including gay rights activist Harry Hay. Radical Faeries reclaimed the traditionally pejorative name in order to identify with queer, gender variant sacred outsiders devoted to resisting traditional notions of masculinity through periodic performances of drag. Radical Faerie Witchcraft discourse is informed by Marxism, feminism, paganism, New Age and Native American spirituality "spiritual solemnity coupled with camp sensibility, gay liberation, and drag."[9] In addition, Reclaiming Witchcraft was pioneered by ecofeminist and activist Starhawk and has changed much since its beginnings in the late 1970s. This tradition in theory is queer-inclusive and largely rejects "inner female" and "inner male" imagery and "female-male polarization." Starhawk's Reclaiming practice draws upon the principals of the Feri Tradition. The Feri Tradition was founded by Victor and Cora Anderson—who initiated Starhawk into the tradition.[10] Generally, Reclaiming Witchcraft does not solely focus on the Goddess but on a myriad of gods, goddesses, queer identified and gender variant deities. Most forms of Reclaiming Witchcraft operate on eclectic and inventive strategies when creating ritual. This form of Witchcraft is informed largely by feminism, earth based movements, paganism, Marxism and activism. In these traditions I found that belief systems mirrored a postmodern feminist and queer-inclusive approach to religious identity, construction of the divine and religious ritual.[11] Both these traditions questioned the abiding nature of "gender" and "sex" presenting the possibility of fluidity, opened up other modes of representing the divine as well as enacted resistive forms of "techniques of the self" through ritual and magic extending a sacred space in which non-normative practitioners could be represented as variant peoples.[12]

This paper theoretically outlines my path towards queering my practice of Feminist Witchcraft. The reclaimed term "queer", according to Bardella, is used as positive self-identification for individuals who do not ascribe to "assimilations pressures." "The polymorphous ambiguity of the label 'queer' [. . .] enabled the *continual* deconstruction of identity."[13] As such, when using the term "queer" throughout this paper, I am referring to individuals who enact in a continual bending, troubling and dismantling the continuity of gender, sexuality and sex, rather than a mere substitution for "gay" or "lesbian."[14] I have structured this paper according to my own movement away from Goddess Centered Spirituality towards Radical Faerie and a form of Eclectic Reclaiming Feminist Witchcraft, and thus the paper is comparative in nature. I will conduct an analysis of the subversive potential of resistance to dominant forms of representation by both sets of groups and the struggle for new forms of subjectivity and identity through a queer, postmodern feminist paradigm. Throughout this paper I will also draw upon two interviews I conducted with Mandy, a PhD student who identifies with the Feminist Reclaiming Tradition and Sue who is queer identified and practices an eclectic form of Witchcraft (drawing upon principles from both Radical Faerie and Eclectic Reclaiming Feminist Witchcraft). These interviews coupled with my experience as a Witch serve as a very small case study so that I may illustrate my findings through lived experience as well as theoretical analysis. Exploring the construction of identity, the construction and manifestation of the divine as well as the new domains of representation created during ritual and magic in both sets of groups I argue that though Goddess Centered Feminist Witchcraft resists the identity category "woman," as constructed by patriarchy, through enacting other "techniques of the self," its ideologies are still largely reliant on the essentialist patriarchal construction of woman as close to nature, female and nurturing as well as on the exclusion of others that cannot connect directly with these ideologies.[15] Through this comparative analysis I pose that the resistance to dominant domains of representation and identity as well as the possibility for the creation of new fluid identities that are extended representation by the Radical Faerie and Reclaiming Feminist Witchcraft, present gender identity as fluid, open and changeable and thus potentially opening up the domains of representation so that they are no longer constructed and controlled by current heterosexist, patriarchal mechanisms of power.[16]

Identity Reconstruction

Witchcraft is a relatively new religious movement that generally became popular in the late 1970s largely with Western feminists.[17] What is generally known about what a Witch *is* has been through mass media's construction. As mass media acts as a mechanism of power, it has the "authority" to construct what it means to be a Witch. Mass media classifies "the world in terms of the discourse of the dominant ideologies."[18] These representations become accepted as literal translations, as mass media is one of the prime mediums of socialization. Thus, essentialist ideologies regarding identity portrayed in the media not only construct the way we perform identity, but also shape and naturalize and thus internalize these dominate ideologies.[19] However, "there is always at least some resistance to the imposition of any particular form of subjectivity, and thus resistance is concomitant with the process of subjectification."[20] This form of diffused resistance is enacted by Goddess Centered Feminist Witches and Reclaiming Witches as they reconstruct and challenge dominant culture's ideologies regarding what constitutes a "Witch" as well as gender identity and what Gayle Rubin terms as the sex/gender system.[21]

In interacting with new people, I am constantly negotiating which aspects of my identity I will reveal and which aspects I keep "closeted." My self identification as a "Feminist Witch" is one of the aspects which I keep closeted, "coming out" as a "Witch" only to selected persons. I have experienced first hand dominant cultural and religious ideologies and constructions of what it means to be a Witch. Here I will examine Goddess centered and the Reclaiming Feminist Witches' counterhegemonic negotiation and "(re)construction" of "Witch" as well as examine how this construction is shaped by each "collectives'" underlying belief systems. In order to examine these "(re)negotiations" of "Witch", dominant cultures' construction of "Witch" will be examined first.

Witch

Mass media portrayals and the creation of the oppositional "not threatening to heteropatriarchy witch" have formed the "bad witch/good witch" dichotomous identity. For example, according to Vikki Godwin, in her analysis of "Witch" in media texts, she outlines that "tales of orgies or sex with animals or demons or lesbianism or lack of interest in male partners casts witches as sexual deviants."[22] These images define heterosexual monogamous sex as the norm and justify punishment for deviating from that norm. Likewise, Witches are constructed as murderers and hunters of men and children. Witches are portrayed as mad cannibals killing for pleasure or food as well. According to Godwin, this portrayal of "Witch" stems from the condemnation of Witchcraft as Satanic worship and sorcery in dominant, traditional Judeo-Christian dogma. This portrayal of "Witch" is evident in the film *Hocus Pocus* released in 1993 by Disney. The film begins in seventeenth-century Salem, Massachusetts where three Witch sisters are executed for transforming one of the villagers into a black cat. The three sisters come back from the dead through a magic book, from which all their powers derive. The three sisters attack the local children during Halloween in order to eat them until they are stopped by a young boy. These Witches are portrayed as mad cannibals, which justifies their execution. According to Godwin, people in power get to impose their metaphors. Thus, Disney as a mass media monopoly is given the power to construct the "Witch" as a deviant, insane, cannibalistic and devil worshiping woman who deserves to be punished for *her* transgressions.[23]

This "symbolic annihilation," that is media texts' trivialization or condemnation of "woman," is also evident in the media portrayal of what Godwin describes as "the media Witch." Here Witches are portrayed as "sexually attractive young women" who use their "power" to chase after heterosexual men, and to carry out acts that aid them in accomplishing their gender category.[24] This is evident in the TV series *Sabrina the Teenage Witch*. During the opening credits Sabrina is shown changing her outfits with the twitch of her finger. She also repeatedly uses spells and potions to attain her love interest's attention. Though Sabrina is portrayed as the postmodern independent "woman," this media portrayal constructs the Witch as the ultimate metaphor affirming the "woman within." However, it is evident that this "woman within" that must be "liberated" is actually a heterosexual masculinist constructed image.[25] This portrayal of the "media Witch" makes evidence that Susan Faludi's theorized *backlash* never went away. Thus, mass media texts' portrayal of "Witch" constructs *her* as a sexually deviant, cannibalistic, Satanic worshiper that must be disciplined or is trivialized as a heterosexual young "woman" who uses her "powers" to *perform* normative femininity well.

These two representations of "Witch" in mass media perpetuate cultural condemnation or trivialization of this religious identity, which can be internalized by practitioners. In my interview with Sue, a queer identified practitioner of an eclectic form of Witchcraft, this internalization was made apparent when she stated "As I got older, a number of things began to conflict with my understanding of and experience with Wicca/Witchcraft...I began to see much of my spiritual practice as irrational, self-deceptive, or even pointless." It is possible that these dominant notions of Witchcraft as "irrational" and "pointless" could partly stem from the constructions of "the media Witch" as it trivializes and presents Witchcraft as fluffy, imaginative play with no authentic political or spiritual component. Goddess Centered Feminist Witches resist these mass media text constructions through resignifing this dominant notion of "Witch."

In her book, *Drawing down the Moon*, regarded as one of the many influential books within Goddess Centered Feminist Witchcraft, Margaret Adler explains that:

> [t]he Witch, after all, is an extraordinary symbol—independent, antiestablishment, strong, and proud. She is political, yet spiritual and magical. The Witch is woman as martyr: she is persecuted by the ignorant; she is the woman who lives outside society and outside society's definition of woman. In a society that has traditionally oppressed women there are few positive images of female power. Some of the most potent of these are the Witches.[26]

Adler identifies "Witch" as aggressive, strong, independent and powerful, emblematic of *female* power. This construction of "Witch" also subversively performs "woman" in resistance to the normative, masculininist construction which is one who embodies the characteristics of "delicacy, dreaminess, sexual passivity, and charmingly labile and capricious emotionality."[27] Adler's construction resists the "media Witch" described formerly and transforms portrayals of the 'bad Witch' into positive, affirming attributes. However, though the "Witch" Adler describes does not normatively align itself with the characteristics which constitute the "woman" identity, it is not exactly "outside" this identity either. In her critique of feminism Judith Butler states that "the category 'woman', the subject of feminism, is produced and restrained by the very structures of power through which emancipation is sought."[28] Adler describes a set of criterion which constitutes what it means to be a "Witch." This criterion places Goddess Centered Feminist Witches into a structured category. Though this resignification of "Witch" resists dominant notions of femininity and media portrayals, it essentializes the "Witch subject." Adler's description creates a domain of representation that sets out criterion by which the practitioner is formed. Though the "Witch" identity, described by Adler resists dominant media portrayals of "Witch", this resistance is restrictive as it produces the very subjects that it claims to represent.

Resistance is also enacted by Reclaiming Feminist Witchcraft which attempts to not only resist dominant notions of "Witch" but also to dismantle its very construction as a stable universal identity. According to Judith Butler, the body is a situation which is culturally signified and maintained through self imposed disciplinary practices. These "practices" mark the body and style the flesh to produce a body that fits into a particular domain of representation, a body that is "intelligible." These same "practices" can be used to parody identity as natural and abiding thus performing unintelligible identity.[29] In her dissertation, "Shape-Shifting 'Religion': Witchen Identities as Post()Modern Exemplum," Detrixhe describes her experience as an ethnographer at a Witch Camp, which serves as an annual gathering place for the Reclaiming eclectic community. She terms this particular community who gather together at the camp "Mud Pie Labyrinth." Detrixhe describes how the campers "mark themselves and thereby shift from 'everyday reality to ritual reality.'"[30] When arriving at the Witch Camp, campers change from their everyday clothes into what Detrixhe terms "Witchy-wear." For example, Detrixhe describes "gender bending men-in-skirts," and "women" wearing overtly, almost painfully, colorful clothing and dresses."[31] According to Claudio Bardella in his article "Queer Spirituality," *Queer Spiritual Discourse* proposes a theoretical template for the articulation of alternative "queer" identities in the study of New Age, Witchcraft and Eastern Spiritualities. Within this discourse, a particular form of identity *performed* that is pariodic and deconstructive is called "camp." "Camp" is described as "what constitutes the limit of a thing—too far out, too much, too low, too bad, too outrageous, too rough, too cultured, too aggressive, too sexual."[32] "Camp" is also considered an aesthetic that employs humor, bad taste or irony. This aesthetic can be used to challenge culture by forcing a confrontation with its own perceptions. For example exaggerating stereotypical feminine attributed such as fragility and emotionality is done to undermine the credibility of naturalness of those presuppositions. When these Reclaiming Witches "put on" their Witch identity, they reveal identity as an ever changing performance or a prosthetic that can be put on and taken off. This performance of "Witch" and gender variant identity also makes evident that one's gender performance does not always follow from one's sex.[33] However, some could argue that this "camp" performance does little to resist or transgress normative ideologies regarding the construction of "woman." Detrixhe placed these campers in a gender and sex category according to their performance of both. Focusing specifically on the Reclaiming Witches she *could* place into this category as they were overtly dressed in feminine clothing or nude, she described a feeling of oddity when looking at these "women", recognizing their over-the-top performances.[34] According to Susan Bordo, the practice of femininity, "[t]oo progressively pursued, practice leads to its own undoing."[35] Detrixhe, did not unknowingly or "naturally" place these "women" in this category but felt very "unnatural" about this placement. This performance reveals "woman" as produced by a set of specific disciplinary practices or "techniques of the self" *repeated* in order to produce the appearance of abiding gender identity. Though it could also be argued that this over-the-top performance of "Witch" through "Witchy-wear" by these Reclaiming Witches, becomes normalized as this kind of "camp" performance is quite popular in Witch Camps and thus no longer acts as a form of Foucaultian resistance. However, Detrixhe describes an incident where a male-identified Witch performed "an interesting reversal of the reversal, Steward, took up the costume challenge and one day wore his government office job suit to his path, jarring his fellow campers with the juxtaposition of deploying the mundane as a magical act."[36] Clearly, the performance of "Witch" is enacted in a "counterhegemonic" manner with a multitude of ways to be represented.[37] This "Witch" identity is queered and these individuals enact in "the *continual* deconstruction of identity."[38] The portrayals of the "media Witch" by dominant culture are resisted here when Reclaiming Witches perform "camp" gender identity using their overtly feminine clothing. This gender performance parodies "naturalized" femininity revealing the possibility that gender is created through "techniques of the self" rather that inherent and abiding.

Media texts are prime socializing agents, which provide viewers with two portrayals of what constitutes a "Witch," which are generally accepted as natural, that demonize or trivialize "real" Witches. In order to enact a Foucaultian form of resistance against these pervading ideologies, Goddess Centered Feminist Witches attempt to reclaim and resignify the "bad Witch" identity and resist the "media Witch" portrayal. Pickett in his article "Foucault and the Politics of Resistance" affirms that "[t]he purpose of contestation is not the construction of a new, better system [. . .]. Any such system will have similar effects of exclusion, which is why Foucault repudiates the desire to oppose the current law in the name of a new law."[39] By creating and describing new, somewhat essentialist categories, it is possible that Goddess Centered Feminist Witches are recreating a different form of disciplinary categories which they are trying to protest. Feminist Reclaiming Witches resist these media text constructions through an open and fluid representation of "Witch" as well as through "camp," which challenges essentialism and poses that identity is something that is performed and thus individuals can have a multitude of interpretations of what "Witch" means to them.

Resignification/Resistance of "Gender" and "Sex"

In her article "Political Activism and Feminist Spirituality," Nancy J. Finley affirms that despite the diffused nature and diversity of Feminist Spiritualities, such as Feminist Witchcraft, it is evident that there is generally a common focus upon "transformation of self," which can be interpreted and approached differently by each individual. Finley states that "attention is on 'personal responsibility' as the catalyst for alteration and inspiration of behavior."[40] Thus there is an emphasis on personal agency in the shaping of behavior. Foucault affirms that the domains of representation set out criterion by which a subject is formed. However as much as hegemonic criterion shapes and produces individuals through their performance of the former, there is also some form of resistance when power is consciously or unconsciously imposed.[41] However, the underlying ideologies of Goddess Centered Feminist Witchcraft as well as Reclaiming and Radical Faerie Witchcraft emphasize the agency of the subject to resist and transgress the oppressive constraints enforced by dominant ideologies regarding "gender" as well as "sex." To illustrate this point, I will examine the subversive potential of Dianic Witches—a type of Goddess Centered Feminist Witchcraft— enactment of alternative gender identity to actually resist these dominant ideologies. I will then analyze the how this subversive potential is extended by Reclaiming Feminist Witchcraft to also dismantle sex categorization as well as normative gender identity.

In Wendy Griffin's sociological study of the Dianic Covens, Womencircle and Redwood Moon, she observed how the Witches enacted and resisted dominant ideologies of "woman." Womencircle is a radical feminist coven which consists of nine members, of whom four are college educated. Redwood Moon is a radical feminist coven with members who have learned about a radical feminist perspective on gender and power through discussion groups reading assignments. Both groups reject male divinity and honor the female principal and accept "uncritically the belief in pre-historical 'Goddess Cultures' where women and 'women's values' were a major part of the societal ethos."[42] According to Clifford Geertz, rituals, symbols and myths "sum up" what is known about the world and "teach" people how to react to these dominant ideologies. In "reacting" to the patriarchal and heterosexist construction of "woman", these Witches perform alternative femininities which they create through ritual.[43] During a

Womancircle ritual the "Maiden, Mother, Crone" identities were enacted by the practitioners. When the line of "Crones" entered the circle one 22 year old self-identified woman described her reaction:

> It was really exciting, emotional thing. Many of them went back three and four generations. That was amazing. And the power in their voices! In my family the women don't raise their voices and announce who they are. To see such strong women! One said, "If you seek ecstasy with a Crone, seek me." I've never seen older women in a sexual light before. It was really uniting and empowering.[44]

Transgression forces recognition of what restrictive dualistic categories exclude.[45] The Dianic Witches' performance of "Crone," challenges and reconstructs the "woman" identity produced by heteropatriatrchal mechanisms of power systems.[46] Firstly, the speaker recognizes the assertive power from the voice of the woman acting out "Crone" in the ritual. She recognizes that this deviates from the traditional performance of femininity which promotes the "softening or silence of women's voices all together."[47] Secondly, the Crone performer insisted, while addressing a "woman only" circle, that "if you wish to seek ecstasy with a Crone, seek me."[48] The Crone insists, speaking to her coven members, that if they wish to experience the erotic or sexual ecstasy then they should seek out this older woman. It is probable that this statement connotes lesbian sexual experience within and outside of ritual. Thus, not only does this statement challenge the de-sexualizing of older women but it also challenges heteronormativity.

   Another participant exclaimed that this ritual was a clear articulation of "*female* power."[49] Though, the "woman" category is resignified, the emphasis on the *femaleness* of this transgression restricts the transgression itself into the sex/gender system. In my interview with Sue she spoke about her early practice as a Witch as associated with Goddess Centered Feminist Witchcraft. Her entrance into the path of Witchcraft is similar to mine in that I was also involved in Goddess Centered Spiritual practice. Sue described a realization she has after moving away from the ideologies of this tradition stating "critics of Feminist Witchcraft (including myself) charge that it tends to have an essentializing (and therefore anti-trans) understanding of womanhood." She describes the concept of "Women's Mysteries" in Feminist Witchcraft as an illustration of this essentialist understanding of womanhood. In the Womencircle ritual, "woman" category is resignified, but it is still accepted as rigid, essentialist category since "femaleness" is central to being a woman. Thus, these Dianic Witches challenge the rigidity of the "woman" category; however, after transgressing its rigidity they bind themselves to it, inevitably perpetuating its disciplinary power.[50]

   In contrast, Detrixhe describes her experiences regarding gender performance at the Mud Pie Labyrinth Reclaiming Witch Camp. She explains that there are many fluid subgroups (that do not practice exclusivity), who enact the Queer Spiritual Discourse definition of "camp" in their performance of gender, specifically examining a group called the GlitterWhores. She described this group as an eclectic group of people "mostly distinguished by its members' audacity and enthusiastic use of art supplies."[51] Members would dress up in overtly colourful, glittery clothing and act loudly and rude. Laura, a member of the GlitterWhores, described her search for her costume stating "I kept looking at all clothes from a camp perspective . . . does this have enough glitter . . . I even looked at some men's prom fashion to see what might work—a wonderful cummerbund of colours . . . ."[52] It is evident that GlitterWhores moved fluidly from masculine gender display to feminine gender display and back. Utilizing the "camp" style, group members parody the use of dress to construct an abiding gender identity. In looking at the parody of the "woman" identity by the GlitterWhores it is evident that, similar to the Dianics, "women" act aggressively loud and even rude, however it is their use of "camp" dress that is most interesting. Judith Butler, in her examination of drag performance, states that

> [a]lthough the gender meanings taken up in these periodic styles are clearly part of hegemonic, misogynist culture, they are nevertheless denaturalized and mobilized through their pariodic recontextualization. As imitations which effectively displace their meaning of the original, they imitate the myth of originality itself.[53]

The self-identified women members of the GlitterWhores' use of glitter, which is normatively identified as overtly feminine, as well as their use of men's clothing with glitter utilizes the "camp" style of drag. GlitterWhores use their personal agency, not just to overtly mimic one gender or the other, but rather to mix and combine gendered clothing, which they gather in local stores, then "(re)construct" them in order to create a "camp" identity that can be described as queer. Their overt performance in this "Witchy wear," that is dress that campers use to define themselves as Witches, reveals that (gender) identity itself is performative. In addition, the GlitterWhores present a discontinuity of gender identity from sex. Though Detrixhe, does not specify whether she has trouble placing these Witches in a sex category, and thus one could assume that she does not, the Witches "camp" performance reveals that one's gender display does not necessarily follow from the sex category one identifies with.

The GlitterWhores present identities that cannot be placed in either gender category and thus perform an "abject identity." Quoting Butler, Webster states that mechanisms of disciplinary power work through regulating subjects as well as "through the corollary constitution of a domain of unviable (un)subjects— abjects we might call them—who are neither named nor prohibited within the economy of law."[54] GlitterWhores' gender display deviates from the dominant cultural norm, thus, performing the GlitterWhore identity in public space would render their body unintelligible.[55] However, within the Witch camp context, this gender performance is extended sacred representation. The creation of this new identity allows these subjects to be divinely named and thus intelligible.[56]

In conclusion, the Dianic Feminist Witches, a spiritual practice within the Goddess Centered Feminist Witchcraft tradition, described by Griffin, resignify and resist normative ideologies of "woman." However, their emphasis on identifying with the very category that restricts them has the potential to reinstate a new form of regulatory identity that still affirms the sex/gender system. The GlitterWhores, described by Detrixhe, extend this form of resistance in their performance of a fluid "abject" gender identity which is given representation as the "GlitterWhore" identity. This performance disrupts the sex/gender system, dismantles normative femininity, masculinity as well as abiding "nature" of identity itself.

Enacting the Divine

The Body and the Divine

In the depiction of the divine, the representation of the human body is a very powerful way to relate to the viewer. According to Stephen Moore "the more we see a body to be like our own, the more likely we are to feel empathetic, to engage with its suffering."[57] It is evident that when the body of the divine is shown to be similar to our body, according to Moore, we become more deeply and spiritually engaged. What drew me to imagine the divine as the Goddess in my early solitary practice was that I didn't feel like a stranger when I would meditate, pray or do ritual and incorporate the image of the Goddess. However, when I began to question my connection with femaleness, the focus on fertility, vaginal imagery and menstruation in ritual became problematic.

Wendy Griffin affirms "the mythos of God the Father and Creator of everything is a devitalized one which fails to address the experience of women's lives."[58] Many facets of Christianity are addressing this issue, however, Goddess centered Feminist Witches, with whom Griffin engaged at the time, revealed that they could not identify with the patriarchal construction of the divine as something "out there" that must be worshiped, as the sole source of divine power, gendered hegemonically masculine and described as male.[59] Goddess centered Feminist Witches link "what they believe is the divine within them to the divine around them in the natural world. To them, the Goddess is 'the normative image of immanence'".[60] These Witches locate the divine in the material body and the natural world, when they depict the Goddess. In a ritual described by Griffin, one of the coven members performed the Goddess Diana. A woman in her mid 20s, new to this ritual, described her experience.

> Other images of Diana are all sexualized from a male point of view. . . . This was a female who radiated power with her body and costume. Her unselfconsciousness about her body was powerful and the way she walked was almost majestic. . . . *This* was the Diana I want to relate to.[61]

Later, Hypatia, the woman who performed the Goddess Diana, told Griffin that "she neither 'became' nor 'invoked' Diana [. . .] but 'manifested that part' of her that *was* Diana."[62] It is evident that the divine is envisioned as enacted by the body, as the body *is* divine. Clearly, Hypatia could spiritually engage and relate to the Goddess because the divine *was part of* Hypatia. The woman new to the ritual could relate to the femaleness of the enacted divine. This *enactment* of the divine also reveals that the divine "faith" is not something a Witch believes "in" but rather something that a Witch enacts through her body.[63] The "strangeness" Althaus-Reid describes, that is of not being able to relate to the divine, is transgressed here by the construction of the Divine Feminine, to which these women can relate. However, according to Althaus-Reid, though these Dianic Witches reacted against patriarchal, hierarchal religion, they stayed within the sex/gender binaries. By emphasizing femaleness and womanliness through the usage of attributes and characteristics provided by masculinist, heterosexist culture, Dianics also construct the Goddess as heterosexual. Due to pervasive heteronormativity, one assumes the Goddess is heterosexual if her sexuality is not explicitly constructed. Thus, not only are Dianic Witches creating a divine restricted by rigid boundaries, but they are divinely legitimating essentialist ideologies regarding what constitutes a 'real' woman, i.e., vagina, femininity, heterosexual desire.[64] Thus, in perpetuating gender and sex dichotomies as "natural" and divine these Dianic Feminist Witches exclude "others" from the divine realm of representation. This exclusion is made clear in my interview with Sue. She stated "For me personally, it doesn't make sense to imagine divinity as heterosexual, nor as exclusively male or exclusively female (let alone as a hetero couple!) because I'm queer and that kind of imagery doesn't resonate with me." Thus it is probable that practitioners whose identity is other to the construction of the divine do not feel represented by the divine and are thus excluded from that form of representation.

The Reclaiming Witches of the Mud Pie Labyrinth similarly affirm that the divine and "faith" is not something that a Witch believes in but rather is performed or created by the body. In my interview with Mandy she described this as "act as if." When evoking a deity the practitioner would "act as if" they were the deity. In performing the characteristics of the certain deity the deity may actually enter the body of the practitioner. Here Mandy implies the divine as immanent; however, she perceives it as existing outside of the practitioner, not within. Later in her interview she states that the identities of deities are more often than not constructed by the practitioner. Deities thus exist as constructions of the practitioner; performing deities brings these constructions into being. Theologian Don Cupid states that the divine does not exist outside of the people who create it through human activity. He furthers this ideology stating, "We exist in, and only as, the performance we are putting on. We have no being apart from our life."[65] Both Mandy and Cupid suggest that the divine is brought into being through the performance of the body. Reclaiming Witches invoke the divine through human action. Deep relation and spiritual connection to the divine by the practitioner is important in this action. Thus when the practitioners can see themselves in the divine this deep connection becomes more possible. If, as Cupid suggests, the body is only recognizable through performance, then only through the performance of a queer deity, that queer identity become recognizable in the realm of the sacred. Althaus-Reid makes clear that generally there are no queer deities existent in Goddess Centered Feminist Witchcraft. Thus, queer humans have little representation in the domain of the sacred.[66] In Reclaiming Feminist Witchcraft, the construction of the divine is queered in order to provide the opportunity for divine representation to queer-identified practitioners. For example, Detixhe explains that at the beginning of Reclaiming Witch Camp campers get together to cast their first circle to honor the energies of the land as well as ancestors from various cultures. According to Detixhe, the "working characters of the particular myth or theme for the week are also called into the ritual circle as well as the [. . .] Queer ones (those spirits and deities which bend gender and are allies to queer humans who bend gender in this realm)."[67] Here it is evident that "abject" identities as described by Butler, such as the Glitter Whores, are given divine representation also extending divine "nameability."[68]

In her article "Queer Theory and Theology" Althaus-Reid outlines radical feminist scholar Sheila Jeffreys' viable concern that when discourse is transformed from feminist to queer, the focus on woman as a group is decentered, criticized and dismantled. Jeffreys affirms that this results in the dissipation of politics and spirituality that venerate women as a group. When the Goddess, who legitimates women as a group who are othered by traditional patriarchal construction of the divine, is eliminated in the application of a queer paradigm, "women" are no longer able to relate to the divine and thus are no longer represented in the realm of the sacred. Athaus-Reid responds stating "We do not wish to dismiss Jeffreys' concerns or to assume that there is a simple solution when theologians are dealing with these issues [...but] in incorporating queer theory into our theology we hope to expand the area of issues that come under scrutiny and not actually reduce them."[69] Jeffreys' concern and Althaus-Reid's reply is addressed in the Reclaiming ritual described above.

In her introduction to the twentieth anniversary edition of *The Spiral Dance* Starhawk states "[t]oday I don't use the terms *female energy* and *male energy*, I don't identify *femaleness* or *maleness* with specific sets of qualities or predispositions."[70] Later in this introduction she questions the "naturalness" of the two sexed binary and opts for a more fluid understanding of "sex" and "gender." Starhawk revealed the movement from the exclusivity of the Goddess to a more open interpretation of the divine in Feminist Reclaiming Witchcraft. In this ritual the Goddess is evoked and enacted by Feminist Witches *as well as* the Queer Ones, in an attempt to expand the representation of the divine. In their interviews Sue and Mandy both affirmed that it is the *experience* of invoking the divine that makes the divine real. The inclusion of a number of different deities with different identities would allow different human beings to deeply and directly experience the divine. When a myriad of bodies and identities may be enacted when addressing the divine, rather than constructing the divine into one restrictive category, women as well as queer-identified people may still find divine representation.

Enacting the Inner Self: Witches and the "Soul"

In his book *Discipline and Punish*, Foucault discusses the nature of the soul. He writes "It would be wrong to say that the soul is an illusion, or an ideological effect. On the contrary, it exists, it has a reality, it is produced permanently around, on, within, the body."[71] According to this ideology, part of the soul can be described as the inner self, something natural, innate, divine and continuous. The affirmation of this divine inner self is held by Dianic Feminist, Radical Faerie and Reclaiming Witches. According to Wendy Griffin, Dianic Witches, in their spiritual practice, focus upon "topics that are believed to empower women, such as meditation and visualization techniques or discovering the 'Goddess within'".[72] In a Dianic ritual celebrating menstruation, many of the coven members were given red ribbons with special herbs attached, if they were on their "Moon Time." Hypatia, the woman described formerly in this paper who performed Diana, *became* a different face of Diana in this ritual. "Hypatia manifested the strong, independent Maiden that the Witches argue may be found in all women, a natural part of the female self that has been denied and suppressed."[73] The ideology of the "Goddess within" is illustrated here. As a sign, the Goddess represents a new set of criterion, introduced by these Feminist Witches, which is incorporated into the dominant construction of "woman." This new criterion, (strength, independence and power), is viewed by the Witches to have always been a part of the dominant "woman" identity, (nurturance, passivity, emotionality), but was suppressed by patriarchy. When the Goddess is invoked it is these suppressed, "innate" characteristics that are invoked. This belief that "all women" have these innate characteristics is clearly an essentialist ideology regarding gender identity. In my interview with Sue, she expressed that this form of essentialism is what drove her away from Goddess Centered Feminist Witchcraft. "That focus on having to work with and express my 'womanhood' was precisely what turned me off of Witchcraft in the first place, though it took me awhile to realize why I was always so totally uncomfortable at goddess retreats and the like." Sue's experience of the ideology of the "woman within" is similar to my own. I do not feel comfortable identifying with these characteristics nor believe that all "women" embody them. The essentializing of the "woman within," from my experience, is instrumental in the exclusion of others in this tradition. Thus I would like to explore this critique of essentialism for a moment.

In her article "Methodological Essentialism, False Difference and Other Dangerous Traps," Jane Roland Martin reflects upon the use of the term *essentialist* as a term of condemnation that some feminists direct towards each other. In an interview published in an issue of *differences,* Gayatri Chakravorty Spivak said "What I am very suspicious of is how anti-essentialism, really more than essentialism, is allowing women to call names and to congratulate ourselves."[74] Thus, according to Spivak, the accusation of essentialism stunts feminists' intellectual inquiry and creates a regimen of self-denial in the attempt to steer clear of "traps of essentialism."[75] Martin argues that we fall into the anti-essentialism trap which inevitably "rejects one kind of essence talk by adopting another."[76] Here Martin is stating that by critiquing others' standpoints as essentialist one may become trapped in this constant state of essentialist critique. Martin's argument is addressed by Foucault in his analysis of resistance in which he affirms that when limits are placed on resistance, these limits are derived from the very limits of power that the resistance is attempting to overcome. Applying a queer frame of analysis, which utilizes essentialist critique, attempts to fluidly expand categories, rather than produce new rigid ones. Foucault makes evident that the domains of representation allow subjects to become visible within culture. However, these domains of representation also produces criterion by which subjects themselves are formed. Thus, these realms of representation must be malleable and changeable so that individuals have the freedom to invent new forms of identity, and thus serve to potentially give individuals visibility rather than regulate their bodies.

The ideology of the "Goddess within," though it allows woman subjects to enact power and independence, it produces criterion and purports that all women and practitioners embody this inner self. It is possible that this ideology produces these subjects it is supposed to liberate as it sets out criterion in advance by which subjects must abide in order to be visible within that domain of representation. This ideology excludes others who do not identify with this inner self or who cannot fulfill its requirements.

Faerie and Reclaiming Witchcraft hold the belief that there exists a "Divine within, the ultimate, original essence" in each practitioner.[77] According to Starhawk, the Reclaiming tradition adopted this ideology from the Faerie, and thus the ideology itself is synonymous in both traditions. Contrary to the "Goddess within," the Divine self is constantly changing and can take on many forms and thus the divine self is constructed according to identification of the practitioner. To illustrate this I will examine the Radical Faerie ideology regarding the divine self.

The "Gay Soul" articulated in Queer theology emphasizes the similarity and shared experience of lesbians and gay identified individuals. The ideology of a "Gay Soul" poses that lesbian and gay people have *separate* spiritual identities from identified heterosexual people. According to Bardella "only through the realization and appreciation of the unique attributes of an essentialist spirit can gay identified individuals realize their full human potential."[78] These gay identified individuals not only use this ideology as social and spiritual re-empowerment, but also link it to the past, identifying an innate connection to gender-bending deities and shamans. Lesbian and gay identified individuals thus resist religious patriarchal damnation and legitimate their 'otherness' by identifying their identity as something special that accentuates the gifts of healing, empathy, enabling and interpretation.[79] This ideology of the gay soul is articulated in Radical Faerie Witchcraft through the belief of the "fae spirit." According to Hennen, the "fae spirit" indicates the presence of an abiding, ontological and identifiable 'essence' that possibly reveals itself in day to day activities.[80] In Hennen's ethnography of a Radical Faerie Community, he interviewed group member Calliope regarding the "fae spirit." Calliope states "Many of my friends have said, 'Well you are a Radical Faerie, you always have been, you just don't realize to what degree what you are.'"[81] In this context the Faerie identity is presented as fixed and abiding. The Radical Faeries also affirm that this "spirit" is historical and can be linked to spiritual individuals who had alternative identities and sexual orientations. Paradoxically, the enthusiastic performance and embrace of fragmentation and fluidity of identity, which will be elaborated on later, exists alongside this strong emphasis on a fixed Faerie identity. The emergence of this fixed identity, which has now been coupled with a fluid one, emerged from the ideologies of Harry Hay, the founder of the first Radical Faeries, he stated "I propose that we gay folk, who Great Mother Nature has been assembling as a separate people in these last hundred thousand years, must now prepare to emerge from the shadows of history."[82] Thus, similar to Dianic Feminist Witches, the emphasis on the "fae spirit" is birthed from oppression and a resistance movement to transgress and dismantle that oppression. However, this type of resistance, replaces one set of restrictive characterizes with another. The creation of this fixed "soul" does not align with the ideologies within Queer Spiritual Discourse which encourages fluidity.

However, Dianic Feminist Witches and the Radical Faeries' ideology regarding the soul and how the soul is signified are paradoxical. In both traditions the divine is manifested through human action. In the Dianic tradition the "Goddess within" is manifested through enacting power, strength and assertion.[83] In Radical Faerie Witchcraft the "fae spirit" is said to be recognizable when one performs day to day activities.[84] According to Judith Butler "[t]he figure of the interior soul understood as 'within' the body is signified through its inscription *on* the body."[85] The signification of the soul is enacted by the body and thus inscribes itself on the body displacing the dichotomy of the inner/outer divine spirit. Thus the "Goddess within" or the "fae spirit" is neither continuous nor inherent as it only signifies when one enacts the idea. Thus, the essentialist belief of a fixed innate Goddess or Faerie identity is dismantled by the very performative signification of that identity.

The construction of an abiding inner self by both Dianic Feminist Witches and Radical Faerie Witchcraft is both essentialist and performative. However the Dianics' construction of the "Goddess within" prescribes to a set of criterion by which this sign is performed, such as power, strength and assertion, while the performance of the "fae spirit" has somewhat more ambiguous criterion. In comparing the subversive potential of both constructions of the inner self which are constructed in resistance to dominant oppressive ideologies, the Dianic Feminist Witches create the "Goddess within" that contests dominant ideologies of "woman." This form of essentialism pervades all of the Dianic Witches symbols and myths reaffirming dominant sex/gender binaries. However, the Radical Faeries essentialist conception of the "fae spirit" is built on underlying concepts of fluid, ever-changing identity formation and gender-bending, which promotes rule breaking and change. In my interview with Sue she explained that "the notion that we are ever in flux and ever evolving" is a large belief in her practice as a witch, as it aligns with her queer identity. An important difference between the "Goddess within" and the "fae spirit" is that the former insists upon continuity of the self and the latter promotes fluidity and discontinuity as well as continuity of the self. In the Radical Faerie conception of the spirit it is possible for some practitioners to enact the fae spirit in one way or a multitude of ways, thus leaving an opening for interpretation.[86]

The Subversive Potential of the "Abject" and the Divine Space of Representation

Magical Words and Names

Language is a medium of socialization. In turn, words also shape us, giving us names and words to speak about our experiences lending us visibility and representation.[87] Thus, the use of words and names within Witchcraft is given great consideration and is perceived as a site of resistance and rearticulation. According to Luce Irigaray, patriarchal language is restrictive, and linearly structured, which produces, limits and semantically derogates "women." She proposes an engagement with linguistic play in which words are spoken with a multiplicity of meanings until language is somewhat "untranslatable." This approach radically interrogates "'meaning,' which comprises opening discourse to the sense of 'non-sense,' reshaping syntax to suspend its teleological patterns, embracing fragmentation and risking 'incoherence' in order to loosen the resistance of language to the 'female.'"[88] This pluralistic approach was undertaken by some Dianic Feminist Witches in their attempt to resist the semantic derogation of "women" as well as to reaffirm their connectedness. In Naomi R. Goldenberg's article "Witches and Words" she describes this usage of language.

> Why Witches? Because Witches sing. Can I hear this singing? It is the sound of another voice. They tried to make us believe that women did not know how to speak or write; that they were stutterers or mutes. That is because they tried to make women speak straightforwardly, logically, geometrically, in strict conformity. In reality, they croon lullabies, they howl, they gasp, they babble, they shout, they sigh. They are silent and even their silence can be heard.[89]

When I first became interested in Feminist Witchcraft, I found a loosely structured Dianic coven located in Toronto via the internet and requested to attend a gathering. They openly invited me to join them. We met in a basement apartment of one of the members and began to call the corners and cast a circle. After the circle was cast, Goddesses were invoked of whom Kali Ma was the first, one woman began humming. She was joined by another woman who started to create a low beat with her voice, and another who began a soothing sort of yelping. Finally, I gathered the courage and started to hum a song while another woman began a loud clapping and stomping of her feet. The evocation of the Goddess diverged into the multivocal gibberish "song" that we all began to sing. After leaving the apartment I felt renewed and transformed. The fluid structure of this space allowed for a divergence from the "aim" of invoking the Goddesses into this creative, multifaceted song in which new words were created and said at once, producing an incoherent spout of what Naomi Goldenberg terms "witchy words."[90] Using Goldenberg's theoretical template I suggest that Irigaray's use of language could be said to be a use of "witchy words." Through this use of "witchy words," Irigaray affirms that women resist the names and categories in which sexist language places them. In Irigaray's article, "When Our Lips Speak Together" she states that this type of language is distinctly "female." Goldenberg explains this kind of language is not logical, linear or coherent, but emotional, fluid and material.[91] The femaleness of the alternative words used in this ritual was also emphasized by the Dianic coven as they repeatedly affirmed that it was "women" and "females" that were evoking the Goddesses. Although this linguistic play dismantled rigid language structure and allowed for an alternative way of speaking, essentializing femaleness is restrictive and exclusive. The assertion of the "femaleness" of these fluid words as well as emphasis on the emotional and the material reaffirms essentialist, patriarchal notions of what constitutes "woman" and "female" and reinstates the sex/gender system.

In his article "Fae Spirits and Gender Trouble: Resistance and Compliance Among Radical Faeries", Peter Hennen explains that most Faeries take a second name and use it when interacting with other Faeries. Witches often take on magical names, often changing them three or four times and may use them all at once. In Detrixhe's study of Witches at the Mud Pie Labyrinth Witch Camp, the importance of naming held by the Witches was made evident through an interview with Willie/Daniel. Attending Witch Camp, Willie/Daniel was often confused by the myriad of mundane and magical names that people used, which constantly changed. However he stated, "After I started studying Feri and learned the importance of naming in our tradition, since then the practice of shifting identity slightly has become a subtle act of magic for me."[92] It is evident that names have the power to invoke and shape identity. When a subject is given a name, they are also given representation and words to refer to personhood. A person's name may propose that they continuously identify with that name, that there is a continuity of personhood. In my interview with Sue she pointed out that the Witchcraft she practices facilitates the ever evolving and changing aspects of identity, however, she hasn't come across any names that have stood out to her. The Faerie practice of fluid ever-changing naming allows for the expression of other identities by a practitioner.[93] This approach emphasizes that identity is in constant flux and thus is something that is built through relations with others and through experience, rather that something that is continuous, inherent or abiding. This practice of naming extends representation to other identities that may not have had visibility otherwise. It also undermines the use of names to strictly regulate the body and place it into a restrictive category by allowing for visibility of a multitude of shifting unstructured names and identities.[94]

Although Goddess Centered Feminist Witchcraft reshapes and resignifies monolithic language through "witchy words" through ritual in the proliferation of babbling, and incoherent language, the distinct "femaleness," that is attributed to these "witchy words," reinstates masculinist ideologies reapplying restrictions and perpetuating the hegemony of the sex/gender system. The Faerie Witches also attempt to resignify the use of language and naming in their tradition through facilitating the fluidity of identities undermining and revealing the regulatory mechanisms of pervading essentialist ideologies regarding sex and gender.

Ritual Magick and the Representation of the "Abject"

In her book *Powers of Horror: An Essay on Abjection*, Julia Kristeva explains that abjection "disturbs identity, system, order. What does not respect borders, positions, rules. The in-between, the ambiguous, the composite."[95] In Witchcraft, engaging with "the abject," or what is considered to be the "profane," occurs in proliferation. Not only does this engagement, largely through ritual magic, blur the boundary between dichotomized notions of the sacred and the profane, but also challenges dominant ideologies and taboos regarding gender and sexuality. According to Vikki Godwin "Abject behaviors include 'abominations' such as sexual immorality and perversions; corporeal alteration, decay, and death; human sacrifice; murder; the corpse; bodily wastes; the feminine body; and incest."[96] In Goddess Centered Feminist Witchcraft, the abject, which in this case is the "female body" and menstrual blood, is *celebrated as divine* through ritual magic. For example, in a Womancircle ritual, Dianic Witches invoked the Goddess Diana, who was performed by Hypatia. Later in the ritual, Diana asked the circle if anyone was on her "Moon Time." According to Griffin "On these women who were [menstruating], she pinned a spring of herbs tied with a red ribbon."[97] According to Victor Turner, symbolic objects used in ritual shape meanings for particular people, these meanings, may shift the conscious of the practitioner creating a new understanding of the world around them.[98] This "shift in consciousness," is characterized by personal agency called "the Will," that is an individual's agency to change consciousness also called "magic" by many Witches.[99] This ritual is used to divinely legitimate the "female body" and the power of menstrual blood, shown through the tying of the red ribbon on each menstruating woman. One woman described her experience of this ritual stating, "Moon Time! What a beautiful concept! If you were menstruating you were special. You had this incredible gift that your body has given to you, something to be proud of! And we got to wear red ribbons so that everyone else would be proud of you too!"[100]

According to Elaine Willis in her essay "Nothing is Sacred, All is Profane: Lesbian Identity and Religious Purpose," the female body and female sexuality are profane notions in patriarchal religious traditions, she specifically spoke about the dominant traditional Abrahamic traditions and dominant culture.[101] It is evident that the ritual performed in the Dianic Coven transformed ideologies regarding the "female body" and menstruation, divinely shifting them from the "abject"/profane to the sacred. This symbolic shift magically materialized in a shift of consciousness in the meanings given to the body and "abject" fluids illustrated by the excited practitioner. The Goddess centeredness of this space allowed for the creation of this ritual and the divinity given to the "abject." Thus, through this ritual it is evident that resistance is magically enacted against ideologies placing the "female body," "female sexuality" and menstrual blood into the realm of the profane, through celebrating their divinity and worshiping potential fertility. However, it is evident that though the boundary between the sacred and the profane is blurred and recontextualized, not only is "femaleness" essentialized but heterosexuality is also ritually institutionalized.[102]

In some forms of Reclaiming Witchcraft, "dangerous sex" is ritualized and understood as magic. Allison Jasper, describes "dangerous sex" as "sexual acts akin to modern SM and BDSM or to generate and enjoy sexual energies beyond conventional heterosexual coupledom [. . . which has potential] to subvert disembodied orthodoxies and conservative theologies."[103] This type of "dangerous sex" has a special sacred space in the Mud Pie Labyrinth Witch Camp. The Sacred Sexuality Temple, located on camp grounds, is described as a space set aside in order to "transform a cabin into a center of beauty and delight dedicated to the pleasures of the body/mind/spirit. This will be sex-permissive space, meaning that at any time you may find any number of people (from one to . . . oh, use your imagination!) enjoying the pleasures of sexual touch and contact."[104] Witches who support the space will bring materials such as oils, and materials for safe sex to keep the space going.

In her second edition of the *Spiral Dance*, Starhawk affirmed that "erotic energy" is heterosexual, homosexual, bisexual, or even asexual, which celebrates diversity.[105] At Witch Camp what is considered profane or abject, that is bodily fluids and the sexual body, is shifted into the realm of the sacred. This performance of "dangerous sex" transgresses heteronormative ideologies regarding sex prevalent in current culture. "Erotic energies" described by Starhawk are produced within this sacred space and incorporate alternative views of sexuality traditionally viewed as purely for reproductive purposes. Without this focus on fertility, "alternative sexualities" may also be given sacred representation within this ritual space. According to Mary Jo Neitz, author of "Queering the Dragonfest: Changing Sexualities in Post Patriarchal Religion," for queer theorists, an alternative or resistance to heteronormative sexuality is not gay and lesbian "sex" but rather "a fluid and shifting performance of sexual practices, where the enactment of a particular sexual practice does not lock one into a particular sex/gender identity."[106] The anti-structure of the Sacred Sexuality Temple at Witch Camp facilitates alternative, fluid sexualities, not only resignifing the phallocentric concept of "sex," bringing the "abject" into the realm of the sacred, but also transgressing, in the Foucaultian sense, the sex/gender system and rigid heteronormative sexuality, creating a magical shift in consciousness.

According to Judith Butler "oppression works through the production of a domain of unthinkability and unameability."[107] Bodies that enter this realm of unthinkability she calls unsubjects. Butler affirms that the practice of drag or "camp" reveals the performative nature of gender itself. If a male identified person can "pass" when in feminine drag, this could possibly reveal that gender and one's sex category is constructed through social interaction revealing 'sex' and "gender" as ideology. However, when one one's "passibility" is questionable, placing the body into the realm of the unsubject, this disturbs the normative dualist realms of identity as this body cannot fit into either. This troubling and undoing of gender is ritually and divinely legitimated in the Radical Faerie performance of drag. Peter Hennen describes a drag show held at the Faerie sanctuary titled "That's a man? Are you sure?"[108] Though this show placed a premium on illusion and parody of gender identity, there were also parts of the show in which the *real* gender identity of the participants was questioned by the ethnographer. When the question is asked what the *real* gender identity and sex category of the practitioner is, and the question cannot be answered, gender is undone.[109] This space of questionability in which a body cannot be placed into the binary, when the body becomes "abject," reveals the rigidity and the falsity of restrictive gender identity. The "abject" is made divine and given representation in this ritualization of drag performance. This act produces a magical "shift in consciousness" in the creation of alternative domains of representation in which non-normative bodies can exist.

Generally, Witchcraft promotes the blurring of boundaries and the resistance of dominant norms. The boundary blurring between the profane and the sacred occurs in the Dianic Witchcraft "Moon Time" ritual. Here the "female body" and menstrual blood are presented as sacred and divine, resisting normative ideologies resulting in a magical "shift of consciousness" of the practitioners. However, in resisting dominant ideologies the Dianic Witches reinstate and perpetuate essentialist norms, heteronormativity and the sex/gender system. This practice of the blurring sacred and profane boundaries is also enacted by the Reclaiming Witches and Radical Faeries through the negation of restrictions and the emphasis on fluidity of identity though the sacred, ritualistic performance of alternative sexualities and gender identities. This resistance produces a "shift in consciousness" regarding the "naturalness" of gender identity, emphasizing magical agency to transform these essentialist ideologies through action. This practice extends sacred representation to fluid identities that may not gain this type of visibility in society more generally.

Conclusion

Domains of representation allow for identities to become legitimated. Thus the analysis of *representation* is an important endeavor for feminists. Representation can extend visibility to a subject but also regulate a subject according to specific criterion excluding others who do not fit into available categories. Resisting mechanisms of power that facilitate the regulation and/or exclusion of the body is enacted by Goddess Centered Feminist Witches, Radical Faeries, as well as Reclaiming Feminist Witches. Goddess Centered Feminist Witches enact resistance through challenging patriarchal constructions of "woman" and celebrating her as the focus of ritual and practice. However, in doing so Goddess Centered Feminist Witches emphasize femaleness and appropriate characteristics of womanhood thus essentializing gender and sex. The very thing that is resisted thus begins to produce its resistors. Radical Faeries and Reclaiming Feminist Witchcraft resist oppressive mechanisms of power through opening up domains of representation and presenting identity as something that is in constant flux.

The Dianic Witches performance of "Crone" resist and resignify the normative construction of the "woman" identity through challenging the notion that women should be soft spoken, the de-sexualizing of older women and the assumption that all women are heterosexual. However, during this ritual the articulation of *"female* power" is emphasized. Though normative notions regarding "woman" as constructed by patriarchy are resignified, the emphasis on the *femaleness* of this resignification, restricts these individuals to the dichotomous gender/sex system, inevitably perpetuating its disciplinary power. During Detrixhe's study of the Reclaiming Witchcraft camp she made clear that there are many subgroups within the camp that employ a camp style to their performance of gender and identity. For instance the GlitterWhores would mix and match costume accessories to come up with a "camp" outfit that was most defiantly queer. Using Butler's theoretical framework regarding drag, it is evident that the GlitterWhores utilizes and extends "camp" to move fluidly from masculine gender display to feminine gender display which parodies the ideology of abiding gender identity and that gender follows continuously from sex.[110] This form of Witchcraft facilitates the articulation and building of non-normative identities and extends representation and visibility. Contrary to the Dianic's construction of "woman" identity as continuous, this form of Reclaiming Witchcraft promotes the changeability of identity.

In order to relate to the divine or deities it is important that they speak to the practitioner's identity and experiences. Dianic Feminist Witches enact the divine as the Goddess as she relates to their experiences as women. This is evident when Hypatia emphasizes that she did not invoke the Goddess but manifested part of her that was the Goddess. In this instance the Goddess is emphasized as female and is identified as a woman. Though this enactment allows for these women to identify with the Goddess it excludes others in identifying with a deity that relates to their identity. As Sue mentioned in her interview she found that

Goddess centered Feminist Witches tolerate queer people but do not *include* them. Some Reclaiming Feminist Witches attempt to address this problem by including deities such as the Queer Ones and the Mysterious Ones. This allows for queer identified people to connect to the divine directly. It also promotes creating deities that relating to individuals changing identities.

As language is a prime socializing agent and medium of constructing ideology its use plays an important role in Feminist Witchcraft. Within Goddess Centered Feminist Witchcraft words are manipulated and resignifyed through play and song in ritual for example when evoking the Goddess. Here words are slurred and broken or are replaced with humming and cackling. However the distinct "femaleness" and "womanliness" of these words are emphasized. That which is illogical, fluid, emotional and material are linguistic characteristics that are thus attributed to women. Thus essentializing and appropriating patriarchal characteristics of womanhood to apply to all women and female identified people. Radical Faerie Witches extend this use of language through naming. In the Faerie tradition practitioners will take on several names all at once which constantly change to reflect one's ever evolving identity undermining essentialist ideologies regarding sex, gender and identity.

To oppressed people society can often seem alienating and difficult to navigate. For this reason spiritual practice is useful in facilitating self exploration and fulfillment offering sacred tools that can help shape positive identity such as the divine and ritual. Though I currently belong to no particular tradition (I would describe my practice as eclectic and variable) I have begun to incorporate elements from Radical Faerie and Reclaiming Witchcraft into my practice. I have found that these two traditions (or movements) have belief systems that speak to my experience. I have found that currently information available to young people about feminist Witchcraft is generally of the Dianic variety and thus it is difficult for someone who is interested in Witchcraft to find information about these two latter queer-inclusive traditions. In a culture that generally is heterosexist and patriarchal, spaces especially sacred spaces that are queer-inclusive and extend representation and celebration to non-normative and changing identities are scarce. Thus, the availability of a queer-inclusive, variable and eclectic Witchcraft to interested practitioners and beginners is important to allow for the opportunity of a transformative space in which variant identities and facilitated and celebrated.

Notes

1. Judith Butler, *Gender Trouble* (New York: Routledge, 1999), 1-9.
2. Butler, *Gender Trouble*, 134-141.
3. Michel Foucault, "About the Beginning of the Hermeneutics of the Self: Two Lectures at Dartmouth" *Political Theory*, vol. 21, no. 2 (1993): 203-207.
4. Butler, *Gender Trouble*, 32-34.
5. Brent Pickett, "Foucault and the Politics of Resistance," *Polity* (1996): 458.

6. Pickett, "Foucault," 445-466.

7. Cynthia Eller, *Myth of Matriarchal Prehistory: Why an Invented Past Won't Give Women a Future* (Boston: Beacon Press, 2002), 1-37

8. Eller, *Myth*, 1-37; Starhawk, *The Spiral Dance*, Second edition (San Francisco: Harper Collins, 1999), 1-17.

9. Peter Hennen, "Fae Spirits and Gender Trouble: Resistance and Compliance Among Radical Faeries," in *Journal of Contemporary Ethnography* 33 (2004): 501.

10. Starhawk, *The Spiral Dance*, 1-25.

11. Hennen, "Fae Spirits," 499-533; Starhawk, *The Spiral Dance*, 1-17; Pam Detrixhe, "Shape-Shifting 'Religions': Witchen Identities as Post()Modern Exemplum" (PhD diss., 2005): 23-37.

12. Foucault, "About the Beginning," 203-217

13. Claudio Bardella, "Queer Spirituality," *Social Compass* (2001): 119, emphasis added.

14. Bardella, "Queer Spirituality," 117-140.

15. Foucault, "About the Beginning," 199-207.

16. Foucault, "About the Beginning," 201-207; Butler, *Gender Trouble*, 32-34.

17. Vikki Godwin, "Feminist Identities and Popular Meditations of Wiccan Rhetoric" (PhD diss., 2004): 17-32.

18. Godwin, "Feminist Identities," 31.

19. Candace West and Don Zimmerman, "Doing Gender" in *Gender and Society,* ed. Michael Kimmel, Amy Aronson, Amy Kaler, (New York: Oxford University Press, 2008), 91-105; Pickett, "Foucault," 445-466.

20. Pickett, "Foucault," 458.

21. Eve Sedgwick, *The Epistemology of the Closet* (California: University of California Press, 1990), 1-23; Butler, *Gender Trouble*, 32-34; The "sex/gender system," a term coined by cultural anthropologist, Gayle Rubin, describes a set of pervading arrangements through which culture institutionalizes and transforms biological "sex" into how humans are expected to act in day to day life. Thus, for example, a self-identified female, is expected to act feminine and identify as a woman as well as "do" women's work. Assumed heterosexuality also underlies the whole structure of the system.

22. Godwin, "Feminist Identities," 19.

23. Godwin, "Feminist Identities," 17-31.

24. West and Zimmerman, "Doing Gender," 91-94; Godwin, "Feminist Identities," 28-31.

25. Susan Faludi, *Backlash: The Undeclared War Against American Women.* (New York: Doubleday, 1991), 15-21; Godwin, "Feminist Identities," 31.

26. Margot Adler, *Drawing Down the Moon,* (Boston: Beacon Press, 1986), 183.

27. Susan Bordo, "The body and the Reproduction of Femininity" in *Unbearable Weight: Feminism, Western Culture, and the Body*, (California: University of California Press, 1995), 165-184; Butler, *Gender Trouble*, 32-141.

28. Butler, *Gender Trouble*, 32, 134-141

29. According to Butler "intelligible" bodies are those that are recognizable within particular normative domains of representation, a body that *can be* represented. When one's gender is intelligible this means that there is a continuity of gender identity, sex categorization and sexuality. For example, a body that is feminine, female and heterosexual. Butler, *Gender Trouble*, 32-34, 134-141; West and Zimmerman, "Doing Gender," 95; Foucault, "About the Beginning," 201-219.

30. Detrixhe, "Shape-Shifting 'Religions,'" 75.

31. Detrixhe, "Shape-Shifting 'Religions,'" 73-76.

32. Bardella, "Queer Spirituality," 1-7.

33. Butler, *Gender Trouble*, 13-34, 134-141; Sarah Trimble, "Playing Peter Pan: Conceptualizing 'Bois' in Contemporary Queer Theory" in *Lesbian, Bisexual, Queer, Transsexual/Transgender Sexualities* eds. Burstow and Millward, (2005): 75-80; West and Zimmerman, "Doing Gender," 91-94.

34. Detrixhe, "Shape-Shifting 'Religions,'" 87-88.

35. Bordo, "The body," 180.

36. Detrixhe, "Shape-Shifting 'Religions,'" 76.

37. The term counterhegemonic in this context refers to an alternative interpretation of current social, political or spiritual order. This term refers to a refusal of universal categories and monolithic ways of thinking. Hennen, "Fae Spirits,": 499-533.

38. Bardella, "Queer Spirituality," 4, emphasis added.

39. Pickett, "Foucault," 450.

40. Nancy Finley, "Political Activism and Feminist Spirituality" in *Sociological Analysis* 52 (1991): 350.

41. Foucault, "About the Beginning," 203-217.

42. Wendy Griffin "The Embodied Goddess: Feminist Witchcraft and Female Divinity" *Sociology of Religion* 56 (1995): 38.

43. Griffin, "The Embodied Goddess," 35-48.

44. Griffin, "The Embodied Goddess," 45.

45. Pickett, "Foucault," 445-466.

46. The term "heteropatriarchal" emphasizes naturalized, normative heterosexuality as the main pillar of patriarchal structures. Using this term affirms heterosexuality as ideology, rather than natural or innate.

47. Karina Eileraas, "Witches, Bitches & Fluids: Girl Bands Performing Ugliness as Resistance", *TDR.* (1997): 125.

48. Griffin, "The Embodied Goddess," 45.

49. Griffin, "The Embodied Goddess," 35-48.

50. Bordo, "The body," 179-181; Butler, *Gender Trouble*, 134-141.

51. Detrixhe, "Shape-Shifting 'Religions,'" 98.

52. Detrixhe, "Shape-Shifting 'Religions,'" 100.

53. Butler, *Gender Trouble*, 138.

54. Alison Webster, "Queer to be Religious: Lesbian Adventures beyond the Christian/Post-Christian Dichotomy," *Theology and Sexuality,* (1998): 29.

55. West and Zimmerman, "Doing Gender," 97-105; Butler, *Gender Trouble*, 32, 134-144.

56. Although the GlitterWhores have a structured identity that has a set of rules that one must follow in order to be recognized as such, opportunity to break these rules to create new ones or revise old ones seems to be the norm. Detrixhe, "Shape-Shifting 'Religions,'" 100.

57. Kristy Coleman, "Who's Afraid of 'the Goddess Stuff?'" *Feminist Theology* (2005): 217-230.

58. Griffin, "The Embodied Goddess," 39.

59. Many feminists within the Judeo-Christian tradition have been involved with radical and reform feminist politics beginning in the 1960s and 1970s. Challenging the patriarchal ethos within the Christian tradition, many women have brought about change within their tradition amounting to more gender inclusive language symbolism and ritual. Women such as Rosemary Radford Ruether and Elisabeth Schussler Fiorenza, for example are two prominent women who have challenged patriarchy within their religious tradition which has brought about much change. Finley, "Political," 350; Rosemary Radford

Ruether, "The Normalization of the Goddess Religion," *Feminist Theology* (2004): 151-157.

60. Griffin, "The Embodied Goddess," 40.

61. Griffin, "The Embodied Goddess," 41.

62. Griffin, "The Embodied Goddess," 42.

63. Detrixhe, "Shape-Shifting 'Religions,'" 87-92; Richard Grigg, "Enacting the Divine: Feminist Theology and the Being of God," *The Journal of Religion* 74 (1994): 506-523.

64. Marcella Althaus-Reid, "From Goddess to Queer Theology: The State we are in now," *Feminist Theology* (2007): 265-272.

65. Quoted in Webster, "Queer to be Religious," 36.

66. Althaus-Reid, "From Goddess to Queer Theology."

67. Detrixhe, "Shape-Shifting 'Religions,'" 88.

68. Webster, "Queer to be Religious," 29.

69. Marcella Althaus-Reid, "Thinking Theology and Queer Theory," *Feminist Theology*, vol. 15 (2007): 310.

70. Starhawk, *The Spiral Dance*, 20.

71. Quoted in Butler, *Gender Trouble*, 135

72. Griffin, "The Embodied Goddess," 38.

73. Griffin, "The Embodied Goddess," 43.

74. Quoted in Jane Roland Martin "Mythological Essentialism, False Difference and Other Dangerous Traps," *Signs, (*1994): 630.

75. Martin, "Mythological Essentialism," *Signs*: 630.

76. Martin, "Mythological Essentialism," 631.

77. Starhawk, *The Spiral Dance*, 45.

78. Bardella, "Queer Spirituality," 127.

79. Bardella, "Queer Spirituality," 127-128

80. Hennen, "Fae Spirits," 506-519.

81. Hennen, "Fae Spirits," 508.

82. Hennen, "Fae Spirits," 511.

83. Griffin, "The Embodied Goddess," 45.

84. Hennen, "Fae Spirits," 507-513.

85. Butler, *Gender Trouble*, 135.

86. Hennen, "Fae Spirits," 511-530.

87. Claire Renzetti and Daniel Curran, *Women, Men and Society*, 138-144; Webster, "Queer to be Religious."

88. Luce Irigaray, "When Our Lips Speak Together," *Women in Culture and Society*, trans. Carolyn Burke, (1980): 70.

89. Naomi Goldenberg, "Witches and Words," *Feminist Theology*, (2004) : 204-214.

90. Goldenberg defines "witchy words" as a template of discourse that encourages the continuous deconstruction of language and semantic meanings. As Witchcraft is a counter religious spirituality, it encourages the challenging of dominant patriarchal metanarriatives. She describes the words Witches speak as ones that incorporate continuous deconstruction of language which challenges language used in patriarchal religious dogma and ritual. Goldenberg, "Witches and Words," 204-206.

91. Irigaray, "When Our Lips Speak Together," 70-73; Goldenberg, "Witches and Words," 204-214.

92. Detrixhe, "Shape-Shifting 'Religions,'" 79-92.

93. Hennen, "Fae Spirits," 511-530.

94. Butler, *Gender Trouble*, 13; Pickett, "Foucault," 450.

95. Julia Kristeva, "Approaching Abjection and Semiotics of Biblical Abomination," in *French Feminists of Religion,* eds. Joy, M., O'Grady, K., Poxon, J., (New York: Routledge, 2002), 93-105.

96. Godwin, "Feminist Identities," 5.

97. Griffin, "The Embodied Goddess," 42.

98. John Bowen, "Social Theory and the Anthropology of Religion," in *Religions in Practice: An approach to the Anthropology of Religion,* (2005), 10-23. Marilyn Ferguson describes a process of change called a "paradigm shift." This shift occurs when things are viewed one way, then as new knowledges are introduced, this view changes in reaction to this new information. A paradigm is a set of ideas about something. In this context, there is a shift from the gender paradigm, that relies on the dichotomy of the sex/gender system, used by Goddess centered Feminist Witches to a queer paradigm, which challenges the sex/gender system and restrictive identity categories, employed by Reclaiming Witches and Radical Faeries. Marilyn Ferguson, *The Aquarian Conspiracy* (Penguin Putnam, Inc., 1980), 16-34.

99. Godwin, "Feminist Identities," 4-31.

100. Griffin, "The Embodied Goddess," 42.

101. Elaine Willis, "Nothing is Sacred, All is Profane: Lesbian Identity and Religious Purpose," in *Sex and God,* ed. Linda Hurcombe, (New York: Routledge, 1987), 104-125.

102. Susan Sered, "Ideology, Autonomy, and Sisterhood: An Analysis of the Secular Consequences of Women's Religions," *Gender and Society* (1994): 486-506.

103. Alison Jasper "Dangerous Sex," *Theology and Sexuality* (2005): 10.

104. Detrixhe, "Shape-Shifting 'Religions,'" 72.

105. Starhawk, *The Spiral Dance,* 1-25, 214-263.

106. Mary Jo Neitz, "Queering the Dragonfest: Changing Sexualities in Post-Patriarchal Religion," *Sociology of Religion,* (2000): 389.

107. Quoted in Webster, "Queer to be Religious," 29.

108. Hennen, "Fae Spirits," 516-533.

109. West and Zimmerman, "Doing Gender," 97-105.

110. Judith Butler affirms that the practice of drag reveals the imitational and performative nature of gender for which there is no "real." Drag reveals gender as created by a series of repeated acts which create a stylized body. These acts are taken from a set of disciplinary criterion that, for example, is used to create a feminine and therefore female identified body. According to Butler, drag performance also transgresses the gender/sex system in that sex categorization does not follow from gender display. Butler, *Gender Trouble,* 134-141; West and Zimmerman, "Doing Gender," 97-105.

Bibliography

Althaus-Reid, Marcella, "Thinking Theology and Queer Theory." *Feminist Theology.* Vol. 15 (2007): 302-314.

————, "From Goddess to Queer Theology: The State we are in now." *Feminist Theology* (2005): 265-272.

Bardella, Claudio, "Queer Spirituality." *Social Compass* (2001): 117-140.

Bordo, Susan. "The body and the Reproduction of Femininity." In *Unbearable Weight: Feminism, Western Culture, and the Body*. California: University of California Press, 1995: 165-184.

Bowen, John. "Social Theory and the Anthropology of Religion." *Religions in Practice: An approach to the Anthropology of Religion*, (2005): 10-23.

Butler, Judith, *Gender Trouble*. New York: Routledge, 1999.

Coleman, Kristy. "Who's Afraid of 'the Goddess Stuff?'" *Feminist Theology* (2005): 217-230.

Detrixhe, Pam. "Shape-Shifting 'Religions': Witchen Identities as Post()Modern Exemplum" (PhD diss., Temple University, 2005): 1-260.

Eller, Cynthia. *Myth of Matriarchal Prehistory: Why an Invented Past Won't Give Women a Future*. Boston: Beacon Press, 2002.

Eileraas, K. "Witches, Bitches & Fluids: Girl Bands Performing Ugliness as Resistance." *TDR* (1997): 122-139.

Faludi, Susan. *Backlash: The Undeclared War Against American Women*. Doubleday, 1991.

Ferguson, Marilyn. *The Aquarian Conspiracy*. Penguin Putnam, Inc., 1980.

Finley, Nancy. "Political Activism and Feminist Spirituality." *Sociological Analysis*. 52 (1991): 349-362.

Foucault, Michel, "About the Beginning of the Hermeneutics of the Self: Two Lectures at Dartmouth." *Political Theory*. Vol. 21, no. 2 (1993): 198-227.

Godwin, Vikki. "Feminist Identities and Popular Meditations of Wiccan Rhetoric" (PhD diss., Indiana University, 2004).

Goldenberg, Naomi. "Witches and Words." *Feminist Theology* (2004): 204-214.

Griffin, Wendy. "The Embodied Goddess: Feminist Witchcraft and Female Divinity." *Sociology of Religion*. 56 (1995): 35-48.

Grigg, Richard. "Enacting the Divine: Feminist Theology and the Being of God." *The Journal of Religion*. 74 (1994): 506-523.

Hennen, Peter. "Fae Spirits and Gender Trouble: Resistance and Compliance Among Radical Faeries." *Journal of Contemporary Ethnography*. 33 (2004): 499-533.

Irigaray, Luce. "When Our Lips Speak Together." trans Burke, Carolyn. *Signs*. Vol. 6, no. 1 (1980): 69-79.

Jasper, Alison. "Dangerous Sex." *Theology and Sexuality* (2005): 7-10.

Kristeva, Julia. "Approaching Abjection and Semiotics of Biblical Abomination." In *French Feminists on Religion*. Ed., Morny Joy. New York: Routledge, 2002.

Neitz, Mary Jo. "Queering the Dragonfest: Changing Sexualities in Post-Patriarchal Religion." *Sociology of Religion* (2000): 369-391.

Pickett, Brent. "Foucault and the Politics of Resistance." *Polity* (1996): 445-466.

Radford Ruether, Rosemary. "The Normalization of the Goddess Religion." *Feminist Theology* (2004): 151-157.

Renzetti, Claire and Daniel Curran. *Women, Men and Society*. Person Education, Inc, 2003.

Sedgwick, Eve. *The Epistemology of the Closet*. California: University of California Press, 1990.

Sered, Susan. "Ideology, Autonomy, and Sisterhood: An Analysis of the Secular Consequences of Women's Religions." *Gender and Society* (1994): 486-506.

Starhawk. *The Spiral Dance*. Second edition. San Francisco: Harper Collins, 1999.

Webster, Alison. "Queer to be Religious: Lesbian Adventures beyond the Christian/Post-Christian Dichotomy." *Theology and Sexuality* (1998): 27-41.

Willis, Elaine. "Nothing is Sacred, All is Profane: Lesbian Identity and Religious Purpose." In *Sex and God.* Ed., Linda Hurcombe. New York: Routledge, 1987. 104-124.

Chapter Three:
Bound in the Spiral Dance: Spirituality and Technology in the Third Wave

Anna Mercedes and Jennifer Thweatt-Bates

Two women at thirty and thirty-one, we are the daughters of the second-wave generation. And yet, our age alone does not make our spirituality indicative of a third-wave feminism; it is possible to be young and yet to identify most strongly with the politics and spiritualities of the vigorous second-wave. Likewise many activists of the second wave are now also participants in a "third wave," and have in their mentoring and written work described for us the contours of the feminism that we now carry. It was the feminists of the eighties and early nineties who were shifting feminism, while we were still navigating the poignancy of adolescence, both of us then white middle-class girls in North Carolina towns.

One such herald of the third wave is Donna Haraway, who in the late seventies began to complicate feminist discourse from the angle of technology and science. In this article we contemplate the ways in which the technological complexity of contemporary women's lives retextures the claims of previous feminisms regarding the female body and spirituality, particularly in dialogue with Haraway. We will return throughout to the example of childbirth, and particularly to our own recent experiences of labors both natural and technological, as the discourses of feminism, embodiment, spirituality and technology coalesce at this vivid focal point.[1]

In the 1985 "Cyborg Manifesto," Haraway builds on a critique of feminist essentialism, in which the identity of woman *qua* woman is assumed to be self-evident and unchanging, positing that the logic operative in challenging patriarchal and colonial essentializing tendencies in defining self and other leads to the conclusion that *all* claims of identity based on a natural or organic standpoint are suspect. Identifying herself as "cyborg," then, is Haraway's symbolic shorthand for the rejection of any attempt to define identity on the basis of "nature." This basic stance is the key critique of posthuman discourse on human nature, breaking down the dichotomy between nature and culture, or nature and technology. The cyborg is both, or neither, natural and technological, simultaneously.

In this resounding "no" to any essentialism in second-wave feminism, Haraway positions herself as a vanguard of the new generation. She concludes her manifesto with the announcement that she would "rather be a cyborg than a goddess."[2] The choice at first may sound like a decision between incommensurable options. "Goddess" evokes spiritual power superseding isolated embodiment; "cyborg" calls to mind technological function bound to a machine-body, whether R2D2, the Terminator or the sexier possibilities of the new *Battlestar Galactica* Cylons.[3] The cyborg appears precisely to lack the spiritual; its wavelengths are instead electronic. Yet the cyborg is not merely machine; it is a hybrid, a seamless melding of organism and machine whose existence challenges the easy dichotomy of the technological and the natural, the material and spiritual. Thus, simultaneous with her contestation of essentialism, Haraway says "yes" to the second wave's emphasis on the importance of embodiment. The cyborg is not a flight from the body nor does it mark the disappearance of embodiment; rather, the cyborg stands as evidence of the multiple possibilities of embodiment that cross the boundaries of identity politics.

This yes-and-no to the second wave is characteristic of third wave feminism as it continues to wash ashore new forms of difference contesting who and what the female is, and what is the "nature" of her spirit. It remains difficult to speak of a "third wave" in monolithic terms: such is the recognition of plurality inherent in third wave criticism of second wave feminism. At the same time, it is important to try to speak about the third wave, even if we recognize it as diverse and fragmented, partly because in the age of the third wave many of our experiences are rapidly becoming global even as we recognize them as partial and local. Not only negotiating difference among women (black and white, gay and straight, colonizers and colonized), the third wave also negotiates with technology. There is no longer any feminism untouched by technology: so far as women's lived experience is the primary source of feminism, the third wave is populated by technological women. This is not to say that we are "computer-savvy" women, but rather that we are "posthuman" women, with synthetic fibers now rebuilding the bones of Ezekiel's valley.

What exactly is a "posthuman?" Defining the term, while a necessary academic prerequisite, is a contentious undertaking; however, broadly speaking, we can say that the term posthuman has emerged in recent scholarly discourse as a way to describe the new appreciation for the plasticity and flexibility of "human nature" spurred by discoveries in, and new techniques of, biotechnologies and virtual, information and communication technologies. It therefore functions as an umbrella term, covering a span of related concepts: the genetically enhanced person, the artificial person, the downloaded consciousness, the cyborg and the chimera (that is, the mechanically or genetically altered person). It is therefore, in a very real sense, inaccurate to speak casually of "the" posthuman, as if humanity were part of a steady progress to a universally agreed upon and clearly evident particular posthuman end. Rather, plurality is built into the very concept of posthumanity. Posthuman discourse has crystallized around two very different possibilities: Donna Haraway's cyborg, and transhumanist "uploads." These two visions mark a bifurcation of possibility and embody radically differing philosophical and ethical commitments; in this article, we will be using "posthuman" and "cyborg" synonymously, casting our philosophical lot decisively with Donna Haraway, N. Katherine Hayles, Elaine Graham and other cyborg women.

In posthuman discourse, the human body becomes a site of technological possibility, of alteration and enhancement, the natural boundaries increasingly permeated by external devices. That which is bodily is as hard to circumscribe as that which is spiritual. To what extent are these words of ours on this page (or screen) before you our bodies? Does Jen's voice in Anna's mailbox convey her spirit? Are the emails that travel to our parents' "blackberries" extensions of our flesh: physically produced words that then travel through the air, across the miles, connecting the spirits of parent and child? In this generation, feminists may still insist on a spirituality grounded in their bodies, yet meanwhile their bodies are hemmed by more and more invisible, illusive edges, and their spirits are tangibly embodied in multiple technologies.

We are bodies that circle the globe on satellite soundwaves, bodies with plastics from other continents embedded in our tissues, with cycles regulated by moon and chemical. We are bodies permeated by electromagnetic fields and "artificial" preservatives; we are mended with Teflon, clothed in polyester blends. Embracing, we negotiate the jumpdrives stored in our lovers' pockets. We are bodies bearing our young by muscle and by knife, and commending our dead and our machines to the same earth, dust to dust.

Embodied Spirit

In myriad ways second wave feminists stress the embodiment of their spiritual experiences. Women's spirits are woven into their flesh; the body can be a source of spiritual wisdom rather than an impediment to be transcended on the spiritual quest. Especially for women who have long been taught by religious authorities that they embody the profane and not the sacred, the voices of second wave feminism encourage expressions of spirituality seated in goodness of the female body.

One of the legacies of second wave feminism that most strongly reveals the integral experience of spiritual and bodily power is the natural birth movement. Ina May Gaskin's *Spiritual Midwifery* records numerous narratives of women's passage through the labors that brought forth new being. In the throngs of the intense experience of childbirth, the women at the "Farm," Gaskin's Tennessee intentional community, do not distinguish between the spiritual and bodily. "I felt like I'd made love with God and was grateful and humble from the experience," Mona remembers of her Erinna's birth.[4] Of the moment of her son's birth, Shirley Ray writes "I made a noise—thought I'd explode into a thousand billion pieces—and his head was out. The most wonderful moment. Then he slipped out, wet and warm. . . . Extraordinary peace pervaded my whole existence."[5] And Debra gives this advice: "If you decide that you want to keep yourself together and get high on the energy of your kid being born and have that agreement with your man and the midwives, it can easily be the most Holy day of your life."[6]

Our daughters' birth stories provide examples both of our continuity with the embodied feminist spirituality that has preceded us and of our location within a new wave of feminism. Our daughters were born within two months of each other; we experienced our pregnancies together. Both of us were drawn irresistibly to the discourse of natural childbirth, with its insistence on the power and goodness of the female body, its resistance to the relegation of the female body to the position of passive object. Natural childbirth resists modern medical technologies, viewing them as interference with the integrity of the female body's own process of laboring and delivery; the dichotomy of natural versus technological could not be more stark. The goodness and integrity of the female body is set in opposition to a masculinized technology which invades and obstructs, sometimes literally, in unnecessarily frequent pelvic examinations and episiotomies, and sometimes more figuratively, in the insistence upon the primacy of the technologically mediated, neutral, observer-knowledge in the legal mandate of electronic fetal monitoring.[7] And natural childbirth is repeatedly portrayed, not simply as an empowering experience, but a spiritual one.

One of us did indeed experience an ideal "natural" birth. Entering the hospital 15 days post-date, only an amniotomy was needed to nudge her body into active labor. Labor was quiet, almost serene; even transition seemed to encourage the deep dive inward of spiritual meditation. Yet it was no solitary experience; leaning back into supportive arms, lover's, then mother's, the connections between us were more than tactile, but spiritual. The solid satisfaction of a really good push, then the realization that this was it, this was the moment. The moment of birth was a startling epiphany, followed by an inversion of reality: the inward was outward, the squirming daughter felt for months suddenly visible, hefty, there at the breast. Through it all, the most highly technological tool employed was needle and thread—what in medieval times was instead the midwife's one long fingernail, later portrayed as the witches' mark.[8] The female body seemingly unaided was the interface between worlds, between spirits, between bodies, in that unequaled moment of the advent of a new woman into the world.

The entry of our daughters into our lives, however, pushed us to integrate the new textures of embodiment present in this new generation of feminist spirituality. While not negating the truths contained in natural birth discourse and in the second wave's insistence on the power and spirituality of female embodiment, we question the simplicity of this picture of the woman's body, and the "natural" process of childbirth. In the complicated dance of bodies that is childbirth—mother, baby, birth partners—the lines between where one body ends and another begins is blurred; no less so, in many instances, is the line between bodies and technologies.

Haraway introduced the cyborg to feminist discourse to counter the second-wave tendency to "see deepened dualisms of mind and body, animal and machine, idealism and materialism in the social practices, symbolic formulations, and physical artifacts associated with 'high technology' and scientific culture."[9] In defining its relationship to technology, feminism need not reconstruct the dualisms it has long criticized. Yet as our generation of feminists encounters pregnancy, just such a dualism confronts us. The natural birth movement places the natural and the medical in direct opposition to such an extent that even subtle cooperation with medicine spells betrayal: a woman choosing to give birth in a hospital, even without drugs, must lack confidence, must not be at home in her own body, must not trust her own power.[10]

In poignant counterpoint to the ideal "natural" birth experience recounted above, the other of our daughters was born through a process that extended her mother's concept of the natural. At 16 days postdate, no vigorous dance or potent drug could trigger labor. The chemicals in cervical gels used to induce labor mimic those in a male lover's sperm: one is used in medically managed births, the other encouraged by the sages of natural birth. Here both chemicals would fail. In a similar mimicry, could the surgeon's knife then also reproduce the mother's power? As it happened, the surgeon on-call was a she, and a mother of three, with confidence in her step and her steady eyes exuding trust in the intimacy of birth and the power of women's bodies. Spiritual connection, somehow, welled up in the cesarean room, despite all hopes for a different birth outside hospital walls, hopes for a spiritual, sexy process of water and blood and muscle. A dad, a midwife, three doctors, and four nurses, monitors, tubes, plastic, and steel, all incorporated into the body of mother-with-child. The maternal body was expanded through so many IVs, the team of people, the multiple drugs and tools. Yet which of these was not the extension of human muscle or earthly matter? Where does embodiment end? At which point would this birth become unnatural?

In this case the icons of medical and natural birth merged in the persons of the surgeon and midwife, who presided together over open flesh, over a split gut, a cut no longer serving the death-for-life economy of the disemboweled Tiamat.[11] As strong female hands managed this birth, an unexpected sexiness entered in as tingling nipples responded to the movement of hands inside the womb: an internal relationality at once concrete, gory, and life-giving. Their arms joined their strength to the energy of the uterine contractions: a vigorous and messy full-room heave, chasing a baby out into the open, with mom's body shoved way down and rebounding up again. And then, with an angry scream, came the climax of this posthuman birth: "Sylva," named for the trees. Afterwards the surgeon presented a healthy placenta in a plastic tub. A finger pressed curiously into its blood joined this mother to birthing women everywhere, and to the plastic tub, which will outlive us all.

Haraway writes that "the cyborg is a matter of fiction and lived experience that changes what counts as women's experience in the late twentieth century."[12] Both our births count as women's experience; neither are natural or both are natural, depending on one's definition of the "natural." The IVs of the cesarean mom mark her as more obviously cyborg, but the vaginal birth was not devoid of human skill and technical know-how; the technologies differ, in degree if not in kind. The experiences diverge in the specific paths toward the ultimate outcome and the reintegration of the technologically mediated spiritual experience of giving birth. Yet owning both our experiences together, we provide example that as cyborg we do not somehow transcend the vaginal and replace it with the surgical machine. Our technologized, distributed embodiment did not undermine the holiness of our birthing. Counter to the message of the natural birth movement, an elusive "return to nature" was not necessary (indeed not possible) for the thriving of our bodies and spirits.

This is not to depict "medicalized" birth as the wave of the future; to do so would simply be to choose one side of a dualism over another. Rather, our daughters were both born into an impure matrix, confused by many extensions of the natural, a wide spectrum of technologies. Another option would be to imagine one of our births as successfully pure and natural, leaving the other of us consigned to sad exclusion from the Natural, too weak and too scarred for membership (she didn't make the cut; she got cut). Our births in counterpoint better express a posthuman feminism. Neither was pristine; both were impure, as impure as the "natural" milk our breasts would soon leak.

Haraway hopes that "a cyborg world might be about lived social and bodily realities in which people are not afraid of their joint kinship with animals and machines, not afraid of permanently partial identities and contradictory standpoints."[13] One of the birth narratives from the Farm records just such a kinship with animals: Mary writes, "I was brought up with the idea that people had an animal nature and a spiritual one; and that your animal nature was lower. But then I felt One with the monkeys and everything that brings forth new life. It felt very Holy."[14] But life on the Farm would have resisted kinship with machine. Indeed, for the one of us whose "birth plan" was most redirected, the integration of spiritual and physical "kinship with animals and machines" took time, as tears fell over the loss of a birth like those in *Spiritual Midwifery*.

In coming to peace with posthuman embodiment, breastmilk paved the way. The body's milk production bespoke the vivacity and power of the female body. Especially where the wounds of incision were present, nursing provided a sort of regeneration for the scarred maternal body, a reassertion of powerful embodiment, albeit altered.[15] For us nursing itself was a spiritual practice, a truth only underscored by the eventual necessity of the introduction of the breast pump, as the technologically mediated possibility of continuing this spiritual practice, as well as the frank pleasure of watching the milk mount steadily up, to feed and protect and deepen bonds even in physical absence. Our breastmilk also symbolized for us the web of relations joining baby with animal with machine: breastmilk is a fluid unmistakably mammalian, yet also peppered with heavy metals and other residues of our industrialized era. In breastmilk, ocean pollution flows into the female body and out of it; care for the earth's waterways becomes a spiritual commitment to the connected, hybridized bodies of earth, mother and child.[16]

The juxtaposition of our birth narratives, and our claim that both are simultaneously spiritual and cyborg, problematize Haraway's own reluctance to connect the cyborg with the discourse of birth. Instead, for Haraway, cyborgs, "not of Woman born," have "more to do with regeneration and are suspicious of the reproductive matrix and of most birthing...We require regeneration, not rebirth."[17] This rejection of birth for the alternative metaphor of regeneration tempts one toward a reading of Haraway which rejects the maternal altogether, in favor of a genderless reproduction outside the narratives of patriarchy and essentialist feminism; Katharyn Privett reads Haraway thus: "As she insists that: 'cyborg replication is uncoupled from organic reproduction,' Haraway strips the liberated cyborg of what she names as: 'reproductive politics [as the cyborg is] not of Woman born.' In an effort to resist maternal essentialism, Haraway creates a material corporeality that excludes the maternal as one possible element in a feminist constituency."[18]

Yet if cyborg hybridity dismantles the dichotomy of nature/technology, there can be no subsequent opposition of the cyborg and the natural. Haraway's consistent concern with multiple, complex, hybrid embodiment precludes this as a possible reading, for this comes too close to the technologically produced "masculine brain children" mocked in "The Virtual Speculum"[19] and longed for in transhumanist discourse.[20] Rather, Haraway's rejection of birth is a rejection of the patriarchal narrative of birth and rebirth within the "origin story" of which the cyborg has no part; connected both to "salvation history" and to heterosexual normativity, the nuclear family and the "natural" ties of blood kinship, birth, in this story, functions as the naturalizing, normative entry of Man into the world. This birth must be rejected, yet in such a way that avoids recourse to a romanticized version of the notions of Nature and Woman present in that narrative. This is the function of the language of "regeneration."[21]

And yet, for us it has precisely been our experiences of childbirth that have provided us with our most intense experiences of spiritual, cyborg embodiment *and* with the desire to move out of pure politics (in this case Natural or Medical) in order to advocate a healthier birth culture. Thus, as we describe technological embodiment in conversation with Haraway, we continue to employ the language of birth, choosing to reclaim it from masculinist meaning as a fecund metaphor for feminist spirituality.[22] It is not, after all, the hybrid natural-technological births described here that Haraway is rejecting. Like breastmilk, which "is not nature to the culture of Nestle's formula,"[23] neither is birthing nature to the culture of regeneration. It cannot, therefore, be theorized as the opposite of birth, despite Haraway's hyperbolic rhetoric here, for if the cyborg to function as the fusion of categories, she too must be birthed. The answer is neither natural birth nor artificial wombs, but a stubborn insistence on the both/and of posthuman genesis, unafraid of the technologized, fleshy births which are no return to the pristine natural.

Ultimately, Haraway does not dispute birth from women, but from Woman: Woman as that canal through which the masculine passes on its way to autonomy. There is birth for the posthuman, but it departs from the metaphors of birth defined by violence and patriarchal domination. Haraway claims that

> there is another route to having less at stake in masculine autonomy, a route that does not pass through Woman, Primitive, Zero, the Mirror Stage and its imaginary. It passes through women and other present-tense, illegitimate cyborgs...who refuse the ideological resources of victimization so as to have a real life.[24]

Grace Jantzen, another third wave feminist who emerged from the second wave generation, describes a new horizon that may be a contender for this sort of alternative route with "less at stake" in a masculinist symbolic. Jantzen articulates an alternative to the violence inherent in the Western imaginary in her proposal of a fecund and fleshy "imaginary of natality" that beckons our "becoming divine."[25] Jantzen claims, seemingly in contradiction to Haraway, that "there can be no other selves than selves of woman born."[26] Yet in concert with Haraway, she notes, "It would not be possible, working within an imaginary of natality, to think of ourselves as disembodied minds, to climb up into our heads and try to leave our bodies behind."[27] Such a conceptual world involves our bodies, our sex, and sometimes babies—little embodied strangers:

> an imaginary of natality leads to a symbolic which takes seriously our embodied, sexuate selves, situated in communities, limited, finite, but connected with all other animals, with the past and with future generations, and with the universe itself. It points toward a focus on flourishing, and on acting for love of the world, to nurture its natals, who join us as little strangers and take it up when our portion of infinity is done.[28]

Haraway offers the cyborg as an image for the hybrid identities through which we can join together in coalitions (not homogeneous identity campaigns)[29] in "acting for love of the world." Though Jantzen does not meditate upon technology, her "little strangers" sound curiously like natal cyborgs.

The spiritual vivacity of the birthing of our own little strangers demonstrates to us that technology and spirituality need not be at odds. Haraway chooses the cyborg over the goddess, but this need not signal a choice between opposites. Indeed, Haraway recognizes this: the full text of the famous last line of her Manifesto being, "Though both are bound in the spiral dance, I would rather be a cyborg than a goddess."[30] To identify as cyborg does not entail an abandoning of the spiritual in favor of the machine, nor certainly a replacement of female spirit with masculine technology. The cyborg represents neither pure spiritual being nor pure mechanics, and the cyborg troubles gender constructions.[31] It does not seek the pure, or the false privilege of innocence. The cyborg is hybrid, through and through, a diversity saturating feminist subjectivity to the core, appropriate to the third-wave. "The cyborg is our ontology; it gives us our politics."[32] The cyborg is also the matrix of our spirituality. Posthuman bodies draw the deep breath of spirituality in lungs both fleshy and fabricated.

Women have long incorporated earthly elements into spiritual ritual; in a posthuman generation the technological is similarly integrated, not as deviation from but as continuation of the same earthly matter that has long grounded our spiritual alchemy. We encounter new earthly matter, and as with the new chemistry of plastics, this matter can work for good or ill, mending or poisoning. Like the plastic baby Jesus in a modern crèche, can we feminists cradle our new technological incarnations, regarding the spiritual possibilities of new bodily forms? Can we circumscribe sacred circles to include the bodies born from scientific manipulations of earth, wind, fire, and water? May prayer shawls be woven also with wires, the rub of the *tzitzit* connecting us like a click on hypertext?

Spirit of Coalition

Our emphasis on the spirituality of our cyborg embodiment departs somewhat from Haraway's emphasis. Haraway cautions against disembodied politics of masculinist autonomy: in the same moment that she claims the cyborg as our ontology, she acknowledges the cyborg's dubious history as "the awful apocalyptic *telos* of the 'West's' escalating domination of abstract individuation, an ultimate self untied at last from all dependency, a man in space."[33] Haraway alludes here to the etymology of the word "cyborg," originally coined by scientists contemplating a means for "mankind" to conquer the interstellar vastness of the universe: a man in space, indeed. The solution to the quandary of meeting the physical needs of the human body in such an inhospitable environment was to negate those needs, to re-engineer human embodiment as to dispose of physical dependency on air, warmth, gravity—in short, an escape from Mother Earth.[34] How can such a vision morph into an icon of female embodiment and spirituality?

Haraway's answer points to the transgression of boundaries: the cyborg, in its hybrid existence, renegotiates the human-animal, organic-mechanical, physical-nonphysical boundaries which have set the terms for conceptualizing identity and being. Thus, the cyborg is not (necessarily) doomed to exile from the body, but rather has the capacity to redefine it: "The main trouble with cyborgs, of course, is that they are the illegitimate offspring of militarism and patriarchal capitalism, not to mention state socialism. But illegitimate offspring are often exceedingly unfaithful to their origins. Their fathers, after all, are inessential."[35] As bastard child, the cyborg speaks an emphatic "no" to the disembodied dreams of its inessential fathers. (The cyborg's relationship to Mother (Nature) remains more complex.)

Given this context, it is unsurprising that Haraway is unconcerned with the category of "spirit." Cyborgs are about bodies, and how different bodies make a difference; and "spirit" seems akin to the fathers' notions of disembodied souls. "These ontologically confusing *bodies*, and the practices that produce specific embodiment, are what we have to address, not the false problem of *dis*embodiment."[36]

The question is, then, what do we mean, what can we mean, when speaking of posthuman feminist spirituality? First of all, though technology may seem counter to embodiment, we speak of a spirituality resolutely and complexly embodied, a spirituality pulsing vitally through our tissues, even our synthetic ones. This is not the only possibility that the posthuman offers; the cyborg is after all firstly the product of "the womb-brain of its war-besotted parents in the middle of the last century of the Second Christian Millenium," and this heritage would seem to predispose it toward the destruction of bodies and spirits.[37] The feminist challenge remains, then, to honor the spirituality inherent in embodiment, and as we move forward into an increasingly complex and technologized posthuman world, to maintain the second wave's increasingly vital insight, "our bodies, ourselves; bodies are maps of power and identity."[38] N. Katherine Hayles writes,

> I view the present moment as a critical juncture, where interventions might be made to keep disembodiment from being rewritten, once again, into prevailing concepts of subjectivity. . . . If my nightmare is a culture of posthumans who regard their bodies as fashion accessories rather than the ground of being, my dream is a version of the posthuman that embraces the possibilities of information technologies without being seduced by fantasies of unlimited power and disembodied immortality, that recognizes and celebrates finitude as a condition of human being, and that understands human life is embedded in a material world of great complexity, one on which we depend for our continued survival.[39]

The spiritual practice of listening to and caring for one's own body widens as the boundaries of one's body widen and envelop, however temporarily and partially, material bits of the world, geographically distant but technologically proximate, genetically foreign but technologically kin. "Why should our bodies end at the skin, or include at best other beings encapsulated by skin?"[40] As we realized while suckling our young ones, the mercury of the ocean pollutes the flow of our own bodies; our physical bodies are not tightly contained within the boundaries of our skins. Our bodies are more fluid, and more metal.

"By the late twentieth century, our time, a mythic time, we are all chimeras, theorized and fabricated hybrids of machine and organism; in short, we are cyborgs."[41] We live with our daughters in an age where the elderly woman next door wears a machine inside to restart her heart when it stops and where a woman on the news is reported to have "detonated herself." But it is not only those of us who, for better or worse, have direct contact with the communications technologies, biotechnologies, or nanotechnologies who can claim cyborg ontology; for, as Haraway pointed out presciently in the 1985 Manifesto, "these tools embody and enforce new social relations for women worldwide."[42]

This leads to our second point. Posthuman bodies, bound together in surprising and counterintuitive ways, show us in yet another way that the connections between us overflow the biological bonds of identity and the ties evident by proximity allowing us to recognize our hybrid kinships, allowing for a generation of new subjectivities and a recrafting of our bodies. These recrafted bodies are counterintuitive: via technologies termed "invisible" for their ubiquity and ease of use, embodiment expands rather than disappears into the virtual world of the Net (or cyberspace, or the MetaVerse, or what have you—the dream worlds of male science fiction).[43] The shifting, temporary but real connections, made through the mediation of ever-evolving communication technologies, teach us that we cannot take for granted any simple notion of where my body ends and yours begins. Thus posthuman embodiment reiterates the feminist critique of atomized individuality. Our bodies become distributed, extended, global—even while remaining located, partial, and particular. These things are not necessarily mutually exclusive, and in fact in the age of hypertext are rarely so. Technology becomes another umbilicus connecting us across distance and despite difference, linking us together, distinct bodies but interdependent, a collectivity encompassing all kinds of humans and nonhumans, all kinds of natural creatures and technological creations. At the same time, we recognize that this, too, is not a given; technology can be an umbilicus, or it may mark precisely the ability to create without the guts of female form. The cyborg, for all its possibility, remains ambivalent in its possibilities and spiritualities.

The third wave, grappling with the myriad differences that make "metanarratives" suspect and with the technologies that complicate our embodiment, is at the same time faced with global crises and delicate interconnection. We recognize our complicated difference from one another in the same era in which we know a profoundly interconnected ecology and a technologically hybridized globe. We speak with our particular voices, but the challenges facing our spirits face us precisely because they are ours, not only "my" issues: ecological crisis and technological de/construction face so many in so many cultural contexts. The information age confronts us ever more rapidly with the reality of each other: at once with our interrelation and our difference.

Thus we have a heightened awareness of hybridized global embodiment, a sense of "hypertextured relationality." Haraway writes that "cyborgs are needy for connection."[44] This need for connection results from both the lack of natural, given connectedness and the heightened possibilities for connections that exist with the advent of technologized posthumanness. "Hypertext" is the ultimate metaphor for this cyborg connectedness, for "making connections is the essence of hypertext."[45] But hypertext is also "an instrument for reconstructing common sense about relatedness."[46] That is, in claiming that posthuman bodies and spirits are global, we do not simply reiterate the vision of female bodies reconnecting with the natural, earthy, spiritual power of the Goddess. The third wave reconstructs this sense of connection. There is no pristine natural Earth to tap into; as we ourselves are hybridized organic-technological posthumans, so our earth is a hybrid matrix of nature and culture.[47]

Cyborgs understand this, without lament. Technology is bane and boon; endangering aspects of our world, it also provides the means for making the connections which can heal. In ways both metaphorical and literal, cyborg identities provide the opportunity for constructing communities based on the common goal of making life liveable. Michelle Bastian argues, correctly, that Haraway's motivation in the Manifesto was not to meditate upon technology, but to employ the cyborg as a figuration which enabled "coalition building" for effective action without the false necessity of identity politics.[48] The point was not ontological navel-gazing, but to construct a way out of the dilemma of the paralyzing "endless splitting and searches for a new essential identity."[49] As a figuration, the cyborg frees us to form "vulnerable, on-the-ground work that cobbles together non-harmonious agencies and ways of living that are accountable both to their disparate inherited histories and to their barely possible but absolutely necessary joint futures."[50] This coalition for justice describes a second texture of posthuman feminist spirituality. In posthuman identities, ever shifting, always permeable and overlapping, new doors are opened for global care, beyond the stagnations encountered at the rigid boundaries of identity politics. The posthuman allows an imaginary of a body recrafted not into a new One, a false whole (as in the essence of some Womanhood) but a rather hybridized and temporary collaboration.

Thus connected by these technologies for good or ill, our mutual task, as Haraway and others would remind us, is to make them work for good. Acknowledging our cyborg existence is but the first step of the process; "We must cast our lot with some ways of life on this planet, and not with other ways."[51] This is not simply a political or ethical challenge; just as the cyborg gives the lie to the boundaries of natural/technological, Man/Woman, so, too, does it confuse the boundary of physical/spiritual in all of its versions. Escape from world and body, via the *Deus ex Machina* of transhumanist technology, or the *Left Behind* Rapture of evangelical pop theology—neither dream is for cyborgs. Cyborgs are uninterested in a transcendent, clean, passive, inward spirituality; they are interested in action, a spirituality at work in a hybrid techno-natural world.[52] The spiritual cannot be compartmentalized away from the physical: feminists have long made this claim, but technology precludes such compartmentalization as well.

Our claim that spirituality and technology are bound in common embodiment does not intend an unabashed celebration of technoscience. Such a claim would be naïve: the dangerous imbalance of the ecosystems in which we live is deeply related to technology. Haraway's own use of the cyborg image conveys not some festival of robotics but rather the hope that the sort of embodied subjectivity that is cyborg might be a position from which to challenge technological destruction. Accordingly, Haraway hopes that the cyborg might recraft the destructive programming of military science. "The cyborg skips the step of original unity, of identification with Nature in the Western sense. This is its illegitimate promise that might lead to subversion of its teleology as star wars."[53] She provides an example of such a subversion: "The convention of ideologically taming militarized high technology by publicizing its applications to speech and motion problems of the disabled/differently abled takes on a special irony in monotheistic, patriarchal, and frequently anti-semitic culture when computer-generated speech allows a boy with no voice to chant the Haftorah at his bar mitzvah."[54]

Echoing the "incredulity of metanarratives" characteristic of postmodernity,[55] Haraway explains that "there is no drive in cyborgs to produce total theory, but there is an intimate experience of boundaries, their construction and deconstruction. There is a myth system waiting to become a political language to ground one way of looking at science and technology and challenging the informatics of domination—in order to act potently."[56] This potent action is the intention of Haraway's metaphor of cyborg subjectivity. The "intimate experience of boundaries," their overlapping, their failures, their fissures, heightens the possibility of selfhood that can work together, finding a common ground where dichotomized identity boundaries would otherwise separate. The cyborg "does not seek unitary identity and so generate antagonistic dualisms without end (or until the world ends)."[57] Rather, "the cyborg is a kind of disassembled and reassembled, postmodern collective and personal self."[58]

To return to the example of our childbirths, joined in the common space of cyborg childbirth, we are freed from the constraints of any particular birthing campaign and the antagonism of Natural versus Medical. We can focus our energies instead on the holy marvel of sex and gestation and offspring, and on the politics that still render the experience of birth persistently unjust in contemporary society. As Bastian explains, "Political groups can be released from both the pressures of unity and the frightening prospect of a homogeneous enemy, focusing instead on developing the skills to become more able to handle unstable, pragmatic coalitions that focus more on attaining specific goals than on proving the group's common identity or innocence."[59] Though it may seem that the best way to further just reproductive health is to pick a side, rallying behind either the natural birth movement or the more medical model, the cyborg women laboring in the muddle of this dichotomy—that is, most all laboring women today—bear witness to another truth: cyborg births are holy. Let's give up the fight over which births are natural and get on with making them healthy. As Haraway writes, "the point is to make a difference in the world, to cast our lot for some ways of life and not others. To do that, one must be in the action, be finite and dirty, not transcendent and clean."[60]

Echoing the confusion of the Pentecost narrative in the book of Acts, Haraway explains that the cyborg myth

> is a dream not of a common language, but of a powerful infidel heteroglossia. It is an imagination of a feminist speaking in tongues to strike fear into the circuits of the supersavers of the new right. It means both building and destroying machines, identities, categories, relationships, space stories.[61]

We see this "speaking in tongues," this heteroglossia of cyborg subjectivity, as an expression of feminist spirituality. For example, in her meditation on "the virtual speculum in the New World Order," Haraway expresses feminist "yearnings,"[62] yearnings particularly for reproductive freedom and for change in the worldwide economies that result in devastating infant mortality. She writes: "I long for models of solidarity and human unity and difference rooted in friendship, work, partially shared purposes, intractable collective pain, inescapable mortality, and persistent hope."[63] Such is spirituality in the new generation of feminism.

Among her many birth narratives from the Farm, Gaskin records the story of Anita. Anita had given birth in the hospital but subsequently gave birth on the Farm. Anita writes, "Being relaxed and comfortable in bed at home in my own familiar surroundings was nothing at all like being shaved, sterilized, poked, and strapped down. . . . Surrounded by strangers, blinded by bright lights. . . ." In contrast, Anita writes to one of her Farm babies: "You came into the world riding on the wave of the best we could do, the highest hopes we could intend, the cleanest, most compassionate vision we could generate at that point in time and space."[64]

We hope that cyborg subjectivity might position women to experience the natural/technological hybridity of contemporary childbirth as the "most compassionate vision" we can generate, and to recraft it such that it is the wave of the best we can do for our next generation. Technology need not entail the dehumanizing experience Anita encountered in the hospital; recrafted by women and other cyborgs it can be an expression of our humanity. As with Mona, who in childbirth on the Farm felt that she had made love with God, might we find also in technologically complex embodiment that we have encountered the divine? Might our coalitions work toward that possibility for women around the globe? Looking at the dry bones in our global valleys, we rightly wonder with Ezekiel, "Can these bones live?" The cyborg prophesies the possibility of recrafting our powers toward the invocation of life rather than the filling of more mass graves.

Our generation of feminists lives in a time when the technological and the bodily have already come together. We are not simply contemplating a marriage: the technological and the spiritual already join in our hybridized bodies. Our generation of feminism still has work to do in spiritually integrating this new and complicated aspect of our relational embodiment. Coming into greater spiritual congruence with our cyborg selves, seeing the creative potential of our broken boundaries, we are ready to recraft the world, *tikkun olam*. We experience our relational identity in a heightened way. Refusing to serve the patriarchal route to autonomous identity, we labor for another future, letting down our cyborg milk to nourish a new generation, speaking in many tongues with a passion for justice.

In sum, the cyborg is both our embodied reality and a metaphor to the coalition to and for which our embodiment invites and enables us. The diverse spiritualities of the third wave need not be adversarial to technological embodiment, seeking an illusive transcendence of it or a cleansing from it (as seen with the natural birth discourse). Coming to peace with technological embodiment, that is living into the permeability, temporality, and inconsistency of our identities, our spirituality draws its breath in impure bodies, without lament, such that we might be positioned to take responsibility for the unclear air we breathe, and all the devastating problems of our world. We "cast our lot" with particular others, forming a new subjectivity, a new sense of self and a new political body. This recasting of ourselves characterizes our spiritual practice, resonating with and yet reforming the trajectories of many ancient religious traditions.[65]

The third wave complicates feminism's second wave with *difference*, a current rushing in upon the waters of the second wave and infusing it with new biochemistry, producing a richer, thicker feminism. Our cultures, our lovemaking, our global positions: these things make us different, too different for any monolithic political agenda. The myriad voices of the third wave have made this clear. Our diversity, however, is not only related to class and race and sexuality: we are also each of us cyborg. Our biochemistry is implanted and extended through plastics and electronic cells. These become our skin. The commitment of feminism to an *embodied* spirit means in the current time a commitment to a technologically complex embodiment, a commitment therefore to ecology. Those who work for the thriving of women's spirits are pressed to also care for the healthfulness of our food sources, our computer networks, our medical technologies, our plastics. To tend to these diverse systems is to nourish the cyborg spirit of a third-wave feminism.

We pollute our bodies and spirits in the industrial air that chokes our lungs and our children's, in the processed and nutrient-poor food available to the poorest among us, in all the ways that our technological evolution makes "natural" selection an increasingly class-driven process. Yet we also nourish our spiritual selves in a wide physical body: in a Community Supported Agriculture garden, in online communities, with a lighter "environmental footprint," with pray-as-you-go podcasts on commutes, with an ever widening awareness of how daily decisions in marketplace and home affect not only our bodies and spirits and our daughters', but women and generations far away and yet near.

As to the placenta in plastic, it made its way onward who knows where. A friend who is a Wiccan priestess encouraged burying it in protected land that will not be developed. The friend is right: what better way to honor the sacred power of that sustaining organ? Perhaps, though, the alternate sacred journey that was the end of this particular placenta can demonstrate the expansive spirituality of the third wave. It's not clear where that placenta went: most hospitals incinerate them with other medical "waste," some sell them to cosmetic companies.[66] Whether mingling with the ashes of others or supplementing another woman's face, the placenta's spiritual power is released to the complex world in which our daughters grow. Across the miles, they watch videos of each other on their toddler blogs, and laugh.

Notes

1. Haraway writes that "reproduction has been at the center of scientific, technological, political, personal, religious, gender, familial, class, race, and national webs of contestation for at least the past twenty-five years. Like it or not, as if we were children dealing with adults' hidden secrets, feminists could not avoid relentlessly asking where babies come from." Donna J. Haraway, *Modest_Witness@Second_Millennium.Femaleman © Meets_Oncomouse™: Feminism and Technoscience* (New York: Routledge, 1997), 1027.

2. The famous concluding statement of her "Cyborg Manifesto," first published as "Manifesto for Cyborgs: science, technology and socialist feminism in the 1980s," *Socialist Review* 80 (1985): 65-108. The text quoted here is the revised version: Donna J. Haraway, "A Cyborg Manifesto: Science, Technology and Socialist-Feminism in the Late Twentieth Century," in *Simians, Cyborgs and Women: The Reinvention of Nature* (New York: Routledge, 1991), 149-181.

3. Of these images, Michelle Bastian reminds us that when discussing the cyborgs of Donna Haraway, "the figure presented here is not the technoborg that we are most familiar with but rather the coalition cyborg, who remembers her beginnings in U.S. third-world feminism." In contrast, however, Bastian explains that the cyborg of popular culture emphasizes a hyper-masculinism, violent and autonomous, quite different from Haraway's proposals. See Michelle Bastian, "Haraway's Lost Cyborg and the Possibilities of Transversalism," *Signs: Journal of Women in Culture & Society* 31, no. 4 (2006): 1033. Indeed, for this very reason Haraway has moved on from the cyborg into work on companion species, and completely disavows the term "posthuman" because "human/posthuman is much too easily appropriated by the blissed-out, 'Let's all be posthumanists and find our next teleological evolutionary stage in some kind of transhumanist technoenhancement.'" See N. Gane and D. Haraway, "When we have never been human, what is to be done? Interview with Donna Haraway," *Theory Culture & Society* 23, no. 7-8 (2006).

4. Ina May Gaskin, *Spiritual Midwifery,* 4th edition (Summertown, TN: Book Publishing Company, 2002), 108. This book was first published in 1975 in the most active period of the Farm.

5. Gaskin, *Spiritual Midwifery,* 127.

6. Gaskin, *Spiritual Midwifery,* 134.

7. Rayna Rapp, "Real-Time Fetus: The Role of the Sonogram in the Age of Monitored Reproduction," in *Cyborgs & Citadels: Anthropological Interventions in Emerging Sciences and Technologies,* ed. Gary Lee Downey and Joseph Dumit (Santa Fe: School of American Research Press, 1997), 33. Rapp observes a similar role played by technology in the ubiquity of 20-week ultrasounds; at the same time, she notes that the opposition between "male medicalization" and "maternal experience" is an oversimplification, one which often obscures the privileged location of the dispute.

8. Tina Cassidy, *Birth: The Surprising History of How We Are Born* (New York: Atlantic Monthly Press, 2006), 32.

9. Haraway, *Simians, Cyborgs, and Women,* 154.

10. Indeed there is an overuse of medicine in contemporary North American births, and a lack of recognition precisely of the *spiritual* power seated in women's bodies. The U.S. cesarean rate, for example, is currently over twice that of the recommendations of the World Health Organization (See Sheila Kitzinger, 348-49). Yet technological systems are not inherently antithetical to that embodied power. They *may* work against the body and many examples of the destructive power of technological systems could be named; however, these systems may also be integral to bodily power. Expressing this same point in converse, trees, winds, and waters, long recognized as natural and powerful, are not inherently congruent with a woman's bodily health, although they *may* be integral to it.

11. In the Babylonian creation epic the *Enuma Elish,* the world is created from the split-open body of Tiamat.

12. Haraway, *Simians, Cyborgs, and Women,* 149.

13. Haraway, *Simians, Cyborgs, and Women,* 154.

14. Gaskin, *Spiritual Midwifery,* 80.

15. Sadly, a strongly drug laden childbirth can interfere with healthy lactation. Here a coalition of women outside the strong camps of Natural and Medical can together speak a word about technological embodiment: the medically managed woman can still nurse (sometimes). She has not transcended her body upon entrance to the hospital. In Anna's

experience of nursing after cesarean, the returned bodily strength in lactation functioned somewhat like the regeneration of the salamander's limb in Haraway—perhaps not monstrous, but potent indeed. See Haraway, *Simians, Cyborgs, and Women*, 181, and footnote 21 below.

16. Haraway's own meditation on breastfeeding (Haraway, *Modest_Witness*, 203-11.) characterizes it as technical, skillful, embodied practice enmeshed in economic and political discourses as well. Haraway analyses the high infant mortality due to dehydration following the loss of breastfeeding practice among women in the slums of Brazilian town studied by Nancy Scheper-Hughes; here the loss of lactation is related to the loss of knowledge and culture of breastfeeding among women, as well as to Nestle's exploitive practices, and unexpectedly, to the affirmation of paternity in the one who brings home the (artificial) milk. She describes the import of this complex milk: "In several senses, computers in financial centers in Geneva, New York, or Brasilia are reproductive technologies that have their bite in the breast of marginalized women and the guts of their babies" (Haraway, *Modest Witness*, 208). Haraway also alludes to a coalition familiar to natural birth discourse in the following passage about knowledge of lactation: "Women can lose, regain, or improve the natural-technical knowledge necessary to breastfeeding, just as young elephants can lose the ability to find water in long droughts when most of the older, knowledgeable animals are killed by poaching or by inexpert culling of herds. That comparison is not a naturalization of women but an insistence on the shared natural-technical matter of living as intelligent moral creatures on this planet." (Haraway, *Modest_Witness*, 209).

17. Haraway, *Simians, Cyborgs, and Women*, 150, 177, and 181.

18. Katharyn Privett, "Sacred Cyborgs and 21st Century Goddesses," *Reconstruction* 7, no. 4 (2007): 5.

19. Haraway, *Modest_Witness*, 186. Privett misreads Haraway on this point because of a larger interpretive error, viewing the cyborg as strictly autonomous and disembodied, rather than the connection-needy, coalition-building, hybridly embodied cyborg Haraway describes.

20. As in, for instance, James Hughes' outrageous claim that all women really want artificial wombs "as an alternative to the burdens and risks of pregnancy and delivery, and to allow a level of control, purity and optimization of the uterine environment impossible in a woman's body." See James Hughes, *Citizen Cyborg: Why Democratic Societies Must Respond to the Redesigned Human of the Future* (Cambridge, MA: Westview Press, 2004), 87. We do not want to claim here that somehow artificial wombs are categorically not "spiritual," for that would again inscribe the nature/technology dichotomy in yet another form. We do, however, want to emphasize the way in which Hughes' transhumanist claim for the superiority of technology rests on disdain for the maternal body, and views pregnancy and birth as burdensome rather than a possible site of revelation and pleasure.

21. It is worth commenting upon that the image Haraway chooses to elucidate regeneration, a salamander regrowing its damaged limb (*Simians, Cyborgs, and Women*, 181), is a "natural" one rather than a "technological" one—natural, at least for the salamander, if not for the human being. This is a subtle indication that the nature/technology dichotomy Privett sees at work in the birth/regeneration contrast is not present in Haraway; also, the salamander serves as a reminder of Haraway's argument that the mutability evident in salamander-like regeneration is a token of possible kinship that extends both across the human/animal boundary as well as the human/machine.

22. As does Grace Jantzen, discussed below.

23. Haraway, *Modest_Witness*, 209.

24. Haraway, *Simians, Cyborgs, and Women*, 177.

25. Grace Jantzen, *Becoming Divine: Towards a Feminist Philosophy of Religion* (Manchester: Manchester University Press, 1998).

26. Jantzen, *Becoming Divine*, 141.

27. Jantzen, *Becoming Divine*, 194.

28. Jantzen, *Becoming Divine*, 194.

29. Bastian describes "Haraway's political technique of developing visions of unsure, heterogeneous, desiring, noninnocent, leaky, situated actors. These visions are not abstract theories but 'performative images that can be inhabited.'" Here Bastian quotes Haraway, *Modest_Witness*, 11. Bastian, "Haraway's Lost Cyborg," 1029.

30. Haraway, *Simians, Cyborgs, and Women*, 181.

31. Haraway writes: "Cyborgs might consider more seriously the partial, fluid, sometimes aspect of sex and sexual embodiment. Gender might not be global identity after all, even if it has profound historical breadth and depth." Haraway, *Simians, Cyborgs, and Women*, 180.

32. Haraway, *Simians, Cyborgs, and Women*, 180.

33. Haraway, *Simians, Cyborgs, and Women*, 150-1.

34. M. Clynes and N. Kline, "Cyborgs and Space," in *The Cyborg Handbook*, ed. Chris Gray (London: Routledge, 1995), 29-34. Their article was originally published in the September 1960 *Astronautics*.

35. Haraway, *Simians, Cyborgs, and Women*, 151.

36. Haraway, *Modest_Witness*, 186.

37. Haraway, *Modest_Witness*, 51.

38. Haraway, *Simians, Cyborgs, and Women*, 180.

39. N. Katherine Hayles, *How We Became Posthuman: virtual bodies in cybernetics, literature, and informatics* (Chicago: Univ of Chicago Press, 1999), 5.

40. Haraway, *Simians, Cyborgs, and Women*, 178.

41. Haraway, *Simians, Cyborgs, and Women*, 150.

42. Haraway, *Simians, Cyborgs, and Women*, 164. We would be remiss to not address the obvious dependence of access to technologies on social location for women worldwide, as if everyone had ready access to internet and cell phone. Yet the image of cyborg is not intended primarily as one which describes women literally engaged with technologies, but how technologies restructure social relations for everyone, in differing ways dependent on social location. Indeed, Haraway offers us a paradigm of cyborg activism far from the desktops of academic feminist practice: "These cyborgs are the people who refuse to disappear on cue, no matter how many times a 'Western' commentator remarks on the sad passing of another primitive, another organic group done in by 'Western' technology, by writing. These real-life cyborgs (for example, the Southeast Asian village women working in Japanese and US electronics firms described by Aihwa Ong) are actively rewriting the texts of their bodies and societies. Survival is the stakes in these play of readings" (*Simians, Cyborgs, and Women*, 177). Yet, as Michelle Bastian points out, Haraway's cyborg is also "a response to the criticisms women of color have made of hegemonic feminism. Accordingly, the cyborg lays the primary responsibility for this sort of identity work in the hands of those who may not currently be experiencing intense

oppression and domination" (Bastian, "Haraway's Lost Cyborg,"1038). Such is the role of the "Modest Witness" (cf. Haraway, *Modest_Witness*, 270).

43. Noted briefly by Haraway, the "invisibility" of modern communications technologies is discussed in detail by Andy Clark, *Natural-Born Cyborgs: Minds, Technologies, and the Future of Human Intelligence* (Oxford: Oxford University Press, 2003).

44. Haraway, *Simians, Cyborgs, and Women*, 151.

45. Haraway, *Modest_Witness*, 126.

46. Haraway, *Modest_Witness*, 125.

47. Rita Lester, "Ecofeminism and the Cyborg," *Feminist Theology: The Journal of the Britain & Ireland School of Feminist Theology*, no. 19 (1998): 31.

48. Bastian, "Haraway's Lost Cyborg," 1029.

49. Haraway, *Simians, Cyborgs, and Women*, 155.

50. Bastian, "Haraway's Lost Cyborg," 1027. See also Donna J. Haraway, *The Companion Species Manifesto: Dogs, People, and Significant Otherness* (Chicago: Prickly Paradigm, 2003).

51. Haraway, *Modest_Witness*, 51; cf. *Modest_Witness* 36 and 270.

52. Haraway, *Modest_Witness*, 36.

53. Haraway, *Simians, Cyborgs, and Women*, 151. Similarly Haraway writes on the same page: "The cyborg would not recognize the Garden of Eden; it is not made of mud and cannot dream of returning to dust. Perhaps that is why I want to see if cyborgs can subvert the apocalypse of returning to nuclear dust in the manic compulsion to name the Enemy."

54. Haraway, *Simians, Cyborgs, and Women*, 247.

55. See Jean-François Lyotard, *The Postmodern Condition: A Report on Knowledge* (Minneapolis: University of Minnesota Press, 1984), xxiv.

56. Haraway, *Simians, Cyborgs, and Women*, 181.

57. Haraway, *Simians, Cyborgs, and Women*, 180. Similarly, Haraway declares that the dichotomies ruling the Western imagination since Aristotle "have been cannibalized, or as Zoe Sofia (Sofoulis) might put it, they have been 'techno-digested'" (*Simians, Cyborgs, and Women*, 163).

58. Haraway, *Simians, Cyborgs, and Women*, 163; cf. 212: "the cyborg is text, machine, body, and metaphor..." After her "manifesto," Haraway's work shifts away from the cyborg image to other "figurations" that more easily convey a hybrid subjectivity (see footnote 3 above). These impure subjectivities enable coalition. Here Haraway's vision of coalition resonates with Bruno Latour, *Politics of Nature: How to Bring the Sciences into Democracy* (Cambridge, MA: Harvard University Press, 2004.) and Michael Hardt and Antonio Negri, *Multitude: War and Democracy in the Age of Empire* (New York: Penguin Press, 2004).

59. Bastian, "Haraway's Lost Cyborg," 1036; cf. Haraway, *Simians, Cyborgs, and Women*, 176.

60. Haraway, *Modest_Witness*, 36.

61. Haraway, *Simians, Cyborgs, and Women*, 181.

62. Haraway, *Modest_Witness*, 191-2.

63. Haraway, *Modest_Witness*, 265.

64. Gaskin, *Spiritual Midwifery*, 84.

65. For our diverse religious traditions, cyborg subjectivity indicates both vital specificity and impure boundaries.

66. Cassidy, *Birth*, 220-21.

Bibliography

Bastian, Michelle. "Haraway's Lost Cyborg and the Possibilities of Transversalism." *Signs: Journal of Women in Culture & Society* 31, no. 4 (2006): 1027-1049.

Cassidy, Tina. *Birth: The Surprising History of How We Are Born*. New York: Atlantic Monthly Press, 2006.

Gane, N., and D. Haraway. "When We Have Never Been Human, What Is to Be Done? Interview with Donna Haraway." *Theory Culture & Society* 23, no. 7-8 (2006): 135-158.

Gaskin, Ina May. *Spiritual Midwifery*, 4th edition. Summertown, TN: Book Publishing Company, 2002.

Haraway, Donna J. *Simians, Cyborgs and Women: The Reinvention of Nature*. New York: Routledge, 1991.

———.*Modest_Witness@Second_Millennium.Femaleman©_Meets_Oncomouse™: Feminism and Technoscience*. New York: Routledge, 1997.

———. *The Companion Species Manifesto: Dogs, People, and Significant Otherness*. Chicago: Prickly Paradigm, 2003.

Hayles, N. Katherine. *How We Became Posthuman: Virtual Bodies in Cybernetics, Literature, and Informatics*. Chicago: Univ of Chicago Press, 1999.

Jantzen, Grace. *Becoming Divine: Towards a Feminist Philosophy of Religion*. Manchester: Manchester University Press, 1998.

Kitzinger, Sheila. *The Complete Book of Pregnancy and Childbirth*, 4th revised edition. New York: Alfred Knopf, 2004.

Lester, Rita. "Ecofeminism and the Cyborg." *Feminist Theology: The Journal of the Britain & Ireland School of Feminist Theology*, no. 19 (1998): 11-33.

Privett, Katharyn. "Sacred Cyborgs and 21st Century Goddesses." *Reconstruction* 7, no. 4 (2007): 1-27.

Rapp, Rayna. "Real-Time Fetus: The Role of the Sonogram in the Age of Monitored Reproduction." In *Cyborgs & Citadels: Anthropological Interventions in Emerging Sciences and Technologies*, ed. Gary Lee Downey and Joseph Dumit, 31-48. Santa Fe: School of American Research Press, 1997.

Chapter Four:
Fandemonium and Spirituality

Gena Meldazy

A popular family legend that my siblings and I like to recount is the one where Leon Trotsky, at the beginning of his exile from Russia, stayed on a family farm in Mount Forest, Ontario with great-cousins of ours who identified as anarchists. Trotsky stayed with the cousins for a time and then presumably left for Mexico, where the rest is history. My cousins, likewise, eventually left for the States to join an anarchist commune and the growing anarchist movement. Whether or not this family story has any kernel of truth, I have a very strong sense of pride in my speculative lineage to these black-flag waving reprobates.

This period of my family history has played a fundamental role in how I understand the notion of spiritual substance and spirituality. Especially as a woman, this sense of spirituality is beyond the pale, and the relationship of anarchy to authority has something to do with this. Any moral, ethical or political boundary connoted through an authoritative presence is immediately de-centered with anarchistic interjection. My cousins practiced a philosophy which sat off the radar of the status quo, which acted as a guiding principle for them, and which brought meaning and wholeness to their lives. The current irony of this is that anarchist philosophies and ideas—a long intellectual tradition which some historians date back to the eighteenth-century Enlightenment—have since been integrated into the popular culture; as they are integrated, they become subsumed as a branded and marketable commodity.[1] This interjection into the hegemonic structure presents itself as an option for appropriation from the popular culture.

Statement of Purpose

This paper expresses a nascent philosophy about the popular culture, notions of spirituality, and feminism. My initial aim with it is to discuss the aestheticization of demarcated spaces, between 'self' and 'other' specifically within the realm of current Western pop culture. A secondary aim of mine is to discuss the need for the inclusion of non-religious beliefs in the study of feminism and spirituality. I ask the reader to bear in mind that this paper is an abstraction that is still in development, and warrants discussion and criticism.

The title of this piece, *Fandemonium and Spirituality*, is at first glance contradictory and inaccessible. Fandemonium is a word that conjures connections to fandom and celebrity culture. Likewise, for those who read the sports section of the newspaper, you may have come across this term before as a reference to acts of fandom in the audience; again, it brings a familiar sense to the word. Both of these examples refer in part to my intended use, but are not fully encompassed within it. Fandemonium is a word which can be applied to what I see as a relationship within the popular culture that is contributing to the assembly of a unique brand of spirituality. Instead of trying to define a meaning of spirituality which is inclusive, and confirm that these relationships in the popular culture *are* spiritual, I would rather question their potential to present spiritual substance through there construction. If yes, why? If not, why not? In an effort to bring new vocabulary to the discourse of feminism and cultural studies, this re-defined term sits somewhere on the margins between social relevance and fraudulent semantics. It is a word I have appropriated and am re-defining for the purpose of expressing these questions, and though related to feminism, is not limited to this discourse for analysis.

Fandemonium is, above all else, the aestheticization of the demarcation between self and other; that is Fandemonium is a re-signification of the image of otherness as difference, into a commodity of sameness. Through the process of aestheticization, whether human, geographic, celebrity, or theistic in form, otherness becomes an obsessive target and the act of looking becomes tantamount to daily living. The relationship of aesthetics and spirituality becomes interesting when marketable commodities are included. As mentioned before, this form of spirituality is not just limited to the incorporeal, as in traditional understandings of spirituality.

Fandemonium expands beyond the scope of the cult of celebrity, yet is intrinsically tied to the mass media and Western popular culture. Fandemonium is also assisted by the multi-sensorial world in which we now live, including audio and visual mediums such as the internet, television, and material objects.

I imagine Fandemonium as working in partnership with visual and audio mediums, along with the democratic structure of media and journalism, as well as spatial constructions and geography. This relationship could amount to an inter-systemic model through which Fandemonium constructs itself. Imagining that this model has three spheres, sphere 'One' would represent the general concept of Fandemonium, as a process of aestheticization and branding of spirituality. Sphere 'Two' would represent a variety of visual and audio mediums which we have come to rely on in Western culture for our news and information, including within this the democratic participation of the masses in media and journalism. Sphere 'Three' is the spatial and geographic element, which allows us to locate these media images within an imaginative space. This model which I have laid out is not concrete in its taxonomy, but the relationship between aesthetics, media, and geography creates a landscape in which non-religious spirituality resides.

This act of Fandemonium is intertwined with Western popular culture; it is continually re-defined by the pursuit of Western hegemonic power and its gaze, wherever it may rest. Wherein, the popular culture and hegemonic powers that be also continually re-define each other. In this sense, Fandemonium can be linked to an imagined 'global community' and imaginative geographies[2] (to borrow Edward Said's term) that are created through popular culture iconography and language. The idea of a sovereign people as a real community in relation to the creation and positioning of an image of real 'otherness', is an important aspect of this. Where we position these images of otherness is built into the foundation of the belief of the 'people' that this image sought is real, and not a mediated construction. The lenses through which we view our world are colored by this belief/understanding. Likewise, this iconography and spirituality should be discussed as a part of one inter-systemic relationship, not acts distinct in and of themselves. As I propose that this habitual act of looking re-affirms a Western position in the center, I also propose that 'otherness', through its construction and branding as a natural image, presents a relation of spiritual opportunity.

The audio and visual media which are suggested above could also include digital and peer-to-peer forums which use a combination of sound, text, image, performance, and more. The possibilities for this are endless, and not limited to the internet. What's more, these audio and visual media, lacking a concrete physical location, use heterotopic space (figurative space) to construct their message. Though these new media encompass an area of non-physicality, they are embodied within a context that manipulates the media for social purposes which leave a physical mark or delineation. That arena could be described as the *Spatial,* which, indicated above, includes a multi-faceted geography to the non-spatial components of media, one which consists of cultural implications. Likewise, the audio and visual contribute to the construction of these spatial embodiments, and allow us to see these embodiments as more than words on a page.

In Relation to Spirituality

The story of my great-anarchist-cousins in Mount Forest, which informs this essay abstraction, could be summarized as a faith in the freedom to choose and to choose a rational structure through which to situate themselves. That which is considered sacred is not limited to the immaterial, transcendent, or incorporeal;[3] the act of choosing a system of faith constitutes in itself a form of spirituality. I was raised by two very atheistic parents, and this freedom to choose was presented to me as well at a very young age.

In his book *A Brief History of Spirituality,* Philip Sheldrake writes that meanings of the word spirituality have shifted from its Christian roots to a more contextually based understanding.[4] The events, politics, and economics of *now* are continually re-shaping how we understand what spirituality is, and how it is practiced both individually and collectively. Sheldrake writes that "it is possible to suggest that the word 'spirituality' refers to the deepest values and meanings by which people seek to live. In other words, 'spirituality' implies some kind of vision of the human spirit and of what will assist it to achieve full potential."[5] This word has shifted so dramatically from its religious roots, according to Sheldrake, that more than just Christian denominations have embraced it, and in numerous forms.

Similar to Sheldrake, Ursula King writes in the *Encyclopedia for Women and World Religion* that spirituality is neither a fixed nor permanent state of being, but is in constant flux with its surrounding social and cultural conditions. It would be more appropriate to discuss it as a "lived experience", and a state of being that can involve highly tangible material things and products, helping to achieve this self-transcendence, which likewise brings about a greater feeling of wholeness. Thus, spirituality can be individual as well as collective; it can be religious as well as non-religious. It is a word whose definition changes with the social demands of the context in which it is used, and through this is given shape and meaning. For Sheldrake, "'Context' is not a 'something' that may be added to or subtracted from spiritual experiences or traditions but is the very element within which these find expression."[6]

Interactions and Relations

Another term that contributes to what I define as Fandemonium is para-social interaction, from Donald Horton and Richard Wohl's 1956 essay *Mass Communication and Para-Social Interaction.* Where:

> the term para-social interaction is used to refer to relations of intimacy constructed through the mass media rather than direct experience and face-to-face

meetings. This is a form of second-order intimacy, since it derives from representations of the person rather than actual physical contact.[7]

For Horton and Wohl, no longer are "illustrious men", the performers we see on television and through other forms of media entertainment, greeted solely as peers.[8] The audience is responsive to the performer and program, and "the more the performer seems to adjust his performance to the supposed response of the audience, the more the audience tends to make the response anticipated."[9] Though we face these performers face-to-face through entertainment media, Horton and Wohl stress that the spectator and audience members are free to withdraw from this relationship at any time. As well, these interactions provide a framework for fantasy on behalf of the audience, but with no cyclical effect. These performers, then, also begin to take on 'personae' outside of the realm of the performance they enact for the audience.[10]

How do we interact with these personae? Horton and Wohl write that "through direct observation and interpretation of his appearance, his gestures and voice, his conversation and conduct," we are able to establish relationships, as an audience, to the images and personalities presented.[11] Horton and Wohl also suggest that through these continuous and one-sided relations, the audience member "comes to believe that he 'knows' the personae more intimately and profoundly than others do."[12]

These performative personae are created, observed, constructed and mediated from a distance between the audience and the performer. Our relationship with 'otherness', as well, is one-sided and non-reciprocal in a similar fashion. Horton and Wohl's essay yields insight in noting that what we engage in relations *with*, when engaging in audio and visual images, are persona of performative 'otherness' that the self creates, projects, and maintains. We come to know the personae through our voluntary participation in its construction. This participation gives individuals power to conduct a para-social relation with 'otherness', where the performative personae of 'otherness' is established through our non-cyclical intimacy.

Though audio and visual mediums, and their democratic power are important, what about para-social relations with non-'celebrity' personas? The relationship between self and 'other' is usually acknowledged as a demarcation; if one were able to diminish the ideological distance that this implies—while still taking into account its geographic, hegemonic, and popular culture features—'otherness' would become indistinguishable with celebrity. These relations of fandom and imagined intimacy are one-sided, but Fandemonium does not limit para-social relations to the cult of the celebrity. The line between fan and performer can be temporarily erased in a studio environment, but this distinction is also easily acknowledged as a part of the intimate geography that the studio produces. The fan/performer barrier is as to self/other; it is a barrier of performance that requires the fan (the self) and the audience to make relations through a heterotopic space of personae.

The theatrical elements regarding the construction of 'otherness', which allows an arena for looking and acts of Fandemonium, are also ones which require democratic participation from the population to work at their most basic level: television, the internet, journalistic practice, and so on. Consider the style of celebrity reportage which has become standard practice in Western journalism. P. David Marshall writes that a methodically constructed and controlled image of celebrity involves elements of that figures' personal life, moral philosophy, and family time that the public is brought into relation with through contact from daily media outlets.[13] This style of reportage has become "routinized"[14] writing, as both investigative and cultural fluff. The public reception and digestion of these personae, vis-à-vis reputable channels, are methodically framed and engineered as not only a representation of humanity, but as models of human beings. This also requires a public acknowledgment and engagement with the creation, glorification, and framing of these personae. As Marshall writes, one half of this journalism is based on a very public desire to know "what the famous [other] person is *really* like."[15]

As journalism makes this continuous shift towards celebrity reportage, towards a positioning of 'otherness' as an intimate celebrity personae (and celebrity as an intimate personae of 'otherness'), it seems that we are inundated with the possibility of these relations on a daily basis. A non-reciprocal relationship with not only a celebrity but a public figure is one that represents this Western positioning within an 'imaginative geography'.

This non-reciprocal relationship with 'otherness' also makes it possible to name 'otherness' as a cultural target within a specific delineated location. This notion of imaginative geographies presents to "demarcate 'the same' from 'the other'"[16] by positioning the same, the self, within a familiar space. Derek Gregory, in his book *The Colonial Present,* writes that,

> Its [modernity's] constructions of other cultures—not only the way in which these are understood in an immediate, improvisational sense, but also the way in which more or less enduring codifications of them are produced—shape its own dispositions and deployments.[17]

These codified spaces are only one tangent of the construction of the modern 'self'; the aestheticization of the demarcation between 'self' and 'other', as a spiritual brand, begins in these codified spaces. Marc Gobe provides the example of emotional branding; since the mid-1990s, the search for spiritual balance (through things like free time) is one of the biggest growing *consumer* trends in the West.[18] Products, likewise, were manufactured and branded with this in mind. Spirituality shifted, again, from its roots in Christian lexicon to an object of desire in the marketplace, playing specifically off of social needs.[19] Spirituality was visually depicted in a certain way, with Eastern or Oriental themes and undercurrents, in ad campaigns such as make-up, clothing, or bottled water.

This codified space, and the distance that distinguishes it, are not static,[20] just as Sheldrake's spirituality is fluid, and given shape by surrounding cultural and social conditions. A spiritual relation to a personae of 'otherness'—geographic, theistic, celebrity, etc.—is a part of the lived-experience of the self. In Rojek's discussion of celebrity and religion, he notes that fans and audience members project intense feelings onto the personae.[21] Rojek notes other attributes as well: it is as if the performative personae "provides a path into genuine meaningful experiences,"[22] for the fan and audience member.

This is a specific projection of cultural distance, and its spatial qualities are what helps us to locate it and come into relation with it. The image, representative of a body, also locates (embodies) itself within physical boundaries. Entertainment media technologies (the audio and the visual) have bridged the gap of time and space, but not of cultural distance where those times and spaces could be derived. So while entities of Fandemonium that reflect a culture of technology are easily accessible to indulge in, they are spaced-out physically from a physical 'otherness' that these entities may or may not represent: the other as a spiritual relation is also a spiritual relation taking placing within that aesthetisized demarcation. It is reliant on the spatial: for space to be created for its existence.

In Relation to Feminism

The relationship of Fandemonium to contemporary feminist scholarship is vital for a complete understanding of this word. One aim of Fandemonium is to decenter traditional perceptions of spirituality. Feminism plays an important yet understated role in this process. Like Fandemonium, it is contextual, and as much affected by the popular culture as any other area it engages with.

Fandemonium is also, as mentioned at the beginning of the paper, a creative (fraudulent) use of semantics. Consider this example given in Shulamit Reinharz's article *The Principles of Feminist Research: A Matter of Debate,* on the language used by the first feminist scholars. The early women's liberation movements led to insight that all social life was shaped by patriarchy.[23] This thought, in turn, influenced the way that feminism developed research methods, language, and onto what the discourse focused its attention. And as new ways of researching womens experiences were developed, new ways of discussing and approaching their issues of concern were needed as well. Early womens studies began to focus on areas that academia had, until that point, been shoved off as inappropriate, useless, or trivial.

Thus: is pre-established feminist vocabulary still appropriate, or relevant, to discuss our experiences? Or, should women scholars be 'appropriating' new definitions for our feminist lexicon? Words like 'male-stream'—initially used to indicate the feminist position in relation to the male status quo—now appear ironically sexist and counter-productive, in that it is dually alienating. If at one time these words served the purpose of helping feminism to establish itself, it seems that this has shifted dramatically over the last decade. If in the 1960s womens studies refused to play by the rules, and avoided the approval of the bureaucracy, now language like 'male-stream' only nods to establish power, gender, and hegemonic roles through feminist language. It should be noted, and not ignored, that feminism can also help continuously perpetuate an arena where Fandemonium is able to take place.

And while it is important and needed to reserve a space for the voices and experiences of women, working in conjunction with all communities will be more productive for these discussions than completely alienating ourselves, as women, from a popular culture (labeled 'male-centric') that so fascinates our discourse. As a woman, gender issues are affected by every action I take; men's and women's issues have a reciprocal affect on each other. This is to say that they are inter-systemic. On a personal level, I refuse to be 'dually alienated' from the popular culture, by cutting myself off from a society that I feel alienated from. This includes having open dialogue with discourse that is assumed to be, even today, a part of the male-stream. As an extension of this, Fandemonium does not need to avoid or ignore exclusively male forms of study; the same thing can be said for any kind of feminist study to which women take the lead.

Closing Remarks

Referring back to my earlier statement regarding non-religious tendencies, I intended by this term beliefs which are atheistic in nature, or a part of an alternative church or lifestyle which would not be considered in the study of traditional theistic religions. This includes a variety of contemporary schools of thought,[24] though unfortunately there is not room in this paper to discuss them each in more detail. A large area of research could exist for integrating the voices of women who may identify with portions of feminist study, yet who come from non-religious backgrounds (and who do not identify with the discussion of feminism and theism) into the study of feminist spirituality. Feminism must make room for those who do not express a theistic outlook, but find wholeness and meaning in alternative lifestyles. This suggests another larger issue: how do feminists of nondenominational backgrounds discuss spirituality on their own terms? Along with a need to expand the boundaries of feminist study to nondenominational beliefs, the critique of feminism in conjuncture with the entities of spirituality and popular culture is a feature of the discourse that I hope can be expanded and explored in more depth in the future. We have the right to criticize ourselves, our research tactics, and our discourse language to better gender relations and break away from heteronormative identities.

What an understanding of Fandemonium can achieve is a de-construction and shattering of performative personae and images of 'otherness', and through this to de-centre, de-institutionalize, and re-arrange notions of normality, civilization, and celebrity. The assembly of 'otherness' as a spiritual relation, in image, as representative of not only a real manifestation but of a body within the space it embodies, should only exist as a momentary neutral voice before it is dis-assembled. The image and personae is not solid, static, or concrete. To de-centre is not to participate in the preparation of those images, but as a public and as feminists, to be in control of all entities in relation to their creation, life, and death.

The interactive and technologically-based popular culture that comes from audio and visual media presents the possible shape of our next wave, and it will present the obstacle of cultural distance if feminists do not work to learn the geography that has been constructed on our screens. The images produced should be considered for analysis, even if they are not blatantly detrimental to a specific gender group or demographic: spirituality does not always come with familiar labels or in familiar forms. Fandemonium can expose a layer within the popular culture that can provide a new angle which feminist scholarship could move forth with.

Notes

1. In an April 2007 interview I conducted with the UK anarcho-punk band *Subhumans*, singer Dick Lucas touched on this issue briefly in the context of popular music, where the appropriation of rebellious philosophies such as this for marketing purposes is prevalent.
Meldazy: Do you think that these anarchist ideas or these anarchist philosophies, as they participate in music…and through that, participate in popular culture, do they become subsumed in their participation with popular culture?
Dick Lucas: They can be yeah, very much so. Bands that think they can take their anarcho philosophies onto a major record label, I think, are very much self-delusions. And forget that the whole point is, if you wanna beat the system working within it is not going to work. You just become part of it, whether you like it or not. You have to go [through] structures and laws and codes and behavior in order to fit into the music industries shape of the way your musics' gonna be delivered. It will be at the highest priced in the largest music chain stores across the planet. And, so saying "free yourself from the trappings of commercialism" through your lyrics, while those lyrics are only coming out or coming through HMV or Virgin record stores, or whatever is a total contradiction.
2. Derek Gregory, *The Colonial Present* (Oxford: Blackwell Publishing, 2007), 4.
3. Thomas Hobbes wrote in *Leviathan* that there is an arbitrary correlation between the word 'spirit' to incorporeal entities, as a creation of the minds of men: "the opinion that such spirits were incorporeal, or immaterial, could never enter into the minds of any man by nature, because though men may put together words of contradictory significance, as *spirit* and *incorporeal,* yet they can never have the imagination of anything answering to them." (XII, 7) As Antony Flew points out, and it may be also worthwhile to

mention, Hobbes uses the word 'spirit' to act as a kind of substance, or 'stuff'. As words, they are synonymous. (Flew, Antony. "What Is Spirituality" in *Modern Spiritualities: An Inquiry,* 34-35)

4. Philip Sheldrake, *A Brief History of Spirituality* (Oxford: Blackwell Publishing, 2007), 2.

5. Sheldrake, *A Brief History of Spirituality,* 2.

6. Sheldrake, *A Brief History of Spirituality,* 6.

7. Chris Rojek, "Celebrity and Religion", in *The Celebrity Culture Reader* (New York: Routledge, 2006), 390.

8. Donald Horton and R. Richard Wohl, "Mass Communication and Para-Social Interaction: Observations on Intimacy at a Distance", *Psychiatry* 19 (1956), 215.

9. Horton and Wohl, "Mass Communication and Para-Social Interaction", 215.

10. Horton and Wohl, "Mass Communication and Para-Social Interaction", 216.

11. Horton and Wohl, "Mass Communication and Para-Social Interaction", 216.

12. Horton and Wohl, "Mass Communication and Para-Social Interaction", 216.

13. This also begs the question: do consumers believe their media to be reciprocal in nature?

14. P. David Marshall, "Intimately Intertwined In The Most Public Way: Celebrity and Journalism", in *The Celebrity Culture Reader* (New York: Routledge, 2006), 316.

15. Marshall, "Intimately Intertwined in the Most Public Way: Celebrity and Journalism", 316.

16. Marshall, "Intimately Intertwined in the Most Public Way: Celebrity and Journalism", 317.

17. Gregory, *The Colonial Present,* 4.

18. Marc Gobe, *Emotional Branding: The New Paradigm for Connecting Brands to People* (Allsworth Press: NewYork, 2001), 289.

19. Gobe, *Emotional Branding: The New Paradigm for Connecting Brands to People,* 292.

20. Gregory, *The Colonial Present,* 18.

21. Rojek, "Celebrity and Religion", 389.

22. Rojek, "Celebrity and Religion", 390.

23. Shulamit Reinharz, "The Principles of Feminist Research: A Matter of Debate", in *The Knowledge Explosion: Generations of Feminist Scholarship,* ed. Cheris Kramarae and Dale Spencer (New York: Teachers College Press, 1992), 424.

24. Some of these schools may simply include updated versions of past philosophical, commercial, or other movements which open up the floor for more debate on them and their merits: atheism, anarchy, scientology, raunch (or-post) feminism, online social networking, etc.

Bibliography

Antony, Louise M., ed. *Philosophers Without Gods: Meditations on Atheism and The Secular Life.* Oxford: Oxford University Press, 2007.

Flew, Antony. "What is 'Spirituality'?" In *Modern Spiritualities: An Inquiry,* ed. Laurence Brown, Bernard C. Farr, and R. Joseph Hoffman, 31-39. Amherst: Prometheus Books, 1996.

Gobe, Marc. *Emotional Branding: The New Paradigm For Connecting Brands To People*. New York: Allsworth Press, 2001.

Gregory, Derek. *The Colonial Present*. Oxford: Blackwell Publishing, 2007.

Hobbes, Thomas. *Leviathan*, ed. Edwin Curley. Indianapolis: Hackett Publishing Company, 1994.

Horton, Donald and Wohl, Richard R. 'Mass Communication and Para-Social Interaction: Observations on Intimacy at a Distance'. *Psychiatry* 19 (1956): 215-229.

King, Ursula. "Spirituality." In *Encyclopedia of Women and World Religion*, ed. Serinity Young, 942-943, v. 2. New York: Macmillian Reference, 1999.

Marshall, David P. "Intimately Intertwined In The Most Public Way: Celebrity and Journalism". In *The Celebrity Culture Reader*, ed. P. David Marshall, 315-324. New York: Routledge, 2006.

Reinharz, Shulamit. "The Principles of Feminist Research: A Matter of Debate." In *The Knowledge Explosion: Generations of Feminist Scholarship*, ed. Cheris Kramarae and Dale Spender. New York: Teachers College Press, 1992.

Rojek, Chris. "Celebrity and Religion." In *The Celebrity Culture Reader*, ed. P. David Marshall, 389-417. New York: Routledge, 2006.

Said, Edward W. *Orientalism*. New York: Pantheon Books, 1978.

Sheldrake, Philip. *A Brief History of Spirituality*. Oxford: Blackwell Publishing, 2007.

Chapter Five:
Not Pretty Girls? Sexuality, Spirituality, and Gender Construction in Women's Rock Music

Kate McCarthy

The Body Problem

In the second century of Christian history, a Gnostic teacher named Valentinus was condemned as a heretic for teaching that Jesus never defecated.[1] There are two things to note about this largely forgettable moment in theological history. First, it tells us that those with the power to define orthodoxy insisted on the full reality of Jesus' embodiment in human form. Second, and more subtly, it tells us that this issue was momentous and contentious enough to be worthy of theological debate; the church fathers did not go to the mat over just any oddball claim about Jesus. This particular claim and its official condemnation show us just how deeply Christian ambivalence about the human body runs. On the one hand, there is the powerful temptation to deny the association between divinity and our most basic corporeality, between God and shit. On the other hand is the insistence that this is in fact precisely what the Christian doctrine of the Incarnation means: God is intimately involved in the world of human bodies in all their joys and indignities.

Fast-forward to 1995. Rock musician Joan Osborne releases "(What If God Was) One of Us," a Grammy-nominated hit song that invites us to imagine God as "a slob like one of us," "just a stranger on the bus" (*Relish*, 1995). In 1998, former Fugees lead singer Lauryn Hill invokes the doctrine of the Incarnation when she sings of an angel coming to her and announcing the imminent birth of her "man-child." ("To Zion," *The Miseducation of Lauryn Hill*, 1998). These very different but related expressions are part of an interesting array of women's music that brings ancient religious concepts into conversation with contemporary

97

feminism about the meaning of embodied life. Contemporary women's rock music, mostly unknowingly, it seems, gives voice to the intersection of two important intellectual trends—feminist theory's analysis of the cultural construction of female bodies, and feminist theology's reclaiming of embodied experience as a source of sacred meaning and power.[2] In the process, this music is establishing itself as an important, if ambiguous, site of "third wave" feminist spirituality.[3]

It should not be surprising to find women at the forefront of efforts to rethink the dominant culture's assessment of the body. From the Virgin Mary to Barbie, women have been presented with models for their embodied life that fuse asexuality with hypersexuality in bizarre and bewildering ways. And for as long as cultures have been inscribing these meanings on their bodies, women have both facilitated and found ways to subvert their effect, sometimes in the same act. That paradox is illuminated in the spaces where feminist theory, feminist theology, and women's music intersect.

Body Theory and Women's Music

Analyses of the social meanings of the female body are nothing new to feminist theory. In their critiques of violence against women, lack of reproductive autonomy, compulsory heterosexuality, and the beauty system, second wave feminists uncovered the ways in which women's bodies have been used to define and enforce patriarchal constructions of female gender. More recent studies in gender theory, though, suggest the variability and instability of the category of gender itself. It is common in feminist theory today, drawing on the influential work of Judith Butler in particular, to speak of the radically constructed nature of gender; the fiction of gender binaries like male and female or straight and gay; and the playful fluidity of all gender identities.

Increasingly in this context, the female body is presented not (only) as a locus of oppression, but as a kind of performance site, where cultural expectations about gender are rehearsed but also, at least potentially, manipulated and resisted. In this view, the female body is not so much the object of male consumption as a complex social construct, a kind of lived ideology where male domination gets materialized through constant repetition of acts of receptivity, dependence, and vulnerability, but also where alternative acts can subvert that domination.

Central to these analyses of the female body are considerations of women's sexual agency. Women's sexuality, of course, has been a pre-eminent focus of patriarchal anxiety about women's bodies since the ancient period. The reduction of women to sexual objects of male desire and the suppression of the existence, let alone the expression, of female desire has been a mainstay of feminist critique for decades. In her classic essay "This Sex Which Is Not One," Luce Irigaray explains how female sexuality is collapsed into male at the level of the body itself:

In these terms, women's erogenous zones never amount to anything but a clitoris-sex that is not comparable to the noble phallic organ, or a hole-envelope that serves to sheathe and massage the penis in intercourse: a non-sex, or a masculine organ turned back upon itself, self-embracing.[4]

Women participate on a daily basis in the social construction of their bodies as both wholly sexual in terms defined by the culture, and simultaneously asexual in terms of their own agency and desire. A 1994 sociological study of young women's accounts of their sexual behavior summarized the problem well:

Young women are under pressures to construct their material bodies into a particular model of femininity, which is both inscribed on the surface of their bodies, through such skills as dress, make-up and dietary regimes, and disembodied in the sense of detachment from their sensuality and alienation from their material bodies.[5]

One approach to this problem, of course, is to empower women to quit making such inscriptions on their bodies. Those of us who grew into feminism in the seventies are familiar with this effort, often caricatured as mandates to disavow lipstick, shaving, and, ideally, male sexual partners.

Today, using more radically social constructionist views of gender, feminist theorists are drawing increased attention to women's sexual agency as a means of expressing, if not inventing, an irrepressible, because indefinable, female identity. More than just claiming the right to sexual pleasure, feminist focus on women's desire calls forth a new way of being with far-reaching social implications. As Muriel Dimen argues,

Sexuality is not the route to revolution. But it is a prime shaper of desire, and constraint of desire leads directly to self-betrayal and social bad faith. We suffer not from too much desire but from too little. Our failures to rebel, our incomplete revolutions, are rooted in the repression of desire that, essential to sexual oppression, truncates hope.[6]

Because patriarchal societies have so repressed women's desire, it emerges in strange, varied, and often contradictory expressions, none of which stand still long enough to become another's sexual object. The binary of male agency and female objectification is dramatically disrupted in much current feminist writing through playful exploration of countless varieties of women's own pleasure or *jouissance*, that prerational, body-centered joy, passion, and interconnection that "precedes self/other dualisms [and] expresses the continuity of self and other."[7]

In plain terms, this line of thinking says that resisting patriarchal domination of the female body is not a matter of wiping off make-up and stepping out of thongs and high heels. If our gender is radically socially constructed, then these are no more inherently oppressive than unshaven legs and bralessness are liberatory. The mandate, then, is not to embody an alternative gender script, but to resist all scripts, which can be accomplished by donning the body markings (clothes, movements, hair, postures, jewelry, gestures, language, etc.) of an alternative gender, or by combining those of multiple genders in playful or ironic ways.

This theoretical trajectory is traceable in the world of women's rock music, though very few of its producers or consumers have probably ever struggled through a Judith Butler text. Because of rock music's overwhelmingly masculine character, women's very presence within it is marked as gender-significant. It is impossible (as reflected, for instance, in nearly forty years of rock criticism) for a woman rock musician not to be a *woman* rock musician. Given the long association of women with commercial, vocal-oriented pop music and men with the more "authentic," guitar-based rock genre,[8] there is a sense in which simply by picking up a guitar woman musicians are committing the kinds of gender trespass that feminist theory celebrates. Ani DiFranco, who puts out records on her own "Righteous Babe" record label, recalls her early acts of trespassing this way:

> For many, many years, simply walking into a guitar store was almost an act of courage, because it was very much a boy's club. They would kinda look you up and down, and say, "Hi, honey, are you here to get something for your boyfriend?" Now you walk into a guitar store and it's full of teenage girls.[9]

While the link between feminist theory and musical practice is certainly more evident in recent years, when much of women's music has taken on a self-consciously feminist identity, even the earliest women's rock music reflects a challenge to societal gender norms. The so-called "Girl Groups" of the early sixties, even while their lyrics adhered to the conventional gender script of life defined by longing for The Boy (the strong but tender, mysterious and misunderstood loner), nonetheless represent an important female incursion into a masculinist world, one in which the body played a central role. It is important to note that the iconic representation of these groups are black women like Diana Ross, Martha Reeves, and perhaps most significantly, Ronnie Spector. Heavily made-up, mini-skirted, and with a voice that Madonna has called "sexy, hungry, totally trashy" (http://www.ronniespector.com), Spector's self-presentation of raw but innocent sexuality is, among other things, a clear instance in the long history of the American commodification of black women's bodies. Black women singers have had to construct their identities within a racist tradition that has defined them sexually as both deviant and perpetually available, as bell hooks explains:

> Since black female sexuality has been represented in racist/sexist iconography as more free and liberated, many black women singers, irrespective of the quality of their voices, have cultivated an image which suggests they are sexually available licentious. Undesirable in the conventional sense, which defines beauty and sexuality as desirable only to the extent that it is idealized and unat-

tainable, the black female body gains attention only when it is synonymous
with accessibility, availability, when it is sexually deviant.[10]

But there is an important ambiguity here. At the same time that their sexuality
was being defined by male promoters and exploited to sell records, singers like
Ronnie Spector offered via Top Forty radio an alternative for teenage *girls* to the
childlike cleanliness of such cultural icons as Leslie Gore and Sandra Dee, and
established the provocative "bad girl" image that would later be claimed for
more explicitly feminist purposes by white artists like Chrissie Hynde, Madonna,
and Courtney Love. This was, I suggest, a cultural moment in which something
new became possible, when young women (and men) in the dominant culture
encountered an image of female sexuality—in dress, gesture, posture, and
voice—that was raw and powerful, distinctly at odds with the self-abasing lyrics
of the songs themselves.

When they did encounter this music and these images, young girls—black
and white—were also moved to enact its rule-breaking with their own bodies. As
Susan J. Douglas has argued, sixties dancing freed girls from the hold of boys, so
that they were able to use dance as a means of sexual self-expression, alone
and/or with each other.

> So even in songs seemingly about female victimization and helplessness, the
> beat and euphoria of the music put the lie to the lyrics by getting the girl out on
> the dance floor, moving on her own, doing what she liked, displaying herself
> sexually, and generally getting ready for bigger and better things.[11]

It's also important to note that this music was not cheerleading on the sidelines
of American rock; according to rock critic Greil Marcus, "if you were looking
for rock & roll between Elvis and the Beatles, girl groups gave you the genuine
article."[12] But their central and very physical place in the rock music scene does
not obscure the fact that the women of the girl groups had almost no agency in
their own music; "the songwriting, production, and financial rewards still rested
with the production companies and labels."[13]

It would take a second generation of women musicians to claim power and
autonomy in the space made available to them by their sixties predecessors. Janis
Joplin, Patti Smith, Debbie Harry, and, monumentally, Madonna, all helped
create the huge tent under which women's rock music now flourishes. Today,
women musicians are not only making their own records; they are helping to
define western feminism's third wave. Indeed, it has been said that while seventies feminism was text-driven, current feminism is pop culture-driven. As Kylie
Murphy has written, "Third wave feminism is distinguished from the second
wave by a greater literacy in popular culture and technology: this enables both a
critical approach and a willingness to work within systems critiqued for being
patriarchal."[14] Rock music specifically has now emerged as a major vehicle of
this movement. Camille Paglia, ever ready to chide academic feminists, warns:
"Feminists should be concerned about the personalities in rock and roll because

they will be the primary means by which young women get the feminist message."[15] The comments of young women I meet in my university classes and in on-line discussions of women's music at such sites as Rockrgrl.com lend credence to Paglia's and Murphy's claims, as does the growing popularity of such concerts-cum-women's retreats as the Michigan Womyn's Music Festival and its more commercial counterpart, the Lilith Fair. Seen from the textual and political perspective of earlier varieties of feminism, these sites—because commodified and highly interpretive—are extremely ambiguous, but their influence is undeniable and apparently limitless.

It would be impossible to generalize about the type of feminism represented in this music; it is of course as diverse as the musicians themselves. But collectively in the rock music being produced by women today, which runs the gamut from the folk harmonies of the Indigo Girls to the hip-hop soul of Lauryn Hill to the polished punk rage of Courtney Love, at least three themes from contemporary feminist reflections on gender and the body are given vivid expression.

First, it resists the culture's very straightened codes of female beauty not (only) by opting for a genderless presentation of the body, but by ironically adopting, exaggerating or otherwise manipulating, and thereby subverting, those codes. On the cover of their 1994 CD *Live Through This*, for instance, Courtney Love's band Hole offers an illustrative send-up of the dominant culture's construction of female identity in their punk deconstruction of the American beauty queen, complete with Farrah Fawcett hair and mascara-smeared black eyes. Throughout the album, they expose the miserable distortions of young women who are identified (and identify themselves) as so many pretty parts: doll eyes, mouths, arms, and legs.

In much of contemporary women's music, girlishness and its signifiers (dolls, ruffled clothing, high voices, giggling, make-up, barrettes, etc.) are violently rearranged, to powerful effect. As Karina Eileraas explains, "Girl bands call into question the conventional 'props' of gender by performing them as a carnival, offering them up as a funhouse mirror of grotesque reflection and refraction."[16] What comes of these juxtapositions of prettiness and ugliness is, when it works, an exposure of "the violence to and alienation from the body that the obedient performance of 'pretty' femininity entail."[17] If irony and parody are emerging as central strategies of third wave feminism's attack on patriarchal gender constructions,[18] popular music is clearly a major venue for that work.[19]

But the representation of the female body occurs in women's music at levels other than the lyrics of songs and album art. The artists' own self-presentation can be read as a kind of manifesto against the beauty machine. Ani DiFranco, who first came to mainstream attention for her 1995 album called *Not a Pretty Girl,* speaks often in interviews of her own rejection of the ideal of beauty. "If you're female, with long hair and fairly cute, you get plenty of the wrong kind of attention. If a woman is independent, it's not seen as sexy. At one time I remember thinking, 'If this is my only option, I'll be ugly.'"[20] Her body is tattooed, her nose pierced, her head by turns shaved and dreadlocked. "I'm an unglamorous person," DiFranco has said, "and don't have the need to write pretty or be plea-sant."[21] But this woman who insists she is not a pretty girl makes her own power-ful beauty statements through ironic play with symbols of prettiness like short dresses juxtaposed with massive "stompy boots." Similarly, Lauryn Hill, who is a mother of four, producer of her own record, which sold over three million cop-ies and won five Grammy Awards, allows herself to be represented as a little girl with bobby socks and a lollipop and as a cheerleader in magazine photo spreads. The juxtaposition of the autonomy of her life and music with the infantalizing poses makes a parody of the culture's ongoing insistence on representing women as children, in a gesture that at least potentially strips such images of their op-pressive force.[22]

A second way in which women's rock music coheres with current feminist theory on gender and the body is in the self-conscious appropriation of the male rock star's script of sexual aggression and rage. While this is certainly not cha-racteristic of all women's groups, where it does occur it marks a significant vi-olation of the proscription against women's agency and desire, and seems to en-dorse the radically social constructionist rejection of gender binaries. In writing about women's self-defense training, sociologist Martha McCaughey notes that violation of these binaries has important positive consequences for women:

> Our culture is wedded to distinguishing bodies as male and female. One way that sex is materialized is through regulatory norms surrounding the use of ag-gression. Cultural ideals of manhood and womanhood include a cultural, politi-cal, aesthetic, and legal acceptance of men's aggression and a deep skepticism about, fear, and prohibition of women's. . . . When women learn how to re-spond aggressively to thwart assaults, they realize that feminine niceness is a historical effect, not a natural given of women hood. The body-self is trans-formed through rehearsals of aggression that solidify a new embodied ideal.[23]

I believe a similar rehearsal is going on when a female punk band smashes gui-tars and trashes a stage at the end of concerts, when women enter the mosh pit, when Liz Phair sings "I'll fuck you till your dick is blue," ("Flower," *Exile in Guyville*, 1993) and when, for instance, Alanis Morissette verbally calls to ac-counts the partner who has left her: "Did you forget about me, Mr. Duplicity?" The sound and sense of this song, which was the biggest single on Morissette's 1995 album *Jagged Little Pill*, communicate something quite different from the broken-hearted girl's lament of traditional pop music but an in-your-face con-frontation with betrayal. Lyrically, it is an insistence that the one who has left *pay attention* to the mess left behind; musically it is a loud, pounding, purge of rage that we sense leaves the singer (and her listeners) feeling more powerful than before.[24]

The force of these gender code transgressions is evident in the degree to which they overtake the consciousness of (especially male) onlookers. *Rolling Stone* critic Robert Christgau calls musician PJ Harvey "sex-obsessed,"[25] though her lyrics are no match for the phallically fixated tradition of mainstream male rock music. In countless reviews, musicians like Morissette, DiFranco, and Love were tagged as "rock's angry young women." Courtney Love, who has left a wake of wrecked hotel rooms worthy of a male heavy metal band, was called by *Time* magazine a "bratty, tattered tart." These labels, which do not fall on their male counterparts, reflect the high level of cultural anxiety about women's acting out of their assigned demeanors, especially that of sexual passivity. While few feminist theorists would claim acts of public drunkenness, profanity, and throwing microphone stands as important expressions of feminist resistance, these are in fact subversions of essentialized understandings of the female body that can, especially because they are public acts, have significant social ramifications. In a poignant twist on this subversion, Madonna's "What it Feels Like for a Girl" (*Music*, 2000) calls attention to the codes that keep boys from enjoying the alternative pleasures of female scripts, noting that girls are free to adopt male dress codes and hair styles, but that the freedom doesn't go both ways. Her song invites boys to give in to their secret desires to savor the pleasure of twirling their hair or resting their hands on jutting hips, in tune with what may come to be a prominent feature of twenty-first-century gender play.

Finally, we can also see in this era of women's rock music a celebration of the kind of gender ambiguity and instability described by contemporary feminist theorists.[26] Madonna, of course, broke this ground in the 1980s. Reams have been written about the meaning of Madonna for women and for feminism; what seems important to emphasize here is the way that she can be seen as a representation of the line of feminist theory characterized above. Using irony, parody, and always sexuality, "her pieces explore—sometimes playfully, sometimes seriously—various ways of constituting identities that refuse stability, that remain fluid, that resist definition."[27]

Today, this ambiguity is a common theme in feminist analyses of women's music. For instance, Jennifer Rycenga summarizes PJ Harvey's resistance to fixed gender identity this way:

> In her public self-presentations, PJ Harvey adopts a gender-ambivalent form of her name, repeatedly makes provocative comments about gender in interviews, uses her sexuality as part of her artistry, and defines it herself, studiously and self-consciously fitting no one's agenda. She sports a postmodern edge filled with gender ambiguity and repositionings of sexual discourse.[28]

Ani DiFranco expresses similar resistance in both her songs and her public persona. Her rejection of the pretty girl mandate struck chords with countless young fans, who praise her for naming and honoring the ambiguous gender they too inhabit. But DiFranco's frequent metamorphoses (growing her hair, falling in love with a man) have brought charges from some fans that she has sold out the movement. At this she balks and takes every opportunity afforded by interviews to educate her fans about this new variety of feminism. In the title song of her 1998 album *Little Plastic Castle*, she takes to task those who would read lipstick as "a sign of my declining mind," or her self-presentation on any given day as "my statement for all womankind." DiFranco brings this celebration of shape-shifting into her newer work as well. In the title song of her 2003 CD, *Evolve*, she reiterates that her image can't be encapsulated because she has "the kind of beauty that moves." This plea for three-dimensionality coheres with social constructionist theories of the body as text—or, perhaps better, canvas—where meanings have been assumed to be fixed (lipstick equals feminine equals heterosexual equals subordinate) but are better read as smearable, erasable, endlessly revisable.

Gender ambiguity is also expressed in women's music through celebrations of fluid sexual identities. While "women's music" has long been a locus of community and iconic affirmation among lesbians, much contemporary rock music by women presses the very categories of sex and gender identification. DiFranco is described by one reviewer as "ambisexual;" as she puts it, "I'm not a straight girl and I'm not a dyke,"[29] a non-location on the sexual spectrum that consternates fans and critics alike. Even those "straight girl" musicians who do not flip-flop in sexual preference often express this ambiguity in their refusal to be heterosexual in the traditionally scripted way. Claiming sexual desire and expressing sexual agency in ways inappropriate for "nice" girls directly challenge the notion of the female sex as a "non-sex" "hole-envelope" decried by Irigaray. Interestingly, these gestures can be seen as popular expression of the theoretical moves of postmodern feminism that are often deemed irrelevant or even inimical to the lives of real women.

Body Theology and Women's Music

With this kind of music and self-presentation, women musicians are claiming a space in the culture for an embodied feminism that presses the edges of academic feminist theory. What makes this space especially interesting to me as a religious studies scholar is that this space is also widely identified by the musicians and their fans as a kind of *sacred* space. Feminism and religion have never had a very good relationship, so it is striking when their discourses intersect, even more so when that conversation occurs outside their institutional boundaries, that is, in popular culture. From religious images in lyrics to musicians' ironic use of religious symbols as costume jewelry to descriptions of concerts as religious experiences, women's rock music, especially in the past decade, has become an important locus of theological meaning-making. And here, too, the musicians and fans are both embodying and radicalizing the theoretical work being done by their academic counterparts.

Feminist theologians have been at work for three decades now trying to deconstruct and at least in some cases to reconstruct the powerful patriarchal traditions of western religion. Some have abandoned these traditions as hopelessly phallocentric and unredeemable.[30] Others work within or at least on the margins of organized religions to critique and re-imagine the textual and symbolic resources of the traditions. Still others sift though the pre-Christian traditions of ancient Europe and elsewhere to uncover pagan resources for a feminist spirituality. As noted above, the body, especially in its female form, has been particularly troubling for Christian theologians. As the editors of a recent collection of essays on religion and body note, "For a long time the spiritualizing and the control of everything material was central to the history of Christian piety. The body itself was above all the tangible and perceptible place of human sinfulness, exposed to the drives and an obstacle on the way to salvation."[31]

Central to feminist theological work with the body, then, is the critique of the patriarchal theological tradition that has demonized the female body as the primary locus of sin, and the corresponding re-sacralizing of the female body and its desires. Rosemary Ruether analyzes the historical processes whereby the culture of late antiquity turned to a world-fleeing spirituality in which sharply dualistic oppositions—male/female, body/spirit, heaven/earth, reason/passion, supernature/nature—defined the religious quest. In the Greco-Roman philosophical world in which Christian theology took form, ascetic practices that sought to extricate the spiritual from the material became the normative religious pattern, establishing a hierarchical chain of being that, as Ruether points out, is at the same time a chain of command: God → spirits → male humans → female humans → non-human nature → inert matter:

> All that sustains physical life—sex, eating, reproduction, even sleep—comes to be seen as sustaining the realm of "death," against which a mental realm of consciousness has been abstracted as the realm of "true life." Women, as representatives of sexual reproduction and motherhood, are the bearers of death, from which male spirit must flee to "light and life."[32]

A major task of feminist theology, then, has been to pry open the links of this chain and reconfigure it in such a way that women, the body and nature are seen to be in direct, unmediated relation to the sacred. In turn, the sacred (God/dess) is re-imagined as encompassing natural, earthly, female, and embodied elements.

In women's rock music, this theme is widely evident in lyrics that make explicit if subversive use of biblical imagery and symbols; indeed, musicians may well be ahead of the game in the effort to reconnect the female body with the sacred. Madonna broke open the feminist use of religious symbols in pop music in the mid-eighties. Wearing massive crucifixes that dangled into bustiered cleavage, comparing sexual love to prayer, taking as her only name the ultimate symbol of women's ironic status in Christianity, Madonna moved rock music's discussion of religion from an adolescent rant to thoughtful and often faithful reassessments and re-appropriations. More recently, her uses of Hindu and Jewish symbolism[33] in costume, dance, and body art, have added a controversial cross-cultural element to her religious appropriations.

Following Madonna's lead, many contemporary women artists manipulate traditional religious symbols in their attacks on organized religion, and call particular attention to the ways in which those institutions have relegated women and especially their bodies to the world of the unclean and ungodly. Tori Amos, the daughter of a conservative Protestant minister, is perhaps the most thorough-going in her theological deconstructions. She finds the traditional doctrine of God wholly unsatisfactory, singing "God sometimes you just don't come through," In the same song, she quotes Proverbs 31:3, "give not thy strength unto women nor thy ways to that which destroyeth kings," and follows it by asking "will you even tell her if you decide to make the sky fall?" and finally "Do you need a women to look after you?" ("God," *Little Earthquakes*, 1992). In "Cruci-fy," she lays blame for the daily self-crucifixions of women who have been taught that nothing they do will ever make them worthy at the feet of a religion that glorifies guilt and suffering ("Drive another nail in/Got enough guilt to start my own religion") (*Little Earthquakes*, 1992). The music video of this song takes Amos' critique to the level of reconstruction, though, as we see her in the central moment step fully clothed into a bathtub and re-emerge in a long, sexy full-body shot with her dress clinging to her skin. This sensuous baptism sug-gests a cleansing of the old ideology and a rebirth into the body while she sings "never going back again to crucify myself again."[34]

The myth of Adam and Eve in the garden, on which Christian misogyny has drawn for nearly two millennia, is a favorite theme for re-working in women's music. In a 1996 *Rolling Stone* interview, Joan Osborne offers her own fairly sophisticated theological reassessment of the Genesis myth.

> I just don't necessarily see knowledge—being conscious and being an intellec-tual and a sexual creature—as a horrible state. Organized religion presents the Garden of Eden as this ideal of innocence and being sheep in the flock, una-ware, as the goal. To me, that's just too passive; it's less interesting than the more dangerous and confusing but more satisfying state of actually being con-scious—being able to come to God or spirituality with all of yourself, with your brain and your will and your curiosity and your sensuality and everything.[35]

In her own deconstructing of the Eden myth (in "Adam and Eve," *Dilate*, 1996), Ani DiFranco tells a departing lover that she likes apples, has no fear of snakes, and has no interest in the game being played out in the garden.

One of the most effective ways of challenging the dualistic thinking that relegates women's bodies to a world of silence and shame is simply to name and honor bodily reality in public spaces.[36] Feminist theologian Paula Cooey writes:

> For all its wonder, the leaking, heaving, flatulating, needy, vulnerable, finite human body more often than not culturally symbolizes a horrible bondage to natural, social and personal corruption and death in the West. . . . A post-patriarchal understanding of the incarnation must be committed to a redemption of the body. In so doing, it must recognize that the transfiguration of pain be-gins with giving voice or bearing witness to injustice with a view to healing and nurture.[37]

And bear witness DiFranco does in her song "Blood in the Boardroom" (*Puddle Dive*, 1993), in which patriarchal power is symbolized by a boardroom full of record company "suits." Feeling herself "the only part of summer here," she wonders "can these boys smell my bleeding/through my underwear?" Feminist trespassing indeed; the song ends with her leaving a brown bloodstain on their white chair.

Taking their cue from the much older tradition of black sacred music, then, many women artists are today insisting along with feminist theologians that body and soul are not in opposition, that the body has wisdom and power and holy knowledge all its own. In step with feminist theologian Sallie McFague's work on the metaphor of the world as God's body,[38] Ani DiFranco's "Icarus" (*Evolve*, 2003) is didactically clear about deflating the old language. She uses language like "I mean" and "I know" to make explicit her belief that God is a metaphor, a "story that we tell," and that in reality, life and knowledge come from the natural world of which we are a part.

A major focus of this resacralizing of the body among theologians and musicians alike is the (re) discovery of the erotic dimension of spirituality. In feminist theory, Audre Lorde's essay "Uses of the Erotic" has become a classic celebration of the erotic, which she defines broadly and open-endendly as "a resource within each of us that lies in a deeply female and spiritual plane, firmly rooted in the power of our unexpressed or unrecognized feeling;" "a well of replenishing and provocative force to the woman who does not fear its revelation;" "a measure between the beginnings of our sense of self and the chaos of our strongest feelings;" and "the nurturer or nursemaid of all our deepest knowledge."[39]

In Christian theology, the power of the erotic is most closely associated with the work of Carter Heyward, a lesbian feminist Anglican priest. While to many the juxtaposition of God and the erotic is only slightly less shocking than that of God and excrement, Heyward identifies God with the erotic power that draws us into passionate inter-relatedness,[40] and argues that our most christ-like experiences are "our most fully embodied (sensual and erotic) connections in relation to one another, other creatures, and the earth."[41] Heyward insists that our bodies have access to a religious knowledge often hidden from our minds:

> We can know, through our bodies, that making sexual love to a beloved partner and worshipping the sacred Spirit of the worlds, Spirit of life, sacred source of history, alpha and omega of nature, are human experiences with much divinity in common. In our sexuality and our spirituality, we are vulnerable, opening to someone or something we trust to be there for us, holding and comforting us, sharing pleasure and peace. We can know this—intellectually, theologically— because we can learn it from our bodies.

As Christians with a long tradition of sacramental theology, she goes on to argue, this recognition of spirit in the flesh should not be so startling:

Whether in liturgy, in bed, or over a meal, we can know God and ourselves in
relation to God through our feelings, the openings of our bodies, our swellings,
wetness, heat, and cold, our hunger to take into ourselves the very essence of
the beloved—literally to eat and drink the one whom we love. Is this really so
strange a notion for sacramental Christians?[42]

In addition theology draws upon the most foundational doctrine of the tradition—that of the incarnation of the divine in human form—as the basis for a positive affirmation of bodily existence.

It is certainly not strange to many contemporary women musicians. As Susan McClary notes, African-American women have a long tradition of embodied
spirituality in music, one that white women are only just now discovering.
"[T]here are no white equivalents of Bessie Smith or Aretha Franklin—women
who sing powerfully of both the spiritual and the erotic without the punitive,
misogynistic frame of European culture."[43] McClary sees Madonna as a faithful
borrower of this tradition, but there are other prominent examples as well. Joan
Osborne's music can be seen as an effort to hold together the sensual and spiritual experiences that her culture has so emphatically severed. Her style, she says,
is inspired by Etta James, Aretha Franklin, and other "big voluptuous wom-
en...with all this cleavage, squeezing it into these tight little cocktail dresses. But
they're just up there wailing and jamming."[44] Her lyrics celebrate the spiritual
liberation of good sex, as in "Right Hand Man," (*Relish*, 1996), which sacralizes
the experience of walking home in the cool morning air with a grin and wadded
up panties in her purse, as well the erotic satisfaction of good theology—the
"yeah, yeah" following "God is great" in the refrain of "One of Us" turns the
austere Protestant grace into a sexy, satisfied sigh.

Tori Amos' song "Icicle" (*Under the Pink*, 1994) draws the sacred and sexual together in a way that would scandalize many Christians, but that Heyward
and other feminist theologians would no doubt endorse.

father says bow your head like the good book says well I think the good book is
missing some pages gonna lay down gonna lay down . . .
and when my hand touches myself I can finally rest my head and when they say
take of my body I think I'll take from mine instead . . .
getting off getting off while they're all downstairs singing prayers sing away
he's in my pumpkin p.j.s lay your book on my chest feel the word feel the word
feel the word feel it . . .

While few make the connection between female sexual autonomy and satisfaction and spiritual fulfillment as explicit as Amos does here, there is nonetheless a
consistent affirmation that sexuality and spirituality both find legitimate homes
in a woman's body.

A final theme of feminist theological reflection on embodied life that I find
reflected in women's music is the emphasis on alternative spaces for women's
spiritual community outside the structures of patriarchal religious institutions.

While this might at first not seem to bear directly on the issue of the body, I believe there is a close connection. In the traditional worship spaces of Christianity and Judaism, women's bodies have not been welcomed. If women are permitted into the holy of holies, they are required, theologically speaking, to leave their bodies at the door. That is, the female body is either erased or denigrated in public religious activity through such practices as androcentric language, female dress codes, Roman Catholic glorification of the asexual maternity of Mary, and the segregated seating and injunction against female singing in Orthodox Judaism. In response, in settings such as the Catholic-based WomanChurch movement and countless Neopagan communities, women gather together to express and nurture their faith in ways that do justice to their embodied life, including creating rituals for important bodily events—first menstruation, childbirth, menopause, etc.

Women's music venues serve for many women, particularly those with no formal religious affiliations, as this kind of spiritual community. For many women annual events like the Lilith Fair or the Michigan Womyn's Music festival mark the spiritual high point of the year, serving, as do communal religious retreats, as a time to clarify and communally reaffirm certain central values in order to return to the "real world" rejuvenated.[45]

And if these concerts are churches, they are churches where body and soul are reunited, literally through the dancing that is so central to women's concerts, and politically in the prominence of social justice rhetoric in lyrics, extra-musical commentary, and peripheral phenomena like the sale of bumper stickers or the circulation of political petitions. Women's music festivals seem to take seriously Paula Cooey's insistence that a theology that honors the body must begin with defending the earth's most vulnerable and violated bodies.

Commodification and the Limits of Gender Play

The rock music produced and consumed by women today incorporates a varied collection of women's bodies: those that appear in song lyrics, those of female musicians as they appear live and in music videos, and those of their women listeners as they enjoy this music at concerts and in their own living rooms. Analysis of these bodily representations both validates and complicates the theoretical work of contemporary gender theorists and feminist theologians, for while it reveals the "real world" fluidity and manipulability of gender, and the spiritual resources of women's embodied, especially sexual, experience, it also suggests the ambiguity of women's success in reclaiming the body for those purposes.

In spite of the resistance to fixed gender identities and the spiritual liberation reportedly experienced by women in and through this music, its near-complete commodification makes it an awkward site for spirituality and threatens to turn women's bodies back on themselves. Here it is important to recall the

debt much of mainstream feminist rock music owes to its subcultural foremothers in the punk and Riot Grrrl movements, In her comparative study of the press'
treatment of Riot Grrrl bands like Bikini Kill, Bratmobile, and Heavens to Betsy,
and later, more mainstream "angry women in rock," Kristen Schilt shows that the
earlier groups' messages of anger against patriarchal abuse and assertions of
female desire were largely dismissed as immature and unimportant. Performers
like Alanis Morissette and Fiona Apple, on the other hand, were critically lauded
and kept in the public eye by the mainstream music press (which seemed especially interested in their prettiness). Schilt finds the explanation for this different
treatment not in the merits of their music but in the non-threatening presentation
of the so-called angry women:

> Morissette and Apple focused their anger on many of the same issues as Riot
> Grrrl; however, they were carefully constructed as non-threatening and their
> form of female empowerment was something to buy in CD format rather than
> something to actively produce. In interviews, they were well behaved and po-
> lite. And unlike Kathleen Hanna [of Bikini Kill], they did not talk about femin-
> ism or the oppression of women. They simply followed the traditional interview
> procedure of answering questions. This coupled with their pop music style and
> stereotypically feminine appearance, allowed them to be angry without being
> threatening.[46]

The fact that young women find access to these popular forms of feminism and
feminist theology through the commercial medium of the music industry means
that the subversive potential of such feminisms instigate will always be countered by the conservative forces of the market.

In this light, reading female performers' uses of the signifiers of conventional beauty and girlishness as feminist strategies may be too optimistic. Gayle
Wald raises this problem in her analysis of Gwen Stefani, lead singer of the band
No Doubt. In spite of Stefani's "explicit and flippant mimicry of normative femininity," her "girlishly feminine persona—tied as it is to her performance of
gender—potentially furthers the notion that within patriarchal society women
acquire attention, approval, and authority to the degree that they are willing to
act like children."[47] In reality, women rockers who rise to great enough celebrity
to be analyzed in discussions like this, even while they act out ironic and parodic
rejections of "prettiness" as characterized above, are still, by and large, and according to the standards of the dominant culture, *pretty*, i.e., thin, small featured,
shaven, and happy to expose most of their bodies in public. Women who look
like Janice Joplin, I must note, are nearly absent in image-driven contemporary
popular music.

The fine line between subverting and reinscribing definitions of female identity and sexuality begins to emerge when we consider that not all women's music
is read through a women's studies lens; the vast majority of it moves from production to consumption without ever undergoing the kind of critical analysis I've
been presenting here. And the kind of feminism I have been arguing is present in

this music—embodied, playful, sexual, aggressive, unstable—is easily mistaken, when then lens is absent, for old-fashioned exploitation. It is important that much of this music is specifically marketed to very young women, pre- and early teens whose gender identities are in the formative process. Some of the most commercially successful representatives of the kind of playful gender de- and reconstruction I have been describing—Madonna, the Spice Girls, Britney Spears, No Doubt—are hugely popular among this youthful cohort, which may say more about late capitalism's need for younger markets[48] than the currency of feminist theory.

Whatever the feminist potential of these musical expressions, which becomes increasingly difficult to isolate as they are layered with the interests and input of the recording industry, their reception will inevitably be shaped by conflicting social forces. What Eileraas argues with regard to the disruptive "ugliness" of girl bands is also true of the parodic "prettiness" of these performers:

> [W]hatever an artist's intention may be, her work must inevitably fall into an interpretive community in which the work's "true" meaning will be produced, questioned, and recast . . . . Because they investigate archetypes of femininity, girl-band performances of ugliness always risk reinscribing the good girl/bad girl opposition for some audiences.[49]

In other words, Meredith Brooks' half-naked proclamation "I'm a bitch" in her 1997 video may indeed represent feminist play with cultural stereotypes, and the Spice Girls may have championed "girl power,"[50] but they are also selling products to adolescent girls, who may not appreciate the irony. And feminist consumption may have little significance for feminist activism. Schilt makes an important comparison in this context between the feminism of Riot Grrrl movement and the "girl power" Spice Girls: "The main difference is that Riot Grrrl offered ways to practice their feminism, by forming bands, making zines, or starting support groups. The Spice Girls appear to want girls to band together, but to do what? They offer very little in terms of guidance for the young girl who wants to achieve girl power."[51]

The difference between Spice Girls and Riot Grrrl is fairly easy to discern; in the mainstream of progressive women's rock music, however, things are much murkier. It will not be possible (or even useful) to develop a set of criteria for sorting music that advances the social and spiritual agency of women from that which reinforces their object status; the temporal and highly personal way in which we apprehend music make it impossible to apply such clean classifications. But surely there are signs we can look for to help distinguish, say, Britney Spears' sexual displays from those of Tori Amos. In economic terms, while mainstream music is by definition commodified, it makes sense to look for those artists and products that reflect the highest relative degree of self-determination, as indicated by everything from writing one's own music to producing one's own records. While trade in women's bodies will no doubt continue apace in the music industry, something of feminist importance is afoot in women's new if limited *control* over the commodification of their bodies. As Courtney Love insists in the title song of Hole's 1998 album, *Celebrity Skin*, "I'm not selling cheap."

In terms of musical content, it seems possible to reach for an understanding of bodily representation that is more likely than others to serve the feminist projects outlined above. Here the work of Lorde and Heywood on the meaning of the erotic in feminist theoretical and theological discourse is especially useful. Common to both is the insistence that women's sexuality be understood as part of a non-dualistic nexus of body/mind or body/spirit. The western, especially Christian, intellectual tradition that has demonized women has done so through a fiercely dualistic thought system in which sexual feelings are understood as pure sensation, as part of that material, animal, *female* world that it is the telos of the immaterial soul to rise above. When, by contrast, feminist theorists, theologians and musicians seek to reconnect sexual desire with the largest, most socially and spiritually significant longings of human beings, the desire for the sharing of joy and opening to the divine, they work against centuries of deeply ingrained misogyny and are rightly labeled radical. While it is difficult to express systematically, a musical celebration of this kind of sexuality is discernable, I believe, from one that maintains the understanding of sexuality as private bodily sensation.

In this light, we can hear and see in some women's rock music an expression of female sexuality that goes beyond giving women active sexual agency to disclosing an eroticism akin to French feminists' description of *jouissance*. Where this kind of sexual expression can be found in popular music is for artists and listeners to decide. I find it visually in Tori Amos' videos, lyrically in the satisfaction of the smiling woman walking home with her panties wadded at the bottom of her purse in Joan Osborne's "Right Hand Man," and aurally in the way Patti Spiglanin, lead singer of my favorite bar band, the Vagabond Lovers, sings EmmyLou Harris' "Rhythm Guitar" ("don't want to ride no shooting star, just want to play this rhythm guitar").

The religious significance of the erotic element in women's rock music is precisely this power to draw artist and listeners, and listeners themselves, into the present evanescent moment, into the body that receives the music and responds in dance, in the desire for touch that is sexual but not sensational. This is the joyous moment feminist theologians point to in which dualistic categories of past/present, self/other, body/soul, earth/heaven can dissolve, the presymbolic moment that can crack open an ancient tradition of proscribing the sacred from the realm of the senses. At its best, women's music constructs and deconstructs gender and sexuality in ways that facilitate the recovery of this authentic sense of the erotic. In reality, this music will always be an ambiguous site where hierarchical religious and social binaries are reenacted on women's bodies, but also where some women, some times, can experience their bodies as free from all such definition. Women's music may not represent an ideologically pure revolution, but it does indicate that real if slippery progress has been made toward a lived feminism and a real-world theology in which women's bodies are entities to be reckoned with. Whether the twenty-first century, whose popular culture portends unprecedented commodification of women's bodies, will sustain or reverse that progress is a live question.

Notes

1. Paula M. Cooey, "The Redemption of the Body: Post-Patriarchal Reconstruction of Inherited Christian Doctrine," in *After Patriarchy: Feminist Transformations of the World Religions*, ed. Paula M. Cooey, William R. Eakin, and Jay B. McDaniel (Maryknoll, NY: Orbis Books, 1991), 125.

2. For help with the research on contemporary popular music, I am grateful for the assistance of my students, especially Laura Hahn, Kimberly Band, and Holly Compton.

3. The patterns I trace in this essay are at least as clear and often more vivid in subcultural women's music, especially in the seventies punk and nineties Riot Grrrl movements. My focus here is on "mainstream" rock music that has reached and appealed to mass audiences (as measured by such markers as *Rolling Stone* and *Billboard* record charts, prominence in music video programming, size of performance venues etc.) because I want specifically to highlight the presence of ostensibly esoteric themes in feminist theory and theology within the highly commodified world of the dominant American culture, where both the potential and the ambiguity of feminist moves seem very rich.

4. Luce Irigaray, "This Sex Which Is Not One," in *Feminism and Sexuality,* ed. Stevi Jackson and Sue Scott (New York: Columbia University Press, 1996), 79.

5. Janet Holland et al, "Power and Desire: The Embodiment of Female Sexuality," *Feminist Review* 46 (Spring 1994): 24.

6. Muriel Dimen, "Power, Sexuality and Intimacy," in *Gender/Body/Knowledge: Feminist Reconstructions of Being and Knowing,* ed. Alison M. Jaggar and Susan R. Bordo. (New Brunswick, NJ: Rutgers University Press, 1989) , 48-49.

7. Arlene B. Dallery, "The Politics of Writing (the) Body: *Écriture Feminine,*" in *Gender/Body/Knowledge: Feminist Reconstructions of Being and Knowin,* ed. Alison M. Jaggar and Susan R. Bordo (New Brunswick, NJ: Rutgers University Press, 1989), 58.

8. Kristen Schilt, "'A Little Too Ironic:' The Appropriation and Packaging of Riot Grrrl Politics by Mainstream Female Musicians," in *Popular Music and Society* 26 (Spring 2003): 11.

9. Jill Hamilton, "Ani DiFranco," *Rolling Stone,* November 13, 1997, 150.

10. bell hooks, *Black Looks: Race and Representation* (Boston: South End Press, 1992), 65-66.

11. Susan Douglas, *Where the Girls Are: Growing Up Female with the Mass Media* (New York: Times Books, 1994), 94.

12. Greil Marcus, "The Girl Groups," in *The Rolling Stone Illustrated History of Rock and Roll,* ed. Anthony DeCurtis and James Henke with Holly George-Warren (New York: Random House, 1992), 189.

13. Paul Friedlander, *Rock and Roll: A Social History* (Boulder, CO: Westview Press, 1996), 73.

14. Kylie Murphy, "'I'm Sorry—I'm Not Really Sorry': Courtney Love and Notions of Authenticity." *Hecate* 27, no. 1 (2001): 145.

15. Camille Paglia, quoted in Lucy O'Brien, "Singers Embody Both Strength and Sexuality." *Milwaukee Journal Sentinel,* January 10, 1999, Lifestyle, 1.

16. Karina Eileraas, "Witches, Bitches & Fluids: Girl Bands Performing Ugliness as Resistance, 4 *The Drama Review* 41 (Fall 1997): 133-35.

17. Eileraas, "Witches, Bitches & Fluids," 124.

18. See Courtney Bailey's analysis of the alternative magazine, *Bitch: Feminist Response to Popular Culture*, in "Bitching and Talking/Gazing Back: Feminism as Critical Reading," *Women and Language* 26, no. 2 (Fall 2003): 1-8.

19. In her analysis of Madonna's work, musicologist Susan McClary observes that this gender irony also works at the level of the music itself through such strategies as her little girl voice and musical structures that promise then resist narrative closure. "Like her play with the signs of famous temptresses, bustiers, and pouts, her engagements with traditional musical signs of childish vulnerability projects her knowledge that this is what the patriarchy expects of her and also her awareness that this fantasy is ludicrous." Susan McClary, *Feminine Endings: Music, Gender and Sexuality* (Minneapolis: University of Minnesota Press, 1991) 155.

20. J. Poet, "Tattooed Love Girl: Ani DiFranco," *Pulse,* September 1996, 84.

21. Poet, "Tattooed Love Girl," 27.

22. Play with the symbols of beauty can also be seen among the consumers of women's music. At Hole concerts, for instance, one could purchase, among many other things, Hole barrettes, the miniature kind worn by little girls decades ago recently fashionable among young women. Here the juxtaposition is that of a little girl accessory with the huge, raging noise of the female band whose name it bears.

23. Martha McCaughey, "The Fighting Spirit: Women's Self-Defense Training and the Discourse of Sexed Embodiment," *Gender and Society* 12, no. 3 (1998): 280, 297.

24. The limits of this song's feminist perspective are evident, however, in the protagonist's own lack of sexual agency and in the obsessive fixation with a failed relationship. Kristen Schilt queries, "is being unable to let go of a relationship a positive message for young girls?" Schilt, "A Little Too Ironic," 11.

25. Robert Christgau, Robert, "Hot Child in the City: PJ Harvey, *Stories from the City, Stories from the Sea,"* Rolling Stone, November 9, 2000, 128.

26. The temporal, performative quality of music, that is its own inherent instability, makes this mode of expression especially suited to articulating gender fluidity. In this sense, musicians and listeners may have a decided edge on theorists and readers. It's one thing to read a complex analysis of gender constructedness; it's another for that discovery to move through your body as an evanescent apprehension.

27. McClary, *Feminine Endings,* 150.

28. Jennifer Rycenga, "Sisterhood: A Loving Lesbian Ear Listens to Progressive Heterosexual Women's Rock," in *Keeping Score: Music, Disciplinarity, Culture,* ed. David Schwarz et al (Charlottesville, VA: University Press of Virginia, 1997), 217. I am much indebted to Rycenga's analysis of women's music, especially her notion of the "loving lesbian ear," aspects of which I found myself drawing on throughout this project.

29. Poet, "Tattooed Love Girl," 85.

30. Mary Daly's remains the loudest and clearest voice in this movement.

31. Regina Ammicht-Quinn and Elsa Tamez, *The Body and Religion* (London: SCM Press, 2002), 8.

32. Rosemary R. Ruether, *Sexism and God-Talk: Toward a Feminist Theology.* Boston: Beacon Press, 1983), 79-80.

33. Joseph Berger, "A Jewish Madonna? Is That a Mystery?" *New York Times,* June 18, 2004, B1.

34. A fuller theological analysis of this video can be found in Tom Beaudoin, *Virtual Faith: The Irreverent Spiritual Quest of Generation X* (San Francisco: Jossey Bass, 1998), 106-108.

35. Ann Powers, "Holy Roller Joan Osborne Finds Salvation in God and Good Sex," *Rolling Stone,* March 21, 1996, 49.

36. See Karina Eileraas' analysis of girl bands' evocation of bodily fluids in this context. Eileraas, "Witches, Bitches & Fluids."

37. Cooey, "The Redemption of the Body," 109.

38. Sallie McFague, "The World as God's Body," in *The Body and Religion,* ed. Regina Ammicht-Quinn and Elsa Tamez (London: SCM Press, 2002).

39. Audre Lorde, "Uses of the Erotic: The Erotic as Power," in *Women's Lives: Multicultural Perspectives,* ed. Gwyn Kirk and Margo Okazawa-Rey (Mountain View, California: Mayfield Publishing Company, 2001), 156, 158.

40. Carter Heyward, *Touching Our Strength: The Erotic as Power and the Love of God* (New York: HarperCollins, 1989), 94.

41. Heyward, *Speaking of Christ: A Lesbian Feminist Voice,* ed. Ellen C. Davis (New York: The Pilgrim Press: 1989), 22.

42. Heyward, *Staying Power: Reflections on Gender, Justice, and Compassion* (Cleveland: The Pilgrim Press, 1994) 116.

43. McClary, *Feminine Endings,* 153.

44. Powers, "Holy Roller Joan Osborne," 49.

45. See also Bonnie J. Morris, *Eden Built by Eves: The Culture of Women's Music Festivals* (Los Angeles: Alyson Books, 1999).

46. Schilt, "A Little Too Ironic," 11.

47. Gayle Wald, "Just a Girl? Rock Music, Feminism, and the Cultural Construction of Female Youth," *Signs: Journal of Women in Culture and Society* 23, no. 3 (1998), 588.

48. Wald, "Just a Girl?" 591.

49. Eileraas, "Witches, Bitches, and Fluids," 136.

50. Brabazon and Evans offer a good summary of the popular British debate over the feminist significance of the Spice Girls. These authors conclude that, in a limited way, the Spice Girls do "offer a space for a new way of thinking about feminist theory and a new way of living feminist politics." Tara Brabazon and Amanda Evans, "I'll Never Be Your Woman: The Spice Girls and New Flavours of Feminism." *Social Alternatives* 17, no. 2 (1998): 39. Similarly, Dafna Lemish argues that in spite of the Spice Girls' ultimate conformity to most gender conventions, their huge popularity does "reflect something beyond these conventions....an expression of the deep need of young girls for appropriate role models, representing their own inner struggles with their place in a world of changing gender definitions." Dafna Lemish, "Spice World: Constructing Femininity the Popular Way," *Popular Music and Society* 26, no. 1 (2003): 28.

51. Shilt, "A Little Too Ironic," 14.

Bibliography

Ammicht-Quinn, Regina and Elsa Tamez, eds. *The Body and Religion.* London: SCM, 2002.

Bailey, Courtney. "Bitching and Talking/Gazing Back: Feminism as Critical Reading." *Women and Language* 26, no. 2 (2003): 1-8.

Berger, Joseph. "A Jewish Madonna? Is That a Mystery?" *New York Times*. June 18, 2004: B1.

Butler, Judith. *Gender Trouble: Feminism and the Subversion of Identity*. New York: Routledge, 1990.

Brabazon, Tara and Amanda Evans. "I'll Never Be Your Woman: The Spice Girls and New Flavours of Feminism." *Social Alternatives* 17, no. 2 (1998): 39-42.

Beaudoin, Tom. *Virtual Faith: The Irreverent Spiritual Quest of Generation X*. San Francisco: Jossey Bass, 1998.

Christgau, Robert. "Hot Child in the City: PJ Harvey, *Stories from the City, Stories from the Sea*." *Rolling Stone*. November 9, 2000: 128.

Cooey, Paula M. "The Redemption of the Body : Post-Patriarchal Reconstruction of Inherited Christian Doctrine." In *After Patriarchy : Feminist Transformations of the World Religions*, edited by Paula M. Cooey, William R. Eakin, and Jay B. McDaniel. Maryknoll, NY: Orbis Books, 1991.

Dallery, Arlene B. "The Politics of Writing (the) Body: *Écriture Feminine*." In *Gender/Body/Knowledge: Feminist Reconstructions of Being and Knowing*, edited by Alison M. Jaggar and Susan R. Bordo. New Brunswick, NJ: Rutgers University Press, 1989.

Dimen, Muriel. "Power, Sexuality and Intimacy." In *Gender/Body/Knowledge: Feminist Reconstructions of Being and Knowing*, edited by Alison M. Jaggar and Susan R. Bordo. New Brunswick, NJ: Rutgers University Press, 1989.

Douglas, Susan J. *Where the Girls Are: Growing Up Female with the Mass Media*. New York: Times Books, 1994.

Eileraas, Karina. "Witches, Bitches & Fluids: Girl Bands Performing Ugliness as Resistance." *The Drama Review* 41 (1997): 122-139.

Friedlander, Paul. *Rock and Roll: A Social History*. Boulder, CO: Westview Press, 1996.

Hamilton, Jill. "Ani DiFranco." *Rolling Stone*. November 13, 1997: 150-151.

Heyward, Carter. *Speaking Of Christ: A Lesbian Feminist Voice*. Edited by Ellen C. Davis. New York: The Pilgrim Press: 1989.

_____. *Staying Power: Reflections on Gender, Justice, and Compassion*. Cleveland: The Pilgrim Press: 1994.

_____. *Touching Our Strength: The Erotic as Power and the Love of God*. New York: HarperCollins: 1989.

Holland, Janet, Caroline Ramazanoglu, Sue Sharpe, and Rachel Thomson. "Power and Desire: The Embodiment of Female Sexuality." *Feminist Review* 46 (1994): 21-36.

hooks, bell. *Black Looks: Race and Representation*. Boston: South End Press, 1992.

Irigaray, Luce. "This Sex Which Is Not One." In *Feminism and Sexuality*, edited by Stevi Jackson and Sue Scott. New York: Columbia University Press, 1996.

Lemish, Dafna. "Spice World: Constructing Femininity the Popular Way." *Popular Music and Society* 26, no. 1 (2003): 17-29.

Lorde, Audre. "Uses of the Erotic: The Erotic as Power." In *Women's Lives: Multicultural Perspectives*, edited by Gwyn Kirk and Margo Okazawa-Rey. Mountain View, California: Mayfield Publishing Company, 2001.

Marcus, Greil. "The Girl Groups." In *The Rolling Stone Illustrated History of Rock and Roll*, edited by Anthony DeCurtis and James Henke with Holly George-Warren (original editor Jim Miller). New York: Random House, 1992.

McCaughey, Martha. "The Fighting Spirit: Women's Self-Defense Training and the Discourse of Sexed Embodiment." *Gender and Society* 12, no. 3 (1998): 277-301.

McClary, Susan. *Feminine Endings: Music, Gender and Sexuality.* Minneapolis: University of Minnesota Press, 1991.

McFague, Sallie. "The World as God's Body." In *The Body and Religion*, edited by Regina Ammicht-Quinn and Elsa Tamez. London: SCM Press, 2002.

Murphy, Kylie. "'I'm Sorry—I'm Not Really Sorry': Courtney Love and Notions of Authenticity." *Hecate* 27, no. 1 (2001): 139-163.

O'Brien, Lucy. "Singers Embody Both Strength and Sexuality." *Milwaukee Journal Sentinel.* January 10, 1999: Lifestyle 1.

Poet, J. "Tattooed Love Girl: Ani DiFranco." *Pulse.* September 1996: 24-29, 84-86.

Powers, Ann. "Holy Roller Joan Osborne Finds Salvation in God and Good Sex." *Rolling Stone.* March 21, 1996: 44-49, 76.

Ruether, Rosemary R. *Sexism and God-Talk: Toward a Feminist Theology.* Boston: Beacon Press, 1983.

Rycenga, Jennifer. "Sisterhood: A Loving Lesbian Ear Listens to Progressive Heterosexual Women's Rock" In *Keeping Score: Music, Disciplinarity, Culture*, edited by David Schwarz et al. Charlottesville, VA: University Press of Virginia, 1997.

Schilt, Kristen. "'A Little Too Ironic:' The Appropriation and Packaging of Riot Grrrl Politics by Mainstream Female Musicians." *Popular Music and Society* 26, no. 1 (2003): 5-16.

Wald, Gayle. "Just a Girl? Rock Music, Feminism, and the Cultural Construction of Female Youth." *Signs: Journal of Women in Culture and Society* 23, no. 3 (1998): 585-610.

Discography

Amos, Tori. *Little Earthquakes.* Atlantic Records. 1992.

_____. *Under the Pink.* Atlantic Records. 1994.

DiFranco, Ani. *Puddle Dive.* Righteous Babe Records. 1993.

_____. *Not a Pretty Girl.* Righteous Babe Records. 1995.

_____. *Dilate.* Righteous Babe Records. 1996.

_____. *Little Plastic Castle.* Righteous Babe Records. 1998.

_____. *Evolve.* Righteous Babe Records. 2003.

Hill, Lauryn. *The Miseducation of Lauryn Hill.* Sony Records. 1998.

Hole. *Live Through This.* Geffen Records. 1994.

_____. *Celebrity Skin.* Geffen Records. 1998.

Madonna, *Music.* Warner Brothers. 2000.

Morissette, Alanis. *Jagged Little Pill.* Maverick Records. 1995.

Osborne, Joan. *Relish.* Polygram Records. 1995.

Phair, Liz. *Exile in Guyville.* Capitol Records. 1993.

Chapter Six:
Feminist Teaching of the Goddess in Southern Alberta: Students' Responses and Challenges

Glenda Lynna Anne Tibe Bonifacio

Introduction

I hold the belief that each human being has some sense of the divine. To many, this particular sense is expressed in ritualized activities. For others, this is manifested in different ingenious ways of recognizing a supreme reality. Because of the seemingly universal application of the spiritual, regardless of its form and manifestations, religion is often a contentious sphere in our lives. The countless wars waged in human history in the name of religious conflicts, not to mention the current political and ideological divide of the "clash of civilizations"[1] between the Christian West and the Muslim communities visibly marks the importance of this subject.

However, this paper does not delve into religious conflicts. Rather, it explores the continuity of a kind of universality often ignored by mainstream religious traditions. I refer to the goddess often described as the "universal principal of paradox"[2] because she is either One omnipresent divinity or Many.[3] Since its contemporary resurgence, the image of the goddess has created its own ripples of tension amongst mainstream religions especially in the West. With the rise of the feminist movement in the 1960s, the goddess has been rediscovered within existing religious traditions and, following Goldenberg's *The Changing of the Gods*, male-centric religions are in flux.

Religion is, I argue, the last frontier of feminism. While civil and political rights based on the principle of gender equality and social justice have made significant inroads in liberal democracies, although still a struggle in many societies, the patriarchal roots of male authority and female subordination inscribed in the ultimate divine imagery largely remain intact. The symbolism of "who's who" out there in the divine universe demonstrate the ideals of patriarchal culture, for example, Yahweh, Allah, Brahma, Jesus with their male cohorts and associates. An attempt to refocus or shift the divine imagery from male to female through the goddess is controversial, affecting the foundational beliefs of societies but, according to Christ, "symbolize the emerging power of women."[4]

The theoretical engagement of female power lies in the academy. As Women's Studies has become a fixture in many universities so is the discourse on feminist spirituality. This paper highlights the experiential account of teaching a course on the goddess in one of the so-called hotbeds of religious conservatism in southern Alberta, Canada. With the establishment of a new Women's Studies Program at the University of Lethbridge about four years ago, I offered a course entitled *Goddess Across Cultures* under the Sex and Spirituality Series for the first time in 2006 with maximum enrolment, making it one of the most popular upper-division courses of the program to date. I infuse my teaching of this course twice with students' responses towards the subject and the challenges emanating from the use of the goddess imagery in transforming personal lives.

My discussion is divided into three sections. First is an appreciation of the context and locale for the feminist teaching of the goddess is provided by a brief outline of the religion and cultural milieu in southern Alberta. Second is the contemporaneity of the goddess gleaned from students' responses about the relevance of the course and its meaning in their lives. And third is a personal account of the feminist teaching of the goddess and feminist spirituality amidst Christian orthodoxy and the ways in which this renewed vigor can be sustained in the academy for the next generation.

Religion and Culture in Southern Alberta

The southern area of Alberta represent a combination of rural-urban character with Calgary as its metropolitan centre, two medium-sized cities of Lethbridge and Medicine Hat, and contiguous small agricultural towns such as Cardston, Picture Butte, Pincher Creek, and Taber, to name a few. From the ever-stretching plains and the rolling coulees, the southern topography evokes a fresh connection with nature and, at times driving through the thick descent of fog, affirms life's variant rhythms and our place in its cycle. A modern kaleidoscope of towering buildings alongside the cacophony of traffic in Calgary and the stillness of the rural outskirts display the seeming diversity of people in this part of Alberta. While the foreign-born population in Calgary comprised more than 20 per cent in 2001[5] the smaller communities are mainly of white or Anglo-European ancestry.[6]

Historically, as is today, Alberta has been a conservative province with religion as an integral aspect of its socio-political life and formation.[7] The province is commonly referred to as the "Bible Belt"[8] of Canada with 71 per cent of its people declaring themselves Christians in the 2001 census. Alongside established Christian churches are the faith-based colonies of the Hutterites and Mennonites[9] as well as large First Nations communities scattered in different parts of the province.

A closer look at the social landscape outside of Calgary depicts a kind of religiosity seemingly unaltered by time. In a small rural community in Three Hills, twelve churches serve a population of 3500 and the site of the Prairie Bible Institute, one of the biggest missionary schools in North America.[10] Cardston in the southwest is highly populated by members of the Church of Jesus Christ of Latter-day Saints and the site of the first Mormon temple in Canada. The medium-seized city of Lethbridge of 81,692 residents in 2007[11] also boasts of 114 churches and religious organizations in the 2007-2008 Yellow Pages Directory. The hit CBC television series, *Little Mosque on the Prairie*, is an oxymoron. Small towns in Alberta rarely, if at all, have mosques thus far. Muslims in Alberta are concentrated in Calgary and Edmonton comprising 2 per cent of the population in 2001.[12]

Since I arrived in Lethbridge in 2005, the social demographics have become noticeable to me with the number of commentaries about debates related to religion in the *Lethbridge Herald*. Abortion, like anywhere else, is a hotly contested issue that draws instant public response even amongst university students faced with a strong pro-life advocacy group in the community. Other topics with religious slant or issues argued for or against with Biblical references are an interesting read.

The University of Lethbridge is uniquely positioned as the intellectual hub of southern Alberta amidst an associated public known for religious conservatism and a less diverse population compared to Calgary and Edmonton, the sites of two other universities in the province. It is this peculiar societal mix that challenges many university instructors in the delivery of courses, particularly those that offer alternative paradigms like, in my case, the goddess.

Contemporaneity of the Goddess Traditions

Archeological evidences dating back to the Neolithic and the rich folk narratives in Mesopotamia and Minoan Crete suggest a primordial belief in female deities.[13] Much of Old Europe and the Near East have surviving figurines and images of the goddess profoundly akin with the theory of a prepatriarchal society based on the centrality of female worship.[14] However, the physical matter is, to some scholars like Pomeroy and Eller,[15] inconclusive proof of a matriarchal society or what is known as the "lost paradise."[16] The existence of a time when women presumably ruled under the cloak of a female divine superior fuel continued debate in the academy and amongst practitioners of the "craft."[17]

While the debate rages on in western academy, goddess iconography and beliefs have survived in many cultures in Asia, Africa, and Mesoamerica. For instance, Hindu society is replete with varying worship of goddesses from the benevolent Lakshmi to the powerful Durga. In the Brahmanical tradition, the Great Goddess embodies the principles of materiality and energy that transcends into various "multifarious expressions" in particular female divinities.[18] Perhaps there is no other tradition in the non-western world more studied in terms of the goddess in the twenty-first century than in the Indian subcontinent.[19]

In other contexts, the so-called "dark mother"[20] and the goddess Oya are made known by the migration of people from Africa to the western hemisphere.[21] The transformation of indigenous female divinities in the process of colonization and Christianization are marked in present-day rituals of *Santeria* (Way of the Saints) in the Caribbean and in other parts of the world. In countries colonized by Catholic Spain like Mexico, the imagery of Mother Mary served to facilitate pacification or what Ruether calls "the meeting of Aztec and Christian female symbols"[22] in Tonantzin, ancient Mother Goddess, and the Virgin of Guadalupe. The contemporary devotion to the Lady of Guadalupe is perceived by some as the "covert continuation of Mexican goddess traditions."[23]

Throughout the centuries the divine female manifests in many ways in indigenous cultures as "earth mothers" with powers of creation, nurture, and healing.[24] In fact, the richness of human connectedness with the divine is recognized in the ecofeminist movement in Australia, New Zealand, Europe and North America since the 1980s. A sense of urgency awaits among those concerned with the parallelism between the oppression of women and the exploitation of the environment under patriarchal science and capitalism. The ways in which we extract natural resources in the name of development have brought considerable havoc to sustainable progress and the continued marginalization and devaluation of women's work. Ecofeminists and the push toward a partnership with nature resonate in the goddess tradition.

In a world shaped by technology, the goddess traditions find their way into cyberspace and, with the clear absence of hierarchical dogmatic authority, easily reaches out to form one of the many "virtual communities."[25] While its pagan origin is traced back to the dawn of civilization, goddess worshippers are categorized ironically as part of the "new religions" whose ascendancy in the latter part of the twentieth century pose a challenge to mainstream religious traditions. They become the "other" through which many women, a collective marginalized by sacred texts, have come to reclaim their space. According to Starhawk, scholar and prominent leader of the earth-based spirituality movement in the West, the goddess is "the inspiration that comes with an indrawn breath" which connects humans with Her other creations.[26]

The search for women's identity in sacred space has resulted in the concurrent rise of "Neopagan pilgrimages"[27] to Greece and the Mediterranean. Although these spiritual journeys attest to the contemporary interest in the goddess worship, they also occur within an integrated system of consumption and commodification,[28] connecting the tourist traffic to an appreciation of a glorious mythical past. The representation of women's roles in these sacred places, especially sexuality and power, will, arguably, continue to capture a niche among young adherents of alternative religions.

Because the idea of the goddess remains poignant, an academic offering about the near universal worship of goddesses made the *Goddess Across Cultures* one of the first upper-division offering of Women's Studies at the University of Lethbridge to reach its allowable number of 40 students in 2006. *Goddess Across Cultures* is a course that examines the feminine as divine in different cultural and religious traditions of the world including Buddhism, Christianity, Judaism, Hinduism, Taoism, and Sufism. A survey of the evolution, dissolution and recreation of myths, legends and practices attributed to the goddess from the western and non-western histories make the subject of inquiry global in scope. From this course, two female students decided to major in the new Women's Studies Program attesting to its distinct interdisciplinary perspective.

As is my habit of handling any subject for the first time, I listed the insightful responses of students towards enrolling in the course at the beginning of each class. This initial ritual enabled me to follow through the interests of the group in choosing appropriate topics or issues for discussion along the way. Samples of their comments and my analysis of the generation of students taking interest in the goddess course are categorized into two intersecting themes: *knowledge* and *spirituality*.

Knowledge

Learning produces knowledge. The quest for "truths" expands as students' interests grow. At the university level, students have a number of options to enroll in courses that, ideally, give them holistic education. For instance, at the University of Lethbridge, undergraduate students comply with General Liberal Education Requirements (GLER) to complete their degree; that is, they are required to take a certain number of courses in the Humanities, Social Sciences, Sciences, and Fine Arts aimed to "enrich the personal, professional, and public lives" of students.[29] From this GLER component of university education, I have a diverse group of students from all faculties in the Arts, Sciences, Management, Education, and Nursing in *Goddess Across Cultures*.

As most youngsters nowadays would say, new is cool. But there is more to this goddess course than being new in the radar that entices a number of students to register. Granting that it satisfies the GLER curriculum, the following statements selected from my list during the first year provide the non-credit reasons for enrolling in *Goddess Across Cultures*:

> To get a better perspective of the subject that is not popular in its discourse.
>
> I have only ever been presented with the divine in the masculine form.
>
> Explore a topic not normally explored and expanded and to understand the way the image of women has grown.
>
> Being raised in a western male-centered religion, I want to find out more about the feminine role in the world's religions and how different cultures use and create the feminine divine.
>
> To understand more in depth the different goddesses around the world, how they are unique, and the appreciation and acceptance of the different religions out there; to also break down the barrier that "god" equals man and bring forth the 'goddess' that must be known.
>
> Become more aware of the goddess with religions outside of the Catholic tradition.

These statements, undeniably, express both scholarly and practical interests among the students in learning about the goddess in different cultures. It is quite apparent that students recognize a gap in discourse from the absence or lack of visibility of the female divine symbols outside of the Catholic tradition. During the first session of the course, I enquired the names of goddesses from the top of their heads and students well remembered the Greek pantheon of goddesses alongside the gods. Due to a Eurocentric study of goddesses in myths and legends, the rich cultural heritage outside of the West is relatively unknown. My presumption is that the descriptive course *Goddess Across Cultures* opens a new mode of learning.

Students in southern Alberta compare the absence of the divine feminine in Christian-based practices they are aware of to the rich polytheistic traditions in non-western societies. Uncovering the goddess in different cultural traditions demonstrates the beliefs binding primeval cultures. The demise of these goddesses and their consequent rediscovery in the twentieth century through social movements and popular culture connect with the young generation faced with a growing alternative imagery of the divine.

Aside from wanting to understand the goddess traditions in different selected cultural regions, students are able to immediately connect the female divine with women's social situation based on the following statements.

To get a better understanding and background of the goddesses and how they became so, and the ways in which they were treated compared to women in their societies.

I'm just curious about the relationship between aspects of the goddess and their manifestations within society.

Gain more information about the goddess and how she affects her people daily as well as from generation to generation.

Know more the importance of the role of the goddess in women's lives.

Learn about the different goddesses throughout time and throughout the world, and how they have set expectations of the women who have worshipped them. Also, how religions with goddesses as their main figures of worshipping instead of gods differ from our western patriarchal society.

The obvious connection identified in these statements was the relation between the goddess and the status of women in society. In other words, does the goddess worship in particular societies manifest in the lives of women? This is arduous enough to substantiate with evidence from Hinduism, which is still practiced.[30] When looking to ancient societies it is even harder to qualify this relationship. However, a number of scholars point to the rereading of inscribed texts and practices. Hollis, for example, argues that Egyptian goddesses Neith and Hathor relate to the role of queens and the rise of kings in the fourth and third millennia B.C.E. as gleaned from the royal insignia and regalia.[31] The significant role of ancient Egyptian queens appears connected to the relatively high status of ordinary women during this period.

A product of the "third wave"[32] generation under the aegis of globalism, individualism, and liberalism, students in the course *Goddess Across Cultures* are receptive to learning new ideas or rediscovering concepts. Perhaps the magnitude of diverse female iconography and artifacts shown in rituals and festivals in many parts of the world now accessible by satellite television sustains theoretical engagement of *thealogy*.[33] With a continuous flood of information from different media and genre, learning about the goddess is not that difficult to imagine after all.

Spirituality

One surprising reason raised by students in the *Goddess Across Cultures* is spirituality. Some sample statements with spiritual dimension include:

Discover the Goddess's role in my life and where it is shown and how it affects modern day society.

Familiarize myself with the feminine divine and apply this new knowledge to my spiritual life.

Learn as much about the different goddesses in different cultures so that I can have more respect for the Goddess around me and in my own life.

Enlighten myself with spiritual knowledge and understanding of the goddess.

Although credit and grade are desired, these samples of students' responses suggest a non-academic pursuit of "spiritual knowledge" which is quite hard to evaluate. I glean a sense of longing to fill a void through a search for meaning in the lives of students. When an intellectual endeavor is combined with spiritual angst, then the subject of study becomes more than discourse. This is what I refer to as the contemporaneity of the goddess idea. It draws a complex thread between what is known and what is experienced in the lives of the knower, connecting the measurable level of knowledge to the unquantifiable understanding of the goddess beyond the classroom reminiscent of Spretnak's view that the spiritual is also political.[34]

Spirituality is the "process of coming into relationship with reality"[35] involving the transformation of consciousness and our sense of place in the universe. Feminist spirituality through the goddess is far more complex to grapple with as it weaves through the patriarchal consciousness to the salient empowering of women. The intricate ways of transforming personal beliefs of the divine are, according to Althaus-Reid, "mediated by language, culture and levels of human consciousness."[36] Students have individual consciousness and recognition of their own realities. In this case, feminist spirituality is a process of becoming. What is significant though is that a woman-centred idea ushers a more positive spiritual experience in many lives bereft of divine representation.

The complexity of the impact of the *Goddess Across Cultures* or the idea of the Female Divine, in the personal lives of students is beyond teacher evaluation. Though enmeshed in a critical feminist approach of how this comes into fruition in the daily realities of female students particularly, this impact remains personal or privy to individual students unless disclosed.

Postscript

I contacted three former students who enrolled in *Goddess Across Cultures* during the first time it was offered in 2006 through email and solicited their opinion about the relevance of the course in their lives, both personal and academic. A summary of their responses include the following:

Student A: Academically, I have utilized much of the information I learned in the goddess class and applied it in research papers...It seems that the goddess course served as a prerequisite of sorts to my Religion 4110 which is a more focused Hindu Goddess study. I also found it interesting that the art which was depicted on the cover of the textbooks have been discussed in my Art Now course on more than one occasion. Personally, I found it interesting that when watching movies or speaking with friends I have a better understanding of Jewish customs and traditions, Hindu beliefs, and Muslim feminisms. (email February 10, 2008)

Student B: As I am an Anthropology major, this course was very interesting...We not only learned historical accounts, but were also able to apply it to contemporary issues such as the environment, women, empowerment, and religion. ...This course remained significant throughout my studies as I applied the lessons to other subjects, as well as daily knowledge and beliefs. This course offers something special, unique and very interesting (sometimes taboo in our Alberta culture) and I think that is why it should be offered. It appeals to a variety of people and majors and it was a great addition to any liberal arts curriculum. (email February 7, 2008)

Student C: I found this course to be extremely important and relevant in clarifying women's place in history, as well as integrating woman-identified images and concepts of divinity. If only on a personal level, I found the course changed my views about spirituality and opened my mind to the concept of ritual; however, on a larger scale the course also clarified for me women's place in religion and how many people reform and adapt their belief systems in order to create new starting points for resistance, acceptance, creativity, and spirituality. I think the course offers new insight to students in exploring religious tolerance. (email February 7, 2008)

These three students were not enrolled in any of my courses at the time of the email correspondence but were selected because they were critically engaged in the class discussion and made an indelible mark on my memory for having earned top marks. Based on these postscripts, teaching a course on the goddess and feminist spirituality, like other courses, is self gratifying.

Teaching the Goddess: Challenging Orthodoxy

The idea of teaching a course on the goddess came quickly as I did my teaching demonstration in the summer of 2005. With a background in Asian Studies and its cross-cultural approach, I plunged head on to offer *Goddess Across Cultures* in my first year at the University of Lethbridge quite unaware of the challenges ahead, personally and professionally. Never had I expected that the goddess imagery as a critical discourse, once introduced into the southern Alberta community at an invited public presentation, could result in personal harassment.

Looking back into my first community exposure and its subsequent invitation from one of the audience, an ardent disbeliever in the goddess and a self-acclaimed Christian crusader in the Lethbridge area, for an open debate with the "truth" about the goddess and Christianity, I put myself in the place of a reluctant defender of the women's movement in the West, being a new Filipino immigrant to Canada then. Silence was not an effective option towards this invitation during final examination week as I found the same invitation with my name circulated by email throughout the university with no idea how to deal with it. Never had I experienced an invitation that verges on harassment from teaching an academic subject even from my own politically-charged university in the Philippines. It is surprising to note that within the democratic space offered by Canada the goddess imagery is, conceivably, dangerous to some. I guess time heals the "teaching wounds" as I offered the course the second time in 2007.

Goddess Across Cultures is grounded in interdisciplinarity: art, economics, history, philosophy, religion, society and politics. More importantly, the intersection between feminism and religion at the core of the goddess discourse is often ignored in orthodox teaching. Although gender is now recognized as a tool for analyzing social relations, its critical use in religion has just begun.[37] The apparent teaching strategy amongst many male religious scholars is to "add and stir" women into the discussion in relation to normative stories dominated by men. An ingestion of feminism seems unlikely. Stuckey notes that the study of religion in the West is "the study of *male* religious roles, *male* understandings of spirituality, and *male* symbols."[38]

I earlier posed that religion is the last frontier of feminism. Religion is perceived by some as "beyond redemption"[39] and feminist scholars on this subject are mainly divided between reformists and rejectionists. Reformists, or revisionists, attempt to reclaim textual traditions and reinterpret those that convey women's contribution in the formation of particular faith communities. On the other hand, rejectionists deny any possible change towards inclusion of women by established religions and opt to promote separatism. This schism within feminism towards religion is reflective of any social movement that advances societal change. But religion, I argue, unlike the accountability of political decisions, offers various ways to foment transformation albeit sometimes too slow for us to notice. Outside of its hierarchical structure, religion as a practice is left to individuals.

Teaching a course like *Goddess Across Cultures* is one way to instill diversity in perspectives on the once-exclusive domain of patriarchal religions. As feminism has entered the academy, feminist scholars have the opportunity to present alternative visions of the divine and, consistent with the transformative potential of Women's Studies, create the nexus to change—the individual. The medium for this change is in place in many universities; the next task is to sustain it at various levels of engagement: classroom and the community.

The classroom is the bedrock of dialogue with young people and places those facilitating a feminist-inspired topic to be, at best, similarly challenged by the microcosm of minds nurtured in patriarchy. Community is a broad term for any number of persons bounded by shared interest and is context-specific, for example, the academic community. While the discourse on the goddess occurs in the classroom, the students simultaneously represent diverse communities of faith, ethnicity, and other social categories. Through these interlocking communities present in the classroom, the impact of the goddess idea is far reaching.

How then could we sustain the vigor of teaching the goddess and feminist spirituality for the next generation? The answer lies within us. In my case, the first issue is, should I teach or not? But one sure way to keep the goddess as discourse is to continue doing so. Another is to extend the borders of the classroom to be inclusive to other students as part of the wider academic community. This means allowing other students to attend the class discussion based on topical interest. There are students who wish to attend for the simple joy of knowing. Why should we exclude them? Or, why not advertise this topic to the rest of the students, faculty and staff in the university? Extending the classroom to include others creates a learned public.

Teaching in the twenty-first century involves the use of highly animated visuals, videos and internet links with class discussion. Although this may be daunting for many not too adept with the use of technology, it is imperative that we know the effective ways to make a historic trip in time colorful and catchy. This may sound ridiculous since students at the university level are expected to adjust to the teaching styles of their professors. Yet, it is to our teaching advantage, too, to recognize that we are faced with the "digital" generation. For example, no matter how I appear a "technological ignoramus" to much more competent students, I make it a point to make my lectures fully stimulating with internet links to a variety of "googled images" of goddesses in many cultures. Knowing that the attention span of students in lectures is shorter than a sip of coffee, the constant allure of visuals and short video clips bring the topic its needed attention alongside other classroom activities.

Teaching the goddess today is vital to a healthy understanding of everyone's place in this world, especially women. Christ explains that "women need the goddess" to legitimize female power, value female body experiences, and forge bonds among women.[40] In my view, men, too, need the goddess. In *Goddess Across Cultures*, about five male students enroll at one time although I see about three of them remain till the end of the course. While the reasons may be different with women, they are bound to have one. I admit this is quite difficult to address in patriarchal cultures they have been accustomed to. However, the goddess provides a symbol of wholeness and completeness that embraces diversity that speaks more to our lives. By teaching the goddess and inspiring the path to feminist spirituality, we are at that point in pedagogy that asks for more.

Concluding Notes

The goddess is both a concept and a practice; this imagery invites an exploration into its history and manifestations across cultures. Reclaimed as part of the feminist movement in the twentieth century, the goddess imagery is a critical tool to empower women's lives. However, so much debate surrounds it that its significance in today's society is often obscured.

Based on my experience of teaching a course on the goddess in southern Alberta since 2006, I am more convinced not to end it. The benefits for the next generation outweigh the personal harassment that goes with facilitating a topic not well received by mainstream religious traditions. The enthusiasm of students towards this topic gives more meaning to teaching; it does not only impart knowledge but also bridges to something more personal—the spiritual. Responses from students at the beginning of the course, *Goddess Across Cultures*, and two years after demonstrate its relevance in their lives, as students and as individuals. We should, therefore, continue engaging a scholarly discourse that has the potential to shape how lives are lived.

Notes

1. Samuel Huntington, *The Clash of Civilizations and the Remaking of the World Order* (New York: Simon & Schuster, 1998).

2. Jennifer Baker Woolger and Roger Woolger, "Introduction," in *The Song of Eve*, Manuela Dunn Mascetti (New York: Fireside, 1990) 6.

3. See Johanna Stuckey, "Women and Religion," in *Feminist Issues*, ed. Nancy Mandell (Toronto: Pearson Prentice Hall, 2004), 303.

4. Carol Christ, "Symbols of Goddess and God in Feminist Theology," in *The Book of the Goddess*, ed. Carl Olson (Illinois: Waveland Press, 1983), 249.

5. Calgary Health Region, *Healthy Diverse Populations*, http://www.calgaryhealth region.ca.hecomm/diversity/demographics_main.htm#Immigration (1 November 2007).

6. This is inferring on the tendency of visible minorities to settle in cities like Calgary. See Marlene Mulder and Bojan Korenic, *Portraits of Immigrants and Ethnic Minorities in Canada* (Edmonton: PCERII, University of Alberta, 2005), 46.

7. See Michael Jenkinson, "Bible on Teacher's Desk," *Alberta Report*, May 6, 1996; Preston Manning, "Prairie Companions," *Maclean's*, July 1, 2005; Tom Mcfeely, "Religion and Politics Can Mix," *Alberta Report*, April 10, 2000; Kevin Steel, "Moral Exhaustion," *Alberta Report*, June 21, 1999.

8. Donald Aaron Goertz, *The Development of a Bible Belt* (Ottawa: National Library of Canada, 1981).

9. See Dawn Bowen, "*Die Auswanderung*: Religion, Culture, and Migration among Old Colony Mennonites," *The Canadian Geographer* 45, no. 4 (2001), 461-473.

10. Steven Frank, "A Quiet Prayer," *Time Canada*, November 24, 2003.

11. City of Lethbridge, Municipal Census 2007, http://www.lethbridge.ca/home/City +Hall/City+Council/Census/2007+Census/default.htm (September 17, 2007).

12. Statistics Canada, Alberta: Nearly One-Quarter of Population Had No Religion, http://www12.statcan.ca/english/census01/Products/Analytic/companion/rel/ab.cfm (May 31, 2008).

13. See Riane Eisler, "Reclaiming Our Goddess Heritage," in *The Goddess Re-Awakening*, comp. Shirley Nicholson (Wheaton: The Theosophical Publishing House, 1989), 29; Carol Christ, *Rebirth of the Goddess* (New York: Routledge, 1997), 8-21; Marija Gimbutas, *The Language of the Goddess* (San Francisco: Harper & Row, 1989); Kathryn Rountree, "Archeologists and goddess Feminists at Catalhoyuk," *Journal of Feminist Studies in Religion* 23, no. 2 (2007):6-26.

14. See David Kinsley, *The Goddeses' Mirror* (Albany, NY: State University of New York Press, 1989).

15. Sarah Pomeroy, "A Classical Scholar's Perspective on Matriarchy," in *Liberating Women's History*, ed. Bernice Caroll (Urbana: University of Illinois Press, 1976); Cynthia Eller, *The Myth of Matriarchal Prehistory* (Boston: Beacon Press, 2000).

16. Susanne Heine, *Matriarchs, Goddesses, and Images of God*, trans. John Bowden (Minneapolis: SCM Press, 1989),74.

17. Alternatively known as "Witchcraft" to denote one of the modern practices of goddess-centred spirituality in the West since the 1970s. See Wendy Griffin, "The Embodied Goddess," *Sociology of Religion* 56, no. 1 (1995):35.

18. Tracy Pintchman, *The Rise of the Goddess in the Hindu Tradition* (Albany: State University of New York Press, 1994), 3.

19. See Francis Clooney, *Divine Mother, Blessed Mother* (New York: Oxford University Press, 2005); Lynn Foulston, *At the Feet of the Goddess* (Brighton and Oregon: Sussex Academic Press, 2002); Elizabeth Harding, *Kali* (Delhi: Motilal Banarsidaas Publishers, 2004); Devdutt Pattanaik, *The Goddess in India* (Rochester: Inner Traditions International, 2000).

20. Mary Lynn Keller, "Goddesses Around the World," in *She is Everywhere*, comp. Lucia Chiavola (New York: iUniverse), 202.

21. See Judith Gleason, "Oya: Black Goddess of Africa," in *The Goddess Re-Awakening* (Wheaton: The Theosophical Publishing House, 1989).

22. Rosemary Radford Ruether, *Goddesses and the Divine Feminine* (Berkeley: University of California Press, 2005), 190.

23. Ruether, *Goddesses*, 218-19.

24. See Rosemary Radford Ruether, *Women Healing Earth* (New York: Orbis).

25. Wendy Griffin, "The Goddess Net," in *Religion Online*, ed. Lorne L. Dawson and Douglas E. Cowan (New York and London: Routledge, 2004), 189.

26. Starhawk, *Spiral Dance* (New York: HarperSan Francisco, 1989), 92.

27. Maria Beatrice Bittarello, "Neopagan Pilgrimages in the Age of the Internet," *Journal of Tourism and Cultural Change* 4, no. 2 (2006):116.

28. See Adam Possamai, "Alternative Spiritualities and the Cultural Logic of Capitalism," *Culture and Religion* 4, no. 1 (2003):31-45; Douglas Ezzy, "The Commodification of Witchcraft," *Australian Religion Studies Review* 14, no. 1 (2001):31-44.

29. See University of Lethbridge, "A Proposal for a New General Liberal Education Requirement at the University of Lethbridge," GFC General Liberal Education Committee, http://www.uleth.ca/fas/gler.pdf (March 10, 2007).

30. The relationship between the Hindu goddesses and women in society remains contested. While female deities, generally grouped as either benign or fierce, are highly acclaimed, women in Hindu societies lag behind their male counterpart in education, political representation and economic equality. See Stephanie Tawa Lama, "Hindu Goddess and Women's Political Representation in South Asia," *International Review of Sociology* 11, no. 1 (2001): 5; P. Arjun Rao and M. Srinivasa Reddy, "Status of Women: Dimensions of Female Literacy in Andra Pradesh," *ICFAI Journal of Public Administration* 4, no. 1 (2008): 75.

31. Susan Tower Hollis, "Queens and Goddesses in Ancient Egypt," in *Women and Goddess Traditions in Antiquity and Today*, ed. Karen L. King (Minneapolis: Fortress Press, 1997), 210-222.

32. For a lack of a better descriptor of the generational divide of contemporary feminisms, I am using the "third wave" analogy to focus on various interlocking challenges of today's youth.

33. See Melissa Raphael, *Introducing Thealogy* (Cleveland: The Pilgrim Press, 2000).

34. See Charlene Spretnak, ed., *The Politics of Women's Spirituality* (New York: Doubleday, 1982).

35. Carol Ochs, *Women and Spirituality* (New Jersey: Rowman & Allanheld, 1983), 10.

36. Marcella Althaus-Reid, "From the Goddess to Queer Theology," *Feminist Theology* 12, no. 2 (2005): 268.

37. See Elizabeth Castelli, ed., *Women, Gender, Religion* (New York: Palgrave, 2001); Morny Joy and Eva Neumaier-Dargyay, eds., *Gender Genre and Religion* (Waterloo, ON: Wilfred Laurier University Press, 1995).

38. Johanna Stuckey, "Women and Religion," 288.

39. Vanaja Dhruvarajan, "Religion, Spirituality, and Feminism," in *Gender, Race, and Nation*, ed. Vanaja Dhruvarajan (Toronto: University of Toronto Press, 2002), 284.

40. Carol Christ, "Symbols of Goddess and God in Feminist Theology," 248.

Bibliography

Althaus-Reid, Marcella. "From the Goddess to Queer Theology: The State We Are in Now." *Feminist Theology* 13, no. 2 (2005): 265-272.

Bittarello, Maria Beatrice. "Neopagan Pilgrimages in the Age of the Internet: A Life Changing Experience or an Example of Commodification?" *Journal of Tourism and Cultural Change* 4, no. 2 (2006): 116-135.

Bowen, Dawn. "*Die Auswanderung*: Religion, Culture, and Migration among Old Colony Mennonites." *The Canadian Geographer* 45, no. 4 (2001): 461-473.

Calgary Health Region. *Healthy Diverse Populations. Demographics of Diverse Populations in Calgary.* http://www.calgaryhealthreagion.ca/hecomm/diversity/demo graphics_main.htm#Immigration (November 1, 2007).

Castelli, Elizabeth, ed. *Women, Gender, Religion: A Reader.* New York: Palgrave, 2001.

Christ, Carol. *Rebirth of the Goddess: Finding Meaning in Feminist Spirituality*. New York: Routledge, 1997.

————. "Symbols of Goddess and God in Feminist Theology." In *The Book of the Goddess*, edited by Carl Olson, 231-51. Illinois: Waveland Press, 1983.

City of Lethbridge. "Municipal Census 2007." http://www.lethbridge.ca/home/City+Hall/City+Council/Census/2007+Census/default.htm (Accessed 17 September 2007).

Clooney, Francis. *Divine Mother, Blessed Mother: Hindu Goddesses and the Virgin Mary*. New York: Oxford University Press, 2005.

Dhruvarajan, Vanaja. "Religion, Spirituality, and Feminism." In *Gender, Race, and nation: A Global Perspective*, edited by Vanaja Dhruvarajan and Jill Vickers, 273-294. Toronto: University of Toronto Press, 2002.

Eisler, Riane. "Reclaiming Our Goddess Heritage." In *The Goddess Re-Awakening: The Feminine Principle Today*, compiled by Shirley Nicholson, 27-39. Wheaton, Il: The Theosophical Publishing House, 1989.

Eller, Cynthia. *The Myth of Matriarchal Prehistory: Why an Invented Past Won't Give Women a Future*. Boston: Beacon Press, 2000.

Ezzy, Douglas. "The Commodification of Witchcraft." *Australian Religion Studies Review* 14, no.1 (2001): 31-44.

Frank, Steven. "A Quiet Prayer: National Attitudes Toward Religion May Have Changed in the Past 40 Years, But Not in One Alberta Town." *Time Canada*, November 24, 2003, 74.

Foulston, Lynn. *At the Feet of the Goddess: The Divine Feminine in Local Hindu Religion*. Brighton and Oregon: Sussex Academic Press, 2002.

Gleason, Judith. "Oya: Black Goddess of Africa." In *The Goddess Re-Awakening: The Feminine Principle Today*, compiled by Shirley Nicholson, 56-67. Wheaton, IL: The Theosophical Publishing House, 1989.

Gimbutas, Marija. *The Language of the Goddess*. San Francisco: Harper & Row, 1989.

Goldenberg, Naomi Ruth. *The Changing of the Gods: Feminism and the End of Traditional Religions*. Boston, MA: Beacon Press, 1980.

Goertz, Donald Aaron. *The Development of a Bible Belt: The Socio-religious Interaction in Alberta Between 1928 and 1938*. Ottawa: National Library of Canada, 1981.

Griffin, Wendy. "The Goddess Net." In *Religion Online: Finding Faith on the Internet*, edited by Lorne L. Dawson and Douglas E. Cowan, 189-203. New York and London: Routledge, 2004.

————. "The Embodied Goddess; Feminist Witchcraft and Female Divinity." *Sociology of Religion* 56, no.1 (1995): 35-48.

Harding, Elizabeth. *Kali: The Black Goddess of Dakshineswar*. Delhi: Motilal Banarsidass Publishers, 2004.

Heine, Susanne. *Matriarchs, Goddesses, and Images of God: A Critique of a Feminist Theology*, translated by John Bowden. Minneapolis: SCM Press, 1989.

Hollis, Susan Tower. "Queens and Goddesses in Ancient Egypt." In *Women and Goddess Traditions in Antiquity and Today*, edited by Karen L. King, 210-238. Minneapolis: Fortress Press, 1997.

Huntington, Samuel. *The Clash of Civilizations and the Remaking of the World Order*. New York: Simon & Schuster, 1998.

Jenkinson, Michael. "Bible on Teacher's Desk: Logos Finds Room in Five Edmonton Public Schools." *Alberta Report*, May 6, 1996, 42-43.

Joy, Morny and Eva Neumaier-Dargyay, eds. *Gender Genre and Religion: Feminist Reflections*. Waterloo, Ontario: Wilfred Laurier University Press, 1995.

Keller, Mary Lynn. "Goddesses Around the World." In *She is Everywhere: Anthology of Writing in Womanist/Feminist Spirituality*, compiled by Lucia Chiavola, 201-208. Birnbaum. New York: iUniverse, 2005.

Kinsley, David. *The Goddesses' Mirror: Visions of the Divine from East and West*. Albany, NY: State University of New York Press, 1989.

Lama, Stephanie Tawa. "The Hindu Goddess and Women's Political Representation in South Asia: Symbolic Resource or Feminine Mystique?" *International Review of Sociology* 11, no. 1 (2001): 5-20.

Manning, Preston. "Prairie Companions." *Maclean's*, July 1, 2005, 34-38.

Mcfeely, Tom. "Religion and Politics Can Mix (Evangelical Politicians in Canadian Alliance Party)." *Alberta Report*, April 10, 2000, 11.

Mulder, Marlene and Bojan Korenic. *Portraits of Immigrants and Ethnic Minorities in Canada: Regional Comparisons*. Edmonton: PCERII, University of Alberta, 2005.

Ochs, Carol. *Women and Spirituality*. Toronto and New Jersey: Rowman & Allanheld, 1983.

Pattanaik, Devdutt. *The Goddess in India: The Five Faces of the Eternal Feminine*. Rochester, VT: Inner Traditions International, 2000.

Pintchman, Tracy. *The Rise of the Goddess in the Hindu Tradition*. Albany: State University of New York Press, 1994.

Pomeroy, Sarah. "A Classical Scholar's Perspective on Matriarchy." In *Liberating Women's History*, edited by Bernice Caroll, 217-23. Urbana: University of Illinois Press, 1976.

Possamai, Adam. "Alternative Spiritualities and the Cultural Logic of Capitalism." *Culture and Religion* 4, no. 1 (2003): 31-45.

Raphael, Melissa. *Introducing Thealogy: Discourse on the Goddess*. Cleveland, Ohio: The Pilgrim Press, 2000.

Rao, P. Arjun and M. Srinivasa Reddy. "Status of Women: Dimensions of Female Literacy in Andra Pradesh." *ICFAI Journal of Public Administration* 4, no.1 (2008): 75-89.

Rountree, Kathryn. "Archaeologists and *goddess* Feminists at Catalhoyuk: An Experiment in Multivocality." *Journal of Feminist Studies in Religion* 23, no. 2 (2007): 7-26.

Ruether, Rosemary Radford. *Goddesses and the Divine Feminine: A Western Religious History*. Berkeley: University of California Press, 2005.

————, ed. *Women Healing Earth: Third world Women on Ecology, Feminism and Religion*. New York: Orbis, 1996.

Spretnak, Charlene, ed. *The Politics of Women's Spirituality*. New York: Doubleday, 1982.

Statistics Canada. "Alberta: Nearly One-Quarter of Population Had No Religion." http://www12.statcan.ca/english/census01/Products/Analytic/companion/rel/ab.cfm (May 31, 2008).

Starhawk. *Spiral Dance: A Rebirth of Ancient Religion of the Great Goddess*. 10th Anniversary Ed. New York: HarperSanFrancisco, 1989.

Steel, Kevin. "Moral Exhaustion: As Libertine Policies Triumph, Alberta Traditionalists Grow Weary of Politics." *Alberta Report*, June 21, 1999, 12-13.

Stuckey, Johanna. "Women and Religion: Female Spirituality, Feminist Theology, and Feminist Goddess Worship." In *Feminist Issues: Race, Class, and Sexuality*, edited by Nancy Mandell, 287-315. Toronto: Pearson Prentice Hall, 2004.

University of Lethbridge. "A Proposal for a New General Liberal Education Requirement at the University of Lethbridge." GFC General Liberal Education Committee, 2004. http://www.uleth.ca/fas/gler.pdf (March 10, 2007).

Woolger, Jennifer Baker and Roger Woolger. "Introduction." In *The Song of Eve*, Manuela Dunn Mascetti, 6-7. New York: Fireside, 1990.

Part II

Chapter Seven:
Generational Change in Goddess Feminism: Some Observations from the UK

Giselle Vincett

Still feeling sceptical, I talk to Jacqui Woodward-Smith who works in the Home Office. This is her seventh Goddess conference. I ask her how all this can be relevant in the context of modern feminism. It's not cheap to come here—between £175 and £225 (concessions £100), plus extra for accommodation and travel. Isn't it all just middle-class navel gazing? She disagrees. "The Goddess conference stands against patriarchy, so the movement is very political. Coming to the conference shows women how the world could be."[1]

Introduction

This paper seeks to show how Goddess Feminists[2] of different ages exist in different generational contexts which affect not only their feminisms, but also their Goddess spirituality. I will first outline how other researchers have profiled three late-modern generations (Boomers, X, and Y). I will then sketch the context of religion in the UK, and more particularly generational change in religion in the UK. I will summarize what feminist theorists have defined as key differences between second and third-wave feminisms and I will show how Goddess Feminism in the UK leans increasingly toward third-wave type feminism. I will show how recently observed changes in Goddess Feminism in the UK may reflect the growing numbers of X and Y women involved in the tradition, and how these changes also reflect the concerns of third-wave feminism.

In this article I draw upon semi-structured interviews with Boomer, X, and Y Goddess Feminists in the UK, as well as participant observation at Goddess Feminist ritual groups and the Glastonbury Goddess Conference, personal communication with UK Goddess Feminists, and monitoring of Goddess Feminist literature, particularly online literature from the UK.

Contexts

Boomers, X and Y

Pinpointing dates to bracket generations is somewhat arbitrary and different researchers use slightly different dates. For the purposes of this paper, however, I will follow recent work in the UK by Savage *et al.* (2006). Goddess Feminists, founded by second-wave feminists, have been highly influenced by the Baby Boom generation (or Boomers), defined here as being born between 1946-1963/4.[3] However, increasingly, women of the next generation are publishing, leading courses, and facilitating public rituals. These women are part of Generation X (born between 1964/5-1981). Finally, a new generation of young women, often called Generation Y (born between 1982-the millennium), are reaching maturity, encountering Goddess Feminism, and helping to shape Goddess Feminism, particularly through ritual participation and online.

Each of these generations has been defined by "specific socio-historical conditions in common ways."[4] That is, each generation is influenced by "living through and responding to particular historical events, political structures, dominant ideologies and technical developments."[5] The Baby Boomers were born into an economic period of stability and growth and unprecedented access to higher education. They lived through and drove the counter-culture of the 1960s, and the second-wave feminism of the 1970s. Their experiences of the Cold War, government scandals, the large scale strikes of the 70s, and protest events such as that at the Greenham Common military site contributed to them questioning authority in general. The Boomers broke with traditional religion in large numbers, and they have driven the increasing popularity of alternative spiritualities and New Age in the West.[6]

Generation X, on the other hand, the tail end of whom are just approaching 30, has been both positively and negatively influenced by the Boomers. Xers have also participated in the increasing rates of higher education, they are the MTV generation, and have grown up reaping the benefits of the growth of information and communications technologies. However, they also saw divorce rates soar amongst their parents. As a result, they have been called "the lonely generation."[7] They were the first generation to grow up living in an age of AIDS, and have grown up through both economic recessions and booms. Religiously, they are the first generation in the UK for whom a large majority had little or no church family background. Despite many of Generation X having little interest in Christianity, they have also become known for their pluralistic, spiritual eclecticism that in many ways mirrors the third-wave feminism propounded by X feminists.[8]

Generation Y are truly a generation of the technological revolution. The generation of the mobile/cell phone and the Internet, but also of what some have called a "glocal" consciousness,[9] being influenced both by events and phenomena which happen on a global scale, but which are also played out in the local (climate change, 9/11, globalization), as well as fragmented and hybridized cultures. This glocalization "produces the pluralism of today's world" and increasingly brings "into question all traditional modes of authority."[10] Generation Y thus continues trends which have been evident since the Boomers or X. However, unlike Xers, who "remember the promise of a secure life" (career, home, relationships), "Yers were never promised security and so they deal with insecurity with far less self-pity and anger than Xers did." Indeed, they "have emerged into an adult world where only one rule exists—the certainty of uncertainty."[11] Generation Y "is the first genuine consumer generation, a group who started spending and dictating the spending habits of others at an early age."[12] In such a context, we can expect that defining characteristics of Y religiosity or spirituality will be an emphasis on plurality, self-identity construction through personal choices, and mobility.

Feminist Waves

Second-wave feminism (which began in the mid- to late-60s) has been credited (and blamed for) both the flight from traditional religion and the transformation of traditional religion (women's ordination, inclusive language and so forth). Callum Brown argues that women's large-scale move into employment outside the home, together with their fight for more egalitarian relationships between men and women, and for women's right to make choices about their lives, are key factors to understanding larger patterns of religiosity, secularization and sacralization in the West over the last thirty years.[13] Second-wave feminists (like some first-wave feminists) critiqued patriarchal religion and in the process of that critique many left the churches. However, second-wave feminists also sought to shape (or re-shape) forms of spirituality which were liberation-based and which allowed women to define and name themselves and the divine. Linda Woodhead has suggested that the particular stresses and negotiations which women must hold together with regard to gender roles and performance in late-modern life may make self-directed spiritualities especially appealing for women.[14] Similarly, Houtman and Aupers argue that "increasing levels of post-traditionalism drive the spiritual revolution", and that the young are most likely to score highly on measures of post-traditionalism.[15]

The notion of a third-wave of feminism first started to be proposed in the 1990s as young X generation women came of age and sought to differentiate their feminism from their mothers' and from the "post-feminist" backlash of the late 80s and early 90s.[16] These young women were the first generation to grow up with feminism. As Baumgardner and Richards put it, "[for us] feminism is like fluoride. We scarcely notice that we have it—it's simply in the water."[17] Young feminists were not claiming (as others have) that the job of feminism was finished, but that the hard-won achievements of second-wave feminists allowed young women to shift emphases somewhat. Third-wave feminism is usually characterized as emphasizing not just gender but the intersectionality of gender with race/ethnicity, class, geographical positioning, and so forth. X and Y women have claimed that rather than a homogenizing "sisterhood," they stress diversity, to the point that diversity and individual perspectives have become a cohering narrative of third-wave feminism. As Kim Allen writes on the website *3rd WWWave*, "we don't want 'sisterhood'; we want independence, freedom, and as many choices as possible."[18] We should not be surprised by this diversity narrative, representing as it does a continuation of the drive towards the self and away from what Heelas and Woodhead have characterized as "life as" narratives[19] which constrain individualism and personal autonomy (e.g.: life as mother, wife, good Catholic, etc.).[20] The diversity narrative of third-wave feminism is thus part of larger social trends (globalization, pluralization and so forth), which, I argue, also shape some of the new trends in Paganism and Goddess Feminism. Similarly, third-wave feminism has become known for emphasizing individual liberation and personal expression of feminism. That is, there is no one narrative of who or what a feminist is or should be (if there ever was) and the task of feminism now is to live out feminist ideals in one's own life. Third-wave feminism is also characterized by new forms of communication (the internet, email, e-zines) and is focussed on "gendering" the issues of the X and Y generations (e.g.: eco-feminism, gender and globalization).[21]

Gloria Steinem and others have countered that the traits which third-wave feminism claims as its own were present or developed during the 1970s and 1980s.[22] Again, we should not find this surprising. Although X and Y have grown up in different contexts, they are not complete breaks with the past, and in many ways their characteristics are simply intensified ones of the Boomers. For the purposes of this paper, however, it is possible to identify recent changes in Goddess Feminism (and Paganism in general) which may reflect generational change.

"I'm not a feminist, but..."

Huntley found that most young Y people have "internalised feminism to such an extent that many of them question its relevance as a social movement and a way of understanding the world."[23] However, she also found that "a significant percentage of them still identify [. . .] with the goals and ideals of feminism."[24] Several writers have claimed that there are good reasons why young women are turned off by the feminist label. Rebecca Walker early claimed that young women have a "very different vantage point on the world than that of our foremothers,"[25] that they do not want to identify with a movement seen to polarize when their experience of life is full of "contradictions and messiness."[26] She writes, "we find ourselves seeking to create identities that accommodate ambiguity and our multiple positionalities."[27] This sense that the situation is different now, leads to an "ambivalent relationship"[28] with feminism for young women. This is also something that I have found in my own research. Though Jasmine (Y) was happy to use the term Goddess Feminist to describe herself, she stressed that her early "very feminist and Dianic" approach "has kind of mellowed out" to an emphasis on tolerance and difference. In the same way, Alex (X) believes that second-wave feminists performed the task of expressing and "clearing" their anger and resentment at oppression, so that younger generations can pursue "balance." She sees first generation Goddess Feminists as having left a legacy of "spiritual equality" for younger women. She hesitates to use the word "feminist," not because she disagrees with the ideals of feminism, but because she wants to distinguish her feminism from that of a different generation and because she sees the goal of her generation (achieving "balance") as different from second-wave feminism. Many younger Goddess Feminists thus have a troublesome relationship with feminism. At times they embrace it, at others they reject it, but there remains a continuing engagement with many of the issues that second-wave feminists struggled with: authority, self and identity, body, and so forth.

Paganism/Goddess Feminism and Generation Y

The UK is a significantly different situation in terms of religious adherence than either the United States or Canada (where religious participation is much higher). In the UK most people profess to be Christian. The National Census for England and Wales in 2001 reported that 77.7% of respondents identified as Christian.[29] However, only about 7.5% of those people actually go to church.[30] Though Francis found that many young people in the UK profess a belief in God (41%),[31] Savage et al. found that most young people's religious and spiritual beliefs were "fuzzy at best."[32] This is hardly surprising given that in the UK, Y is the generation least likely to have been raised by regular church attenders.[33] The British Social Attitudes Survey of 2005 reports that 52.81% of 18-34 year olds (generations X and Y) claim to have "no religion."[34] However, Lynch points out that a poll conducted for the BBC in 2003 found that 24% claimed to be "spiritually inclined but don't really 'belong' to an organized religion."[35] As

Huntley writes, "on the question of spirituality and ethics, Yers have basically been left to their own devices."[36]

A few quantitative studies have been done on Pagan populations in North America, though not all state age distribution.[37] Berger *et al.* report that their survey indicates that 29.1% of Pagans are between the ages of 20-29, with the majority (34.3%) between the ages of 30-39.[38] The situation is less clear in the UK. Heelas and Woodhead reported that for the "holistic milieu"[39] in their locality study in Kendal, UK, the majority of participants were Boomers (in their 50s).[40] The Office of National Statistics reports that on the 2001 Census 5% of the population claimed to belong to a religion other than those listed,[41] of whom 20% were between the ages of 16 and 34.[42] However, others have insisted that while the majority of young people in generations X and Y "are highly suspicious . . . of traditional religions,"[43] there is a "significant proportion of young people . . . interested in exploring 'alternative' or non-Western religions."[44] Similarly, Beaudoin claims that Xers have a "widespread regard for paganism" and "a growing enchantment with mysticism."[45] He bases this assertion on his own research as well as popular books and music, internet sites, and university courses. Berger *et al.* in their study of US Pagans found that 64.8% of their sample was female, and Reid reported a ratio of three women to every man in her survey of Canadian Pagans.[46] Meanwhile, personal communication with several prominent Goddess Feminist course and retreat/conference facilitators in the UK suggests that the majority of those women on courses are in their 30s or 40s, with the youngest in their early 20s.[47] Kathy Jones, founder of the Glastonbury Goddess Conference, points out that retreat/conference numbers are unreliable since the age differential changes depending on the theme of an event (i.e., for an event which celebrates the Crone one can expect to see more older women than younger). At the least then, we can say that Goddess Feminism continues to attract younger women, though it appears that Generation X women outnumber Generation Y women.

There may be a very good reason why more X than Y young women appear to be involved in Goddess Feminism. Linda Woodhead has written that the disproportionate amount of women involved in what she terms "holistic spiritualities" may be explained by the particular pressures which women feel as they age and try to hold together both career and family responsibilities. She argues that involvement with religion, and especially with forms of religion which "cater for the late modern project of independent, entitled, unique selfhood"[48] may help to ease the burden of the "second shift" which women who have families find themselves working (which is oriented towards an other-referential self).[49] Similarly, Huntley reports that with vastly different attitudes towards (future) housework and childcare responsibilities, "Y men and women are on a collision course."[50] It may be, then, that Y women will increasingly be drawn to forms of religiosity which can help them negotiate and subvert their gender roles and responsibilities.

The Everyday and Self in Process

I am participating in a ritual with several X and Y women. We are using an old cooking pot as a cauldron, stirring red wine within it with a wooden spoon. As we stir, we chant 'She changes everything She touches, and everything She touches changes'. Soon we stand and each of us begins to twirl around the circle as though stirring ourselves. We spin and spin until we fall upon the ground laughing. Later we tell stories about times of change in our lives, changes to our sense of self, as well as decisions about, and changing perceptions of, our bodies.

Paganism and Goddess Feminism accommodate and encourage many Y traits and concerns. In the ritual above, the cauldron is meant to symbolize a woman's body, her menstrual cycle, and her blood in general as a symbol of embodied life; as one informant said of the symbol of the cauldron, it's 'this great pot of life' (Alison, Boomer). It also symbolizes creativity in general and the constant creation of self, not to mention a feminist play on the expression "stirring the pot." The use of a cooking pot in this ritual emphasizes that the cauldron is a symbol of transformation, but also relates the ritual to the everyday. As Lynn (X) said of the cauldron, "really it was just a big pot to cook your dinner in."

Issues surrounding the body, how to celebrate embodied life as a woman, and how to live out and embody new ways of being women are encapsulated in the symbol of the cauldron. Xer Jacqui Woodward-Smith writes forcefully about the need for Goddess Feminist images to reflect the real world of embodiment: "the rot and death, the fucking, the shit and the mud."[51] These things are powerful examples of the Goddess Feminist tendency to thealogize the earth and the life-cycle in all its forms. They force Goddess Feminists to reflect upon what Grosz (in another context) has called our "necessary relation to death, corporeality, animality, materiality"[52] and thus may be seen to symbolize the Goddess Feminist embrace of the unstable subject. The moving, stirred up contents of the cauldron and the twirling, spinning participants in this ritual reflect what Raphael has called the Goddess Feminist emphasis on "unmapped, unfolding being".[53]

Goddess Feminists are well aware of the concerns of recent feminist identity theory on performing self,[54] or a self constantly in process, as well as the stress in third-wave feminism on a self performed through many roles and relationships.[55] Though this view of the self is held by many Goddess Feminists across the generations, it is perhaps an increasingly comfortable position for women of X and Y generations, reflecting as it does the late-modern tendency toward foregrounding "the body" and relating "the spiritual to everyday life,"[56] as well as the notion of a "plastic"[57] self rather than a given or fixed self. Jasmine (Y), for example, was comfortable with the idea of gender performance and transgression. As she said, "[I like] doing kind of special women stuff like honouring menstruation, ...[but] I don't agree with excluding like transgendered people ... I don't think there's a problem if they want to be involved." She also questioned the reification of gender roles when she said, "it annoys me when [in a] traditional [Wiccan] coven it has got male and female working partners and it's all that male and female energy."

Like the cauldron, Goddess Feminists often materialize the notion of a self in process and gender performance through performance of goddesses. Such "performance" can take many forms: at the Glastonbury Goddess Conference women are invited to come dressed up as a goddess at the party on the final evening, but even before then women dress in particular colors associated with goddesses and wear flowered headdresses, and priestesses invoke goddesses in rituals of embodiment.[58] Edward Schieffelin notes that performance "embodies the *expressive dimension of the strategic articulation of practice.*"[59] It is important that such performances are embodied experiences. Within feminism, the body has been a site of constant theorizing, and Lyon contends that a key aspect of the post-modern is "a focus on the body."[60] Given this context, it is significant that Jasmine says that one of the things she likes most about Goddess Feminist ritual is the emphasis on "everything being sensory." These practices potentially create and reinforce strategic "embodied dispositions,"[61] and in the conscious construction of performance, they can lay bare the social construction of gender and self. As Yer Katie Toms wrote in the *Guardian* article with which I opened this chapter,

> In the evening we silently process through Glastonbury and up Chalice Hill in four element groups—earth, fire, air and water. I wear the red of my fire sign. A man calls out: "Excuse me, what's going on here?" "We're Goddesses!" I shout triumphantly. (11/08/06)

Polytheism

"I think the polytheism is desperately important" (Penny, Boomer).

"Specific goddesses represent specific energies of place" (Tara, X).

Above I have referred to what I call the "diversity narrative" of third wave feminism, which corresponds with an increasing pluralism and differentiation of religion in the West.[62] Observers of Paganism (and the New Age) have long emphasized its universalizing aspects, claiming that the divine as a unity is a 'basic assumption' even of polytheist versions of Paganism.[63] However, with other researchers,[64] I see a growing trend in Paganism in the UK toward polytheism.[65] The recent formation of the Association of Polytheist Traditions (APT) in Britain supports this observation. The website for the APT explains, "we see our gods as individual deities, not as 'aspects of the divine' nor as 'avatars' of the Godhead."[66] In my research with Goddess Feminists, participants frequently preferred to use the term "Goddess," rather than "*the* Goddess" to refer to a set of ethics and a way of life which emphasized a plurality of "energies" or goddesses, rather than a single, unifying Goddess. In this way, most Goddess Feminists (even those who are universalists) are *functionally polytheistic*. That is, most Goddess Feminist rituals I have experienced are not directed to *the* Goddess, but to individual goddesses. For the duration of the ritual, those goddesses are treated as autonomous deities or energies. Further, though Goddess Feminism has always relied on multiple visions of female identities (Maiden, Lover, Mother, and Crone), my research indicates a shift to emphasizing the diversity and new meanings within such categories. For example, in one ritual group with whom I worked (made up of both Boomers and X women), the goddess Bloedwedd was invoked at both spring and autumn equinoxes in her materializations as spring flowers (Maiden) and as owl (Crone).

If Cynthia Eller's assertion that women of the Boomer generation who were attracted to the Goddess "wanted to worship a goddess—a big one, bigger than the god of patriarchy"[67] is true, I suggest that a monotheist or henotheist approach amongst these women may stem from a desire not to "dilute" the power of Goddess by polytheism. Further, Boomer women in my research tended to have a Christian family background (or at least attended Sunday School). On the other hand, Y women have grown up with feminism, and the majority in the UK have little church background.[68] Indeed, it was the younger cohort of my research participants who were most likely to say "it makes sense to kind of see male and female [deities]... God is less important for me as a woman, [but] I am not—I mean some Goddess worshippers sort of like [say] there is one Goddess and no God at all" (Jasmine, Y) or, as Tara (X/Y) said of male divinities "I don't deny that." With each generation in the UK "less religious than the last"[69] (i.e., fewer regular church attenders), Savage et al. found that "traditional religious concepts and stories did not seem to have much relevance at all" to young people.[70] In such a context, the necessity for a "big Goddess" to differentiate from the Christian God, is likely to become less important.

Further, for both X and Y women, *choice* has become a second-wave feminist value that has become central in all things.[71] From choosing to op-out of patriarchal religion to choosing from a smorgasbord of deities, the trend toward polytheism in Paganism can be viewed as part of what Grace Davie writes of as an "increasing emphasis on consumption."[72] I do not mean to suggest that such consumer choice is necessarily self-indulgent or shallow. Rather, as David Lyon has proposed, that "consumption plays an increasingly significant role in the way society runs."[73] This plays out in what Woodhead and Heelas have called "post-modern difference," an "affirmatory, even celebratory, stance towards difference." Post-modern difference is "tolerant and provisional. It understands truth as a matter of perspective, relative to different standpoints and different narratives."[74] One of the most prevalent narratives in Goddess Feminism is the narrative of difference and diversity that is modelled by the natural world, by women living out complex gender identities, and the plurality of Goddess(es).

The Glocal

The stereotype of the gap-year traveller backpacking around the world before university or career has added significance for young X and Y women who "have heeded the call of their mothers to get the most out of life before marriage,"[75] and who enjoy an unprecedented freedom of mobility (provided they can afford it). In such a globalized migratory state, Tara says, "that's where [the goddess] Elen of the Trackway[76] has become important to me, I feel I become more connected with the deer, who of course are migratory, and that resonates very strongly with me."[77] Huntley argues that Yers have adjusted to "the world's instability" and their "wanderlust" is a reflection of the way they value "freedom," "flexibility," and "diversity."[78] The very fact that Tara can claim a nomadic identity points to the huge changes in women's mobility over the last 40 years. As Linda Woodhead has written, women's current freedom of mobility "entails occupying public space legitimately and without depending on male permission."[79] Savage et al. point to a "nomadic theme" in contemporary society, but whereas for older generations, this sense of nomadism may be an alienating experience, for Y "it is normal and provides a buzz."[80] Elen of the Trackway becomes then, for Tara, a way to root herself in, even celebrate, rootlessness.

Rather than simply using Elen to reflect post-modern rootlessness, Tara finds Elen also "connects me with ancient [nomadic] communities." The goddess becomes a way to reconceptualize community and identity. The way Tara relates to Elen suggests a plastic, and constantly changing identity, which is key to understanding X and Y ideas of self.[81] However, though it prizes individualism, Goddess Feminism is not an individualistic religion as some have portrayed it. I agree with Graham Harvey when he argues that Paganism is not a "self-religion"[82] but a religion of self-in-relationship.[83] Heelas and Woodhead have argued that in the case of women, there is frequently a concern with relationality which tempers self authority, what they call "relational autonomous subjectivism."[84] As Woodhead has argued, women continue to juggle "two incompatible modes of selfhood—the independent, entitled self and the other-referential, caring self."[85] Elen of the Trackway becomes a way of relating the self to others (ancient communities, other-than-human beings) even as the context (both landscape and self-identity) is constantly shifting.

Savage et al. found that young people find meaning and significance in "this world, and all life in it" and in everyday life[86] and I have discussed above how this can play out with regard to the body and self. Goddess Feminism has always had an immanent thealogy,[87] but I observe an increasing trend in British Goddess Feminism toward emphasizing local deities/energies of place, and only working with "native" goddesses. As Jasmine (Y) said,

> I just feel a bit daft invoking . . . goddesses of the Pacific and stuff when our ocean is nothing like that. Because Paganism has a connection with the land, I think you should try to do that with ritual as well and not sort of import goddesses.

This trend parallels a growing consciousness that working with goddesses from other cultures can be cultural colonialism.[88] The emphasis on the local is held in conjunction with the global consciousness which I discussed above. Tara emphasized, "I think when you are in different landscapes, you need to get to know the goddesses who live there." She spoke of her travels and said that wherever she goes, "when I get there I need to meet the land" and "connect" with local deities. Tara clearly did not import these deities when she returned to the UK. For her, they could not be removed from their ecological context. Tara thus roots herself in the local even as she travels globally. Tara also carries with her the ability to ritually create sacred space wherever she goes, which is a feature of Goddess Feminism's democratized priestesshood stemming from both the drive towards self-authority, and a feminist declaration that women can mediate the sacred *for themselves*.

DIY Spirituality

> The emphasis on personal responsibility I liked—that the church or whatever isn't in charge of you, it's you, you are in charge of your relationship to God or whatever, and with Paganism it is like the connection to nature and a sort of do-it-yourself emphasis [that I like]. (Jasmine, Y)

It is the do-it-yourself (DIY) emphasis that Jasmine insists was an important factor in her original attraction to Goddess Feminism. Jasmine does not simply refer in the quotation above, to "individual autonomy,"[89] she also stresses "personal responsibility." Jordan Paper argues that polytheistic religions in general have a sense of mutual responsibility between the divine and the human.[90] Thus, though the drive towards (functional) polytheism in contemporary paganism may be a reflection of societal consumerism, it does not necessarily imply an irresponsible consumerism. As one informant put it, "it's like a contract I have with my special deities; there's an exchange there" (Helene, Boomer).

Others have commented that this DIY approach is typical of young women's feminism, arguing that although the second-wave institutional approach of legislation and activism has achieved much, that young women feel that they are "*living* feminism" through their personal achievements and in their everyday lives.[91] Young Y women grew up with girl power, an "I can do anything" attitude, which is encouraged by the "freedom" in Goddess Feminism to "make it up" (Kathy Jones, Boomer). Huntley, writing about the politics of Y, claims that Yers prefer "direct democracy," and that they take "a small target approach."[92] She means that young people prefer to approach global issues on the local or even individual level (the glocal). In the same way, Goddess Feminism focuses on politicization through women's re-visioned gender identities that are modelled and supported by their spirituality. The DIY approach towards ritual, Goddess and self in Goddess Feminism mirrors the approach taken by young people towards politics and the approaches of third-wave feminism wherein "the philosophy is more oriented towards individual empowerment."[93] Alex (X) is typical of this personal approach to the political. She says,

> I think the problems of equal rights for women still exist in our society and I think that the power to heal this has to come from women themselves. . . . I think the power to change the world view of women has to be brought about by women. We can stop buying the magazines that promote white, blonde, age 17 years, size 0 as the standard dictation of beauty in the female form. We can do much to our minds and emotions to resolve our conditioning and the conditioning of our mothers and grandmothers.

In a sense, then, critics of both Goddess Feminism and the third-wave are correct when they accuse the movements of being self-obsessed. Both Goddess Feminists and third-wave feminists believe that they must first change gender identities and roles if they are to change the world, that they must develop a sense of self (or selves) which can re-imagine previous dualistic gender identities (i.e., feminine *versus* masculine). In typical Y fashion, Jasmine turns to the internet as a forum to practice her DIY spirituality, running "a website which I do with another girl . . . for teenage Pagans" and moderating several email lists. The DIY approaches of Goddess Feminist ritual and the third-wave (seen in things such as websites, email lists, blogs and zines), allow young women to "critique, question, resist, and reappropriate . . . patriarchal mass culture"[94] by allowing them to focus on their personal, everyday struggle to live out their gender identities using new forms of mass communication. As Lyon summarizes, in late modernity the "creative tension point" lies between the self and broader flows of power.[95]

This tension, in Goddess Feminism, plays out in the conviction that though they start at the level of individual change, Goddess Feminists are convinced that individual change happens in the context of interconnection. As Jasmine said, "I just feel that everything is alive and everything is connected . . . . I definitely like the Gaia hypothesis."[96] Coleen Mack-Canty sees this eco-feminist narrative of interdependence as typical of third-wave feminism.[97] I have argued above that Paganism is a religion of self-in-relationship, which Heelas and Woodhead have claimed is a particularly appealing approach for women who juggle both autonomous and other-referential senses of self. As important to Goddess Feminists, then, as developing a sense of self (or selves), is the notion that the individual only really makes sense in relation to others. Similarly, Rountree contends that Goddess Feminism and feminist witchcraft "provide a theory and experience of connection."[98] As with goddesses, self is understood as always including multiple identities and relationships. When Tara told me that Goddess was a "way of being", she meant, in part, that Goddess *is* relatedness.

Conclusion

This chapter is based upon interviews with boomer, X, and Y women, upon participant observation of ritual groups and the Glastonbury Goddess Conference, and upon observation of web-based forms of communication. It is limited, however, by little generational research on Goddess Feminism in the UK. Instead, I have relied upon evidence from research on Boomers, X, and Y more broadly, including generational differences in religiosity. I have shown how Generation X and Y Goddess Feminists do not represent complete breaks with past generations, but rather a continuation and intensification of societal trends which have been developing since at least the 60s. Most young X and Y women in the UK are not engaged with Goddess Feminism, nor even with religion in general. However, for those who are involved with Goddess Feminism, I have argued that certain characteristics of generations X and Y (formed by particular events and social trends of the 1970s and 80s), as well as third-wave feminist concerns, are mirrored in trends in Goddess Feminism. It can be expected that issues surrounding pluralism, consumerism, identity, self and the body will continue to shape the movement in the years to come.

Notes

1. Katie Toms. "All Hail the Goddesses." *The Guardian*. Friday, August 11, 2006.
2. Goddess Feminism is a term which has slowly gained favor within both academic and practitioner-based circles over the last decade to refer to a segment of contemporary paganism which grew out of the intersection of traditional Wicca, feminism, and environmentalism in the U.S. in the 1970s (see Adler 1986 [1979], Eller 1993) and which later spread to the UK, Europe, and Australia and New Zealand (see Hutton 1999, Harvey 1997, Rountree 2004). Though some observers conflate Goddess Feminism and feminist witchcraft, the women whom I interviewed do not refer to themselves as Wiccans, and only occasionally, and in a specific political context, as witches.
3. Women from previous generations also have a presence in Goddess Feminism. In the UK, two founder Goddess Feminists were part of what has been called the 'Builder' or the 'Silent Generation' (Savage et al. 2006, 5) born between 1925-1945, Asphodel Long and Monica Sjoo. Both women published widely, and Sjoo was a well-known artist.

4. Sara Savage et al., *Making Sense of Generation Y: the World View of 15-25 Year Olds* (London: Church House Publishing, 2006), 5.

5. Savage et al., *Making Sense of Generation Y*, 5.

6. See Wade Clark Roof, *Generation of Seekers: the Spiritual Journeys of the Baby Boom Generation* (SanFrancisco: HarperSanFrancisco, 1993). See also Paul Heelas and Linda Woodhead, *The Spiritual Revolution: Why Religion is Giving Way to Spirituality* (Oxford, UK and Malden, USA: Blackwell, 2005). Of course, not all Boomers have abandoned the churches, and indeed they have also largely been behind the growth in conservative forms of Christianity, especially Pentecostalism (Roof 1993), though I do not have the space here to tease out the reasons for this.

7. Donald E. Flory and Arpi Misha Miller. "Understanding Generation X: Values, Politics, and Religious Commitments," in *GenX Religion*, eds. Donald E. Flory and Arpi Misha Miller (New York and London: Routledge, 2000), 3.

8. See Thomas More Beaudoin, *Virtual Faith: the Irreverent Spiritual Quest of Generation X* (San Francisco: Jossey-Bass Publishers, 1998); Gordon Lynch, *After Religion: 'Generation X' and the Search for Meaning* (London: Darton, Longman and Todd, 2002); Flory and Miller, eds. *GenX Religion*; Rebecca Huntley, *The World According to Y: Inside the New Adult Generation* (Crows Nest, Australia: Allen & Unwin, 2006).

9. David Lyon, *Jesus in Disneyland: Religion in Post-modern Times* (Cambridge, UK and Malden, MA: Polity Press, 2000), 99.

10. Lyon, *Jesus in Disneyland*, 13.

11. Huntley, *The World According to Y*, 15.

12. Huntley, *The World According to Y*, 51.

13. Callum Brown, *The Death of Christian Britain* (London: Routledge Brown, 2001).

14. Linda Woodhead, "'Because I'm Worth It': Religion and Women's Changing Lives in the West," in *Women and Religion in the West: Challenging Secularization*, eds. Kristin Aune, Sonya Sharma and Giselle Vincett (Aldershot, UK and Burlington, VT: Ashgate), 156.

15. Dick Houtman and Stef Aupers, "The Spiritual Revolution and the New Age Gender Puzzle: the Sacralisation of the Self in Late Modernity (1980-2000)," in *Women and Religion in the West: Challenging Secularization*, eds. Kristin Aune, Sonya Sharma and Giselle Vincett (Aldershot, UK and Burlington, VT: Ashgate), 109.

16. Jo Reger, "Introduction," in *Different Wavelengths: Studies of the Contemporary Women's Movement*, ed. Jo Reger (New York and Abingdon, UK: Routledge, 2005), xvii; Rebecca Walker, "Introduction", in *To Be Real: Telling the Truth and Changing the Face of Feminism*, ed. Rebecca Walker (New York: First Anchor Books, 1995).

17. Jennifer Baumgardner and Amy Richards, *Manifesta: Young Women, Feminism and the Future* (New York: Farrar, Straus, Giroux, 2000), 17.

18. Kim Allen, "The Feminist Generation Gap," in *The Third Wave: Feminism for the New Millenium* (http://www.3rdwwwave.com/display_article.cgi?142, 1998), accessed 22/02/08.

19. Heelas and Woodhead, *The Spiritual Revolution*.

20. Feminist scholars have pointed out that second-wave feminism was not the homogenized white-women's movement that some have portrayed it to be, showing that black women (for example) were present in the movement from the beginning (see Reger 2005). However, it is important that third-wave feminists *read* it as such in their effort to

distinguish themselves from the second-wave, and that they have focussed on this *particular* issue, which reflects their social context in so many ways.

21. See Astrid Henry, "Solitary Sisterhood: Individualism Meets Collectivity in Feminisms's Third Wave," in *Different Wavelengths: Studies of the Contemporary Women's Movement*, ed. Jo Reger (New York and Abingdon, UK: Routledge, 2005), 81-96; Dawn Bates and Maureen C. McHugh, "Zines: Voices of Third Wave Feminists," in *Different Wavelengths: Studies of the Contemporary Women's Movement*, ed. Jo Reger (New York and Abingdon, UK: Routledge, 2005), 179-193; Walker, *To Be Real*; Baumgardner and Richards, *Manifesta.*.

22. Gloria Steinem, "Foreword," in *To Be Real: Telling the Truth and Changing the Face of Feminism*, ed. Rebecca Walker (New York: First Anchor Books, 1995); Jo Reger, "Introduction".

23. Huntley, *The World According to Y*, 43.

24. Huntley, *The World According to Y*, 45.

25. Walker, "Introduction," xxxiii.

26. Walker, "Introduction," xxxi.

27. Walker, "Introduction," xxxiii.

28. Henry, "Solitary Sisterhood: Individualism Meets Collectivity in Feminisms's Third Wave," 81.

29. http://www.statistics.gov.uk/CCI/nuggest.asp?ID=984&Pos=6&ColRank=1& Rank=176, accessed 22/02/08.

30. Peter Brierley, *The Tide is Running Out: What the English Church Attendance Survey Reveals* (London: Christian Research, 2000), 27.

31. Leslie J. Francis, *The Values Debate: a Voice From the Pupils* (London: Woburn Press, 2001), 36, 40.

32. Savage et al., *Making Sense of Generation Y*, 19; see also Gordon Lynch, *The New Spirituality: an Introduction to Progressive Belief in the Twenty-first Century* (London and New York: I.B. Tauris, 2007), 4.

33. A. Crockett and D. Voas, "Generations of Decline: Religious Change in 20th-Century Britain." *Journal for the Scientific Study of Religion*, 45(4) (2006): 567-584; David Voas, "Decline in Scotland: New Evidence on Timing and Spatial Patterns." *Journal for the Scientific Study of Religion*, 45(1) (2006): 107-118.

34. http://www.britsocat.com/BodySecure.aspx?control=BritsocatMarginals&add supermap =LBRELIGION, accessed 22/02/08.

35. Lynch, *The New Spirituality*, 3. The poll can be found at http://www.ipsos-mori. com/polls/2003/bbc-heavenandearth.shtml (accessed 26/02/08). The poll interviewed adults aged 16 and over, but does not give information about generational differences.

36. Huntley, *The World According to Y*, 169.

37. See Loretta Orion, *Never Again the Burning Times: Paganism Revived* (Prospect Heights, IL: Waveland, 1995); Danny Jorgensen and Scott Russell, "American Neopaganism: the Participants' Social Identities." *Journal for the Scientific Study of Religion*, 38(3) (1996): 325-338; Helen A. Berger, et al., *Voices from the Pagan Census: a National Survey of Witches and Neo-Pagans in the United States* (Columbia, SC: University of South Carolina Press, 2003); Sian Reid, "The Soul of Soulless Conditions: Paganism, Goddess Religion and Witchcraft in Canada," in *Women and Religion in the West: Challenging Secularization*, eds. Kristin Aune, Sonya Sharma and Giselle Vincett (Aldershot, UK and Burlington, VT: Ashgate, 2008), 119-132.

38. Berger, et al., *Voices from the Pagan Census*, 27.

39. The "holistic milieu" includes Pagans, but also New Age, and participants in activities such as yoga or reiki (Heelas and Woodhead 2005, 156,157).

40. Heelas and Woodhead, *The Spiritual Revolution*, 107.

41. In the 2001 census, the category "Other" was an open category. That is, people had to write in their religious affiliation. It included a wide range of affiliations including Baha'is, Jains and Rastafarians. According to the Office for National Statistics, 31, 000 people wrote in "Pagan" and a further 7,000 wrote in "Wiccan" (http://www.statistics. gov.uk/cci/nuggest.asp?id=954, accessed 26/02/08).

42. http://www.statistics.gov.uk/cci/nugget.asp?id=955, accessed 26/02/08. Meanwhile, Reid found that in her survey of Canadian Pagans "fully 25 per cent of my sample listed something that would not have been coded as pagan [on the census]" (2008, 126).

43. Huntley, *The World According to Y*, 165. Huntley's research was with young Australians.

44. Huntley, *The World According to Y*, 166.

45. Beaudoin, *Virtual Faith*, 25.

46. Berger, et al., *Voices from the Pagan Census: a National Survey of Witches and Neo-Pagans in the United States*; Reid, "The Soul of Soulless Conditions: Paganism, Goddess Religion and Witchcraft in Canada," 119-132.

47. Personal communications from Alex Chaloner (14/01/08, 16/01/08), Kathy Jones (29/01/08), and Cheryl Straffon (28/01/08).

48. Woodhead, "'Because I'm Worth It': Religion and Women's Changing Lives in the West," 156.

49. The "second shift" refers to women's unpaid work in the home which is on top of their paid occupation. Such work includes both material and emotional work, the majority of which still falls to women in most households (Hochschild 1997).

50. Huntley, *The World According to Y*, 51.

51. Woodward-Smith, Jacqui, "The Goddess vs. the New Age: Singing the Sacred Land." *Goddess Pages* (http://www.goddesspages.com/issue1/articles/goddessvsnewage. html, 2006), 4, accessed 26/03/07.

52. Elizabeth Grosz, *Sexual Subversions: Three French Feminists* (Syney: Allen & Unwin, 1989), 73.

53. Melissa Raphael, *Thealogy and Embodiment: the Post-Patriarchal Reconstruction of Female Sacrality* (Sheffield: Sheffield Academic Press, 1996), 251.

54. For example, Judith Butler, *Gender Trouble and the Subversion of Identity* (New York: Routledge, 1990).

55. Walker, "Introduction," xxxiii. I have often been reminded of the wide-ranging reading habits of Goddess Feminists during interviews, and as I have monitored Goddess Feminist email lists.

56. Lyon, *Jesus in Disneyland*, 54.

57. Lyon, *Jesus in Disneyland*, 92.

58. Embodiment ritual is difficult to describe. It is something more than play-acting, but it is not trance possession or channelling.

59. Edward Schieffelin, "Problematizing Performance," in *Ritual and Religious Belief: a Reader*, ed. Graham Harvey (London: Equinox Schieffelin 2005), 130, emphasis in original.

60. Lyon, *Jesus in Disneyland*, 41.

61. Simon Coleman and Peter Collins, "The 'Plain' and the 'Positive': Ritual, Experience and Aesthetics in Quakerism and Charismatic Christianity," *Journal of Contemporary Religion* 15(3) (2000): 318.

62. See Grace Davie, *Europe: the Exceptional Case: Parameters of Faith in the Modern World* (London: Darton, Longman & Todd), 15; Lyon, *Jesus in Disneyland.*

63. Lynch, *The New Spirituality*, 44.

64. For example, see Charlotte Hardman, "Introduction," in *Pagan Pathways: a Guide to the Ancient Earth Traditions,* eds. Graham Harvey and Charlotte Hardman (London: Thorsons, 1995), xii.

65. It should be emphasized that this trend is not limited to young X and Y women, and indeed, there are many young women who prefer a henotheist thealogy.

66. www.manygods.org.uk, accessed 22/02/08.

67. Eller, *Living in the Lap of the Goddess*, 58.

68. Savage et al., *Making Sense of Generation Y.*

69. Voas "Decline in Scotland: New Evidence on Timing and Spatial Patterns," 111.

70. Savage et al., *Making Sense of Generation Y,* 36

71. For a discussion of the post-modern emphasis on *choice,* see Lyon, *Jesus in Disneyland,* 138.

72. Davie 2002, 148.

73. Lyon, *Jesus in Disneyland,* 32.

74. Linda Woodhead and Paul Heelas eds., *Religion in Modern Times: an Interpretive Anthology* (Oxford: Blackwell Publishing 2000), 265.

75. Huntley, *The World According to Y,* 82, 83.

76. Elen appears in the Welsh Mabinogion as a queen and a magical builder of roads across the land. She is treated by British Goddess Feminists as a sovereignty goddess and is connected with the health of the land and the migratory deer.

77. Tara works with Gypsy and Traveller children, which lends another layer to her attraction to Elen of the Trackway.

78. Huntley, *The World According to Y,* 96, 97.

79. Woodhead, "'Because I'm Worth It': Religion and Women's Changing Lives in the West," 149.

80. Savage et al., *Making Sense of Generation Y,* 154.

81. Lyon, *Jesus in Disneyland,* 69.

82. Graham Harvey, *Listening People, Speaking Earth: Contemporary Paganism* (London: Hurst & Company, 1997), 227.

83. Graham Harvey, *What Do Pagans Believe?* (London: Granta, 2007), 20.

84. Heelas and Woodhead, *The Spiritual Revolution,* 105.

85. Woodhead, "'Because I'm Worth It': Religion and Women's Changing Lives in the West," 150.

86. Savage et al., *Making Sense of Generation Y,* 37.

87. See Eller, *Living in the Lap of the Goddess;* Raphael, *Thealogy and Embodiment.*

88. Indeed, in every case where a participant in my research worked with a goddess from a culture other than Celtic/British, they felt the need to justify doing so by emphasizing that the deity had come to them in a vision or some other extraordinary experience.

89. Steve Bruce, *God is Dead: Secularization in the West* (Oxford: Blackwell, 2002), 92.

90. Jordan Paper, *The Deities Are Many: a Polytheistic Theology* (Albany, NY: The State University of New York Press, 2005).

91. Huntley, *The World According to Y*, 47.
92. Huntley, *The World According to Y*, 108 and 113.
93. Naomi Rockler-Gladen, "Third Wave Feminism: Personal Empowerment Dominates This Feminist Philosophy," in *Suite101.com* (http://feminism.suite101.com/article.cfm/third_wave_feminism, 2007), accessed 22/02/08; see also Henry, "Solitary Sisterhood: Individualism Meets Collectivity in Feminisms's Third Wave," 83.
94. Bates and McHugh, "Zines: Voices of Third Wave Feminists," 185.
95. Lyon, *Jesus in Disneyland*, 39.
96. The Gaia hypothesis proposes that the earth self-regulates itself to sustain life on the planet.
97. Colleen Mack-Canty, "Third Wave Feminism and Ecofeminism," in *Third Wave Feminism: Collective Action in a New Millennium*, ed. Jo Reger (New York and Abingdon, UK: Routledge, 2005), 203, 208.
98. Kathryn Rountree, *Embracing the Witch and the Goddess: Feminist Ritual-Makers in New Zealand* (New York: Routledge, 2004), 113.

Bibliography

Adler, Margot. *Drawing Down the Moon: Witches, Druids, Goddess Worshippers, and Other Pagans in America Today*. New York: Penguin Arkana, 1986 [1979].
Allen, Kim. "The Feminist Generation Gap". In *The Third Wave: Feminism for the New Millenium*. http://www.3rdwwwave.com/display_article.cgi?142 (1998). Accessed 22/02/08.
Association for Polytheist Theologies. www.manygods.org. Accessed 22/02/08.
Bates, Dawn and Maureen C. McHugh. "Zines: Voices of Third Wave Feminists." In *Different Wavelengths: Studies of the Contemporary Women's Movement*, edited by Jo Reger. New York and Abingdon, UK: Routledge, 2005.
Baumgardner, Jennifer and Amy Richards. *Manifesta: Young Women, Feminism and the Future*. New York: Farrar, Straus, Giroux, 2000.
Beaudoin, Thomas More. *Virtual Faith: the Irreverent Spiritual Quest of Generation X*. San Francisco: Jossey-Bass Publishers, 1998.
Berger, Helen A., Evan A. Leach and Leigh S. Shaffer. *Voices from the Pagan Census: a National Survey of Witches and Neo-Pagans in the United States*. Columbia, SC: University of South Carolina Press, 2003.
Brierley, Peter. *The Tide is Running Out: What the English Church Attendance Survey Reveals*. London: Christian Research, 2000.
Brown, Callum. *The Death of Christian Britain*. London: Routledge, 2001.
Bruce, Steve. *God is Dead: Secularization in the West*. Oxford: Blackwell, 2002.
Butler, Judith. *Gender Trouble and the Subversion of Identity*. New York: Routledge, 1990.
Coleman, Simon and Peter Collins. "The 'Plain' and the 'Positive': Ritual, Experience and Aesthetics in Quakerism and Charismatic Christianity." *Journal of Contemporary Religion* 15(3) (2000): 317-329.
Crockett, A. and Voas, D. "Generations of Decline: Religious Change in 20th-Century Britain." *Journal for the Scientific Study of Religion* 45(4) (2006): 567-584.
Davie. *Europe: the Exceptional Case: Parameters of Faith in the Modern World*. London: Darton, Longman & Todd, 2002.

Eller, Cynthia. *Living in the Lap of the Goddess: the Feminist Spirituality Movement in America.* Boston: Beacon Press, 1993.

Flory, Donald E. and Arpi Misha Miller. "Understanding Generation X: Values, Politics, and Religious Commitments." In *GenX Religion,* edited by Donald E. Flory and Arpi Misha Miller. New York and London: Routledge, 2000.

Francis, Leslie. *The Values Debate: a Voice From the Pupils.* London: Woburn Press, 2001.

Grosz, Elizabeth. *Sexual Subversions: Three French Feminists.* Syney: Allen & Unwin, 1989.

Hardman, Charlotte, "Introduction." In *Pagan Pathways: a Guide to the Ancient Earth Traditions,* edited by Graham Harvey and Charlotte Hardman. London: Thorsons, 1995.

Harvey, Graham. *Listening People, Speaking Earth: Contemporary Paganism.* London: Hurst & Company, 1997.

Harvey, Graham, ed. *Ritual and Religious Belief: a Reader.* London: Equinox, 2005.

Harvey, Graham. *What Do Pagans Believe?* London: Granta, 2007.

Heelas, Paul and Linda Woodhead. *The Spiritual Revolution: Why Religion is Giving Way to Spirituality.* Oxford, UK and Malden, USA: Blackwell, 2005.

Henry, Astrid. "Solitary Sisterhood: Individualism Meets Collectivity in Feminisms's Third Wave." In *Different Wavelengths: Studies of the Contemporary Women's Movement,* edited by Jo Reger. New York and Abingdon, UK: Routledge, 2005.

Hochschild, Arlie Russell. *The Time Bind: When Work Becomes Home and Home Becomes Work.* New York: Metropolitan Books, 1997.

Houtman, Dick and Stef Aupers. "The Spiritual Revolution and the New Age Gender Puzzle: The Sacralisation of the Self in Late Modernity (1980-2000)." In *Women and Religion in the West: Challenging Secularization,* edited by Kristin Aune, Sonya Sharma and Giselle Vincett. Aldershot, UK and Burlington, VT: Ashgate, 2008.

Huntley, Rebecca. *The World According to Y: Inside the New Adult Generation.* Crows Nest, Australia: Allen & Unwin, 2006.

Jorgensen, Danny and Scott Russell. "American Neopaganism: the Participants' Social Identities." *Journal for the Scientific Study of Religion* 38(3) (1996): 325-338.

Lynch, Gordon. *After Religion: 'Generation X' and the Search for Meaning.* London: Darton, Longman and Todd, 2002.

Lynch, Gordon. *The New Spirituality: an Introduction to Progressive Belief in the Twenty-first Century.* London and New York: I.B. Tauris, 2007.

Lyon, David. *Jesus in Disneyland: Religion in Post-modern Times.* Cambridge, UK and Malden, MA: Polity Press, 2000.

Mack-Canty, Colleen, "Third Wave Feminism and Ecofeminism." In *Third Wave Feminism: Collective Action in a New Millennium,* edited by Jo Reger. New York and Abingdon, UK: Routledge, 2005.

Orion, Loretta. *Never Again the Burning Times: Paganism Revived.* Prospect Heights, IL: Waveland, 1995.

Paper, Jordan. *The Deities Are Many: a Polytheistic Theology.* Albany, NY: The State University of New York Press, 2005.

Raphael, Melissa. *Thealogy and Embodiment: the Post-Patriarchal Reconstruction of Female Sacrality.* Sheffield: Sheffield Academic Press, 1996.

Reger, Jo. "Introduction." In *Different Wavelengths: Studies of the Contemporary Women's Movement,* edited by Jo Reger. New York and Abingdon, UK: Routledge, 2005.

Reid, Sian. "The Soul of Soulless Conditions: Paganism, Goddess Religion and Witchcraft in Canada." In *Women and Religion in the West: Challenging Secularization,* edited by Kristin Aune, Sonya Sharma and Giselle Vincett. Aldershot, UK and Burlington, VT: Ashgate, 2008.

Rockler-Gladen, Naomi. "Third Wave Feminism: Personal Empowerment Dominates This Feminist Philosophy." *Suite101* http://feminism.suite101.com/article.cfm/thrid_wave_feminism (2007). Accessed 22/02/08.

Roof, Wade Clark. *Generation of Seekers: the Spiritual Journeys of the Baby Boom Generation.* SanFrancisco: HarperSanFrancisco, 1993.

Rountree, Kathryn. *Embracing the Witch and the Goddess: Feminist Ritual-Makers in New Zealand.* New York: Routledge, 2004.

Savage, Sara, Sylvia Collins-Mayo, Bob Mayo with Graham Cray. *Making Sense of Generation Y: the World View of 15-25 Year Olds.* London: Church House Publishing, 2006.

Schieffelin, Edward. "Problematizing Performance." In *Ritual and Religious Belief: a Reader,* edited by Graham Harvey. London: Equinox, 2005.

Steinem, Gloria. "Foreword." In *To Be Real: Telling the Truth and Changing the Face of Feminism,* edited by Rebecca Walker. New York: First Anchor Books, 1995.

Toms, Katie. "All Hail the Goddesses." *The Guardian,* Friday, August 11, 2006.

Voas, David. "Religious Decline in Scotland: New Evidence on Timing and Spatial Patterns." *Journal for the Scientific Study of Religion* 45(1) (2006): 107-118.

Walker, Rebecca, ed. *To Be Real: Telling the Truth and Changing the Face of Feminism.* New York: First Anchor Books, 1995.

Woodhead, Linda and Paul Heelas, eds. *Religion in Modern Times: an Interpretive Anthology.* Oxford: Blackwell Publishing, 2000.

Woodhead, Linda. "'Because I'm Worth It': Religion and Women's Changing Lives in the West." In *Women and Religion in the West: Challenging Secularization,* edited by Kristin Aune Sonya Sharma and Giselle Vincett. Aldershot, UK and Burlington, VT: Ashgate, 2008.

Woodward-Smith, Jacqui. "The Goddess vs. the New Age: Singing the Sacred Land." *Goddess Pages.* http://www.goddess-pages.com/issue1/articles/goddessvsnewage.html (2006). Accessed 26/03/07.

Chapter Eight:
Ritual Actions: Feminist Spirituality in Anti-Globalization Protests

Laurel Zwissler

> I think, if you're going to push yourself as an activist, or as a Christian activist, the natural outcome is that you become radicalized, because you're looking at issues of social justice and, once you fully analyze the issues, you're going to end up a radical.
>
> Angel, Catholic feminist activist.

Introduction

Young feminists combine their spirituality and political convictions. They negotiate roles for religion in civic discourse, incorporate religious and spiritual elements into political demonstrations and create rituals to perform in protest spaces. Feminist spirituality is present in global justice protests concurrent with international trade conferences, such as the demonstrations against the Free Trade Area of the Americas (FTAA) in Quebec City in April 2001, the focus of this chapter, and those against the World Trade Organization (WTO) in Seattle, November 1999, in Cancun, September 2003, and against the G8 in Rostock, Germany, June 2007. Such protests have become significant elements of the political landscape around the world, representing frustration about free trade policies and the global dominance of the United States.[1]

This chapter is based on my research about religion among North American feminist activists. It centers on women who identify as political activists and as feminist Catholic, feminist Protestant or feminist Pagan. My main sources are ethnographic interviews with informants in the Toronto area. I also used participant-observation within feminist Catholic, United Church of Canada and Pagan groups: I attended events such as group planning meetings, public demonstrations and religious rituals and, with the explicit permission of each group, participated in their activities for the purpose of better understanding and explaining their experiences in my research.[2]

I sought out three religious traditions that were explicitly present at public demonstrations and with which I was familiar through personal contacts. I chose to investigate specific religious institutions, instead of activists who identified exclusively as "spiritual," in order to address the challenge that religious institutions pose to secularist assumptions within political activist communities, as opposed to a generic "spirituality," which accommodates negative assessments of religion.[3] Two of these groups are Christian: Toronto Catholic Worker[4] and Clearwater United Church.[5] The third, the Yarrow Collective, is Pagan and strongly influenced by Reclaiming Witchcraft.[6] My choices of field study should in no way imply that these are the only feminist, religious groups working on social justice issues. I stress here that there are many active Muslim, Jewish, and Hindu groups in Canada, as well. These particular groups were highly vocal about refocusing their personal religious practices and their congregations' energies on "this-worldly" concerns[7] and promoting incorporation of religious practice with public action, though each also belongs to a larger tradition that does not exclusively involve itself with active social reform projects.

Though many of my participants do fit the category, I include women who do not identify themselves as young. Not everyone involved in the anti-globalization movement is chronologically young; nonetheless, the problems of economic globalization that activists address and the forms of activism in which they engage are recent social developments. I investigate young manifestations of spirituality that are explicitly feminist, rather than focusing exclusively on the spirituality of young feminists. I also urge readers to keep in mind that young feminist women are not isolated from older forms of feminism and activism, even if, in many cases, they may be defining their feminisms in contrast to stereotypes of "the second wave."[8] Within global justice protests, young feminist activists join with people from many different social positions, including older activists. The movement necessarily entails intergenerational interactions.

Moreover, while not all new religious movements, the Toronto Catholic Worker, the Clearwater United Church and the Yarrow Collective embrace feminist practices that can be thought of as "new movements in religion." Feminist Christians explicitly function as reformers, reinterpreting scripture and reworking ritual to emphasis social justice messages at the heart of their traditions. In contrast, feminist Pagans often present their religion as an alternative to Christianity, a relinquishing rather than reformation, an opting out rather than staying to reform oppressive structures from inside.[9] Feminist Witches argue that female symbolism and leadership roles for women have always been a part of Wicca, even if they relied on traditional European understandings of gender and essentialized ideas of women's nature.[10] Nonetheless, feminist Paganisms, particularly feminist Witchcraft and feminist Wicca, can also be seen as reform movements, like feminist Christianities, in that they modify theology, rituals and symbols, particularly from British High Magic roots inherited from Gerald Gardiner among others.[11] In addition, Yarrow members articulate themselves as politically engaged in contrast to other Pagan groups in Toronto, whom they understand to be apolitical.[12]

Ritual is central to how many political activists express their political convictions. For example, activist Louise Leclair compares anti-globalization demonstrations to larger patterns of pre-Lenten Carnival in the West.[13] Human geographer Steven Flusty builds on Mikhail Bakhtin's exploration of *carnival* to explore ways in which anti-globalization demonstrations create "temporary autonomous zone[s]" with alternative social orders.[14] Bakhtin's concept of *carnival*, [15] upon which Flusty draws, involves a ritualized reversal of social structures, akin to Victor Turner's notion of *communitas,* a temporary reversal of accepted social hierarchies through shared communal experience.[16] For Bakhtin, participants in *carnival* constitute a new social organization for the duration of the celebration.[17]

However, rather than mapping a diffuse, implicit ritualization found throughout global justice demonstrations, I explore here the public religion of explicit ritual performances within protest space. An exploration of ritualizing by religiously motivated protesters contributes to understanding the relatively new political phenomenon of mass, anti-globalization protests—in the West generally and in North America particularly—and its relationship with worldviews of feminist spirituality. Further, this exploration augments scholarship concerned with how older patterns of ritual may influence contemporary understandings of spiritual experience and their impact on political expression.

In *Ritual: Perspectives and Dimensions*, Catherine Bell writes:

> While ritual once stood for the status quo and the authority of the dominant social institutions, for many it has become anti-structural, revolutionary, and capable of deconstructing inhuman institutions and generating alternative structures [. . .]. The older conviction that increasing modernization, rational utilitarianism and individualism would inevitably do away with most forms of traditional ritual life has given way to a heroic championing of ritual as the way to remain human in an increasingly dehumanized world.[18]

Many of the feminist Catholic, United Church Protestant and Pagan activists with whom I spoke express this latter sentiment. Through explicit ritual performances within anti-globalization demonstrations they attempt to remind all participants in the event—other protestors as well as police—of the mutual humanity of all involved. They understand religious ritual to help combat political and economic systems that oppress and dehumanize people around the world.

Setting the Stage

For Toronto social justice activists, the April 2001 protest in Quebec City was exciting and important. It was the first major anti-globalization protest in Canada after the 1999 confrontation in Seattle, which marked a new era in global justice organizing for many activists.[19] The Quebec City protest was called to coincide with and disrupt a meeting of world leaders to discuss the Free Trade Area of the Americas (FTAA). In going to the protest, I was joining activists who came from all over the world, but particularly from North and South America, to participate in the political demonstrations and associated activities.

During the protest, Quebec City looked post-apocalyptic. Summit security forces blocked off the entire area, in which the meeting was to take place, with fencing and concrete barricades. Police shut down the highways. Business owners boarded windows and temporarily abandoned their stores to the expected conflict. Groups of protestors roamed around looking for shelter, water, lost friends. Police in riot gear, helmets veiling their faces, were stationed seemingly everywhere. Traffic cameras, continuing to stream to local cable television stations, now focused on blocked-off streets and at night showed clashes between police and a few lone protestors. The two sides scrambled around in black outfits, shadows bathed in the sulphur of the street lights, accompanied by the sounds of breaking glass as protesters lobbed bottles and police launched tear gas canisters and let loose water cannons. Helicopters constantly menaced the city from overhead. Many protestors believed that the helicopters were used deliberately to harass activists and prevent them from sleeping.[20] Toxic billows of tear gas fog permeated everything in the city.

Organizing groups color-coded the geography around the fence and the marching routes according to which demonstration activities were less risky and which were more likely to involve conflict with police: green for safe, orange for slight risk and red for likelihood of confrontation with police and arrest.[21] As a person on a temporary visa to Canada and therefore at risk of deportation, I was anxious to stay out of areas where confrontation with police was more likely. However, the color system quickly broke down as police and protestors engaged in confrontations. There was no place in the heart of the city where activists were sure the police would not rush and no place untainted by tear gas. Over 400 protestors were arrested during the summit.[22]

Every now and then, driven by strategies protestors could rarely determine, the police would charge a street to recover it from demonstrators. It seemed arbitrary and terrifying. One minute, I would be walking along, talking to people about their reasons for coming and their plans for later and the next minute a wave of desperate people would charge, yelling for everyone to run. About the last thing anyone should do in a situation like that is turn and run blindly down a highway ramp or bridge, so everyone would start yelling back, "Walk!" "*Marche!*" and we'd scramble as best we could away from the dangerous area.

Along with the violence, confusion and fear, however, there were also play, creativity and fun. Many different groups brought their messages to the protest and chose to express them in both conventional—placards and chants—and less conventional ways. A major protest event was the People's Summit, named in contrast to the official gathering, "The Summit of the Americas." Beginning April 16 and hosted by the Hemispheric Social Alliance,[23] the People's Summit was tightly organized and offered speakers on issues such as economic justice, environmental protection and responsible development.[24] I attended talks by Naomi Klein and David Suzuki, among others. Throughout the weekend activist groups engaged in less official activities, as well, such as sidewalk art, singing, guerrilla theater, dancing and games. Sometimes specific people planned their actions in advance and rehearsed them; others just happened to meet and created their actions spontaneously.

The color-coding of protest routes was paralleled by different activist groups. Some dressed in specific colors to emphasize their political commitments, such as green for environmentalism. The Pagan Living River, an organizing group of Pagan protestors self-described as "non-violent and confrontational,"[25] dressed in blue both to draw attention to environmental and justice concerns relating to water and also to signal their commitment to non-violence. Activists identifying with the tactics of the black bloc, groups that accept street combat as a legitimate protest tactic[26] and often scapegoated in police statements and media coverage as agitators,[27] dressed in black and red and covered their faces with balaclavas or bandanas to protect themselves from identification. Some groups color-coded themselves to make it easier to keep track of each other in the confusion of actions. Others, like the feminist Raging Grannies,[28] wore flamboyant costumes for fun. One of my favorites was a mixed-gender delegation of York University teaching assistants who dressed up in pink tutus.

Many different individuals and groups came to the protest: co-workers, labor unions, religious groups, classmates and friends. For example, Angel is in her mid-twenties. She identifies as feminist and Catholic and has strong ties with the Toronto Catholic Worker, though she is not in residence there. Her activism focuses on anti-racism, anti-poverty and global justice and she often organizes with anarchist groups. At the time of the Quebec City protest, she was active in OAT (Organizing Autonomous Telecoms),[29] a collective that works to make computer communication technology accessible for grassroots activists and community organizations. A few weeks before the protest, she took the train to Quebec City and stayed with friends. While there, she did advance work setting up communication technologies for the protest marches and actions. During the protests she helped coordinate activists and spent time in the under-pass area, the "anarchist village," where she helped distribute free vegetarian food for Food-Not-Bombs, an organization dedicated to redistributing military spending to instead end global violence, poverty and hunger.[30] After the protest, she waited until the people she knew who were arrested during the protest were released from jail. She then hitchhiked back to Toronto with several friends.[31]

Judy is in her early thirties and identifies as a feminist and a member of the United Church. She is employed by a group that advocates for justice in international economic development. She went to Quebec City in a car with friends and, while there, she slept on a gym floor. While in Quebec, she met up with Catholic co-workers and marched with church coalitions in the official march. She also participated in protest actions at the summit fence, vigils and an interfaith ceremony held at a downtown church mourning global exploitation in the name of free trade.[32]

Lavender is in her early sixties and identifies as a feminist and a Pagan. She is a member of the Raging Grannies, an organization of feisty, older women activists known for their playful protest songs, silly costumes and seizure of the moral high ground.[33] She also belongs to other political organizations and does activist work around anti-homelessness and anti-poverty issues, especially focusing on older women, along with environmentalism, anti-war and global justice. She went to Quebec City with her Pagan affinity group in a rented van.[34]

Affinity groups are consensus-based, intentional communities formed by activists to provide support and protection during protests. Activist Janet Conway describes their history: "Affinity group organizing has its roots in feminist, anarchist and anti-nuclear movements in which small, autonomous groups decide on the nature of their participation in direct action, organizing independently of any centralized movement authority."[35] In forming an affinity group, activists agree to be responsible for each other. For example, affinity groups negotiate about when and where to participate in protest and what direct actions to perform. Ideally, members of an affinity group help each other if they get tear gassed, call a lawyer if members get arrested, and meet them when they get released from holding.

Like many activists, Lavender slept on the floor in the cafeteria at Laval University. She participated in the women's action on Thursday, the official march on Saturday, and "flowed" with the Pagan Living River. Although she decided to only go "green" routes, that is, routes intended to avoid civil disobedience, she often found herself in the thick of confrontations between protestors and police.[36]

Ritual in the Thick of It

The Quebec City women's action took place on April 19, the Thursday night preceding the official opening of the FTAA summit. Reclaiming Witch, Starhawk, wrote the call. Sent out to activist email lists and passed around on flyers in advance of the event, it describes the demonstration as follows:

> We will, as women, weave together our hopes and dreams, our aspirations, our indictments, our testimony, our witnessing, our demands, our visions. We will write on ribbons, on strips, on cloth, on rags. We will draw, paint, knot cords, braid yarn, whisper into pieces of string. And from these materials we will weave our web.
>
> If they ignore our voices and continue their deliberations, the cries of women will haunt them and undo all their plans. Though they erect a fence to stop us, we will twine our web through its mesh to be the visible symbol of the power of women, of the revolution we weave. When they try to wall us out of their meetings, they will only wall themselves in. We claim all of the world beyond their wall.[37]

Groups were encouraged to bring webs from home to incorporate into the larger web, or even to mail in web-work if their group was unable to be physically present at the protest.[38] The demonstration centered on integrating materials into the fence that separated the summit space from the rest of the city and the official delegates from the protestors. The action was designed to incorporate different ritual actions within this larger frame of ritual weaving.

For many participants, the action involved a ritual led by Starhawk that culminating in a spiral dance, a common Pagan practice in which a circle of people holding hands weaves inward in a spiral and back out again, causing each dancer to face all others as they pass. Lavender relates:

> There was a huge puppet of the goddess, Nemesis, which was really great, and there was a woman from the Mothers of the Plaza de Mayo,[39] in Argentina, who spoke to us, before we set off. That was really powerful. Then when we were chanting, we chanted also in Spanish and there was just this feeling of unity as we were trudging up the hill . . . . I felt really good when we went on the Thursday night and we took a web from Toronto, we had done a WomynSpirit ritual. So we [her WomynSpirit group] did that for Quebec City and we took it and we put it up on the fence. And then we created another one there with Starhawk . . . . [and] we put that up on the fence. And did a spiral dance and that was, that was really fabulous. The woman's action was wonderful.[40]

In addition to the ritual that Starhawk led, other rituals took place during the action. For example, Jesse, a Catholic Worker and journalist, relates her experience within the larger action:

> A wail rose up from the five women huddled on the ground as the black cloth settled over them, a wail that grew until the street was filled with its resonant grief and anger. It . . . rang through the nearby security fence . . . grew in my chest until Linzi and I raised up the 6-meter swath of black cloth and pulled it taught between us, freeing the women beneath. Into the waiting silence, we ripped the cloth end from end and ran whooping to weave it into the chain-link fence, the final joyful crescendo of our dance of lament and resistance.[41]

The webs of yarn and cloth woven into the fence during the women's action remained on display throughout the protest weekend. Along with other artistic installations on the fence, like flowers, balloons and bras decorated with anti-FTAA slogans, they contributed to the carnival mood of the protestors and, alternatively, offered stark contrast to the tear gas and police violence that began with the official commencement of the summit.

Why Ritualize?

Religious ritual can serve several functions within global justice protests, for the ritual participants themselves, for different audiences and for others who may not witness the ritual. Activists may use ritual theater to encourage other activists and create a safer and more comfortable social environment. Jenna, a Catholic in her early twenties who works for a non-profit organization focused on justice in economic development, suggested that the art, color and ritual were part of what made the experience positive and exciting for her companions.[42]

Lavender, a Pagan, said that she always tries to get a spiral dance going in areas where violence might break out. "Everyone likes to feel included," she said, and explained that she understands violence as resulting from protestors not knowing what else to do.[43] Spiral dances are light-hearted and sometimes rambunctious affairs; the spiral gets faster and faster until it whips back out into a circle, an activity frequently accompanied by breathless laughter and feelings of camaraderie. She sees the ritual of spiral dancing as providing a positive way to disperse anxious group energy and consciously uses spiral dances to create communities out of motley groups of strangers.

Protestors may employ ritual to signal peaceful intentions to other protestors and to police. For example, in the Quebec City protest, radical Catholics sat down in front of a line of riot police and sang hymns with their hands held open in front of them.[44] Abby, a Catholic Worker in her twenties, relates the following story:

> [W]hat we did is we went to the top of the hill and we followed a group of police in riot squad down the hill towards the fence and we were singing the song "Freedom" and dancing. And then we stopped, the police stopped us, they turned around, and we sang for an hour. Every once in a while the police would come up to our backs and it was really amazing, because I could feel this police person, his legs touching my back, sitting on the ground and I'm like "Oh my God." And we were singing this song, the words kept changing, and we said, "Our hands were made for peace" and we all raised our hands at the same time and the police just backed two feet away from our backs. It was amazing, you know, I was like, "That's just great," because, you know, we all raised our hands, we were all sitting on the ground . . . and we did that for about two hours and then we got a little bit sore in the voice, and then we left . . . . It was just really powerful to see how quickly the song and the prayer just calmed everybody down, including the cops.[45]

Pagan activists participated in a very similar action in which they drummed and read "The Cochabamba Declaration,"[46] a treatise on the sacredness of water, to a line of riot police.[47]

Religiously motivated activists may also use ritual to diffuse tension more generally. Pagan, United Church and Catholic women use ritual for assistance in staying calm and focused within chaotic environments. At Quebec City, one of the downtown churches held an Ecumenical candlelight vigil for peace that was described by several United Church and Catholic activists as a moving and important element in their protest experience.[48] They considered the vigil to have provided a sense of calm and safety in the midst of a chaotic and often violent environment. Jenna said:

> Going to the church and having some kind of service, that was really neat. And they were open 24-hours and it was just kind of nice to feel like there was some safe place there. Still, it wasn't a safe space that was denying the political reality of the day, not like the mall. It was still recognizing that and trying to find a centering there.[49]

Many women of all three traditions recounted stories of Pagan activists arriving at dangerous protest scenes and using ritual to "shift the energy" in order to create an environment where peace and safety are more possible.[50] The Pagan Living River deliberately went to areas of conflict and worked rituals to calm both sides. Catholic activists also referred to moments in which they turned to prayer or meditation to calm themselves in difficult interactions within protests. For example, Angel said, ". . . I've stood in front of riot cops and very quietly said something to myself . . . . I will admit that in really scary situations to center myself I will speak the name of God, but it's sort of under my breath or silently . . . ."[51] Pagan, United Church and Catholic anti-globalization activists with whom I spoke referred to the concept of "grounding" themselves in the midst of the fear and turmoil that protests can generate. For example, Sue, a Pagan peace activist, said, "Religion is really grounding. [It's about] shifting the energy, instead of the agenda being set by the police."[52]

Ritual may also be performed to help alleviate danger for others who are not around to witness its performance. Sabina, a Pagan, environmentalist and member of a sacred dance troupe, relates her experience with her Pagan activist group:

> So it played out like that, that we marched and we weren't in any great danger, and we did some ritual at times, and we were not where the real action was. And we were clear that there were people who were being tear gassed at the center of it, so we formed a circle, and did some visualization and sent energy to people in the thick of it. We also said, "There needs to be"—it was so grim, it was feeling so grim—we said, "There also needs to be vision and life in this," and so we also really were evoking the positive, and other women had flowers, and just invoking a sense of wonder and gratitude and bringing some positive images and offering those up.[53]

Assessments of the utility, or futility, of ritual actions outside the heart of demonstrations vary widely.[54] Nonetheless, Sabina's group understood itself to be using ritual to help specific people in crisis: those getting tear gassed at the center of the protest. They also believed that their use of ritual helped people more generally by working to change the emotional environment of the city.

Evaluating Success and Infelicity

In relating their experiences at the Quebec City protest, a majority of the women
from each of the three traditions discussed the performance of ritual within that
space as a positive thing in and of itself. They understand ritual within protests
to bring variety and creativity to protest actions.[55] They feel good about letting
other protestors know that they are part of the global justice movement because
of religious motivation.[56] They understand religious ritual as signaling to police
that protestors are not out-of-control or mis-socialized, as anti-globalization activists feel they are sometimes stereotyped.[57] Ritual in protest space provides
opportunities for media coverage to depict positive non-violence in contrast to
sensationalized violence.[58] Moreover, these women understand explicit religious
ritual as lending legitimacy to their demands for global justice, not only for police and media but also for world leaders.[59]

Aside from Lavender's disappointment that the police did not pay much
attention in the women's action,[60] I did not receive many reports of infelicitous
ritual performance, to use Ron Grimes' term, that is rituals that did not succeed
in their social or metaphysical aims.[61] There may be several reasons for this.
First, global justice activists are very sensitive to their portrayal in the mainstream media and so, when given an opportunity to represent themselves, may
be less likely to report actions that were inconsequential or that failed.[62] Jenna, a
Catholic, said that, when she returned from Quebec City, there was not a lot of
room even within the Catholic activist community to critique what had happened there.[63] Second, religiously motivated activists often feel invisible or dis-
respected within the larger, more secularly oriented global justice movement, so
the very performance of ritual at all is understood as positive. Assessing ritual
success, especially discussing situations of ritual inefficacy, becomes particularly loaded within a context of dismissal from other activists, who, in a Marxist
vein, may see religion as wasting resources better put towards direct action.[64]
Third, many of the goals for which rituals are performed are long-term and
somewhat abstract. For example, how can a group assess whether it has helped
shift the global attitude towards ecological concern or increased the energy
available for positive change in the world?

On the other hand, there were some rituals that could be assessed on more
concrete terms. For example, Sabina explained that her group did ritual work to
help those in the center of the protest violence. However, she did not assess
whether her ritualizing had a concrete effect for them. This relates directly to her
stated motivation for being at the protest, "I just needed to be really grounded in
the fact that I was there for myself, not to cause an effect, which is what the universe told me: that I wouldn't be doing it in order to save the world, I'd be
doing it because I needed to do that."[65] So, although Sabina could have investigated whether her ritual aided protesters in need by asking friends and col-
leagues in the places where she directed her energy, this was less important to
her than that she attempt to help. Her ritual performance was more powerful for

her than its effects on others, or lack thereof, and she determined ritual success by the effects the performance had on her. An analysis of ritual success or infelicity based on the help and comfort experienced by those at whom the rites were ostensibly aimed—activists in the midst of the protest—might reach different conclusions.

Further examples of rituals that could be assessed as successful or unsuccessful are performances to diffuse general tensions between police and protestors, diffusions described as successful.[66] Finally, there is Abby's sing-in before a line of riot police. Not only did the police back off, but all of their attempts to tear-gas the singers were unsuccessful because of the direction of the wind.[67]

Interpretations of Ritual in Protest Space

There are striking similarities in the ways that feminist Catholic, United Church and Pagan activists understand and use ritual within protest environments. Both United Church and Catholic groups took part in church vigils.[68] Both Catholic and Pagan groups engaged in explicit, though spontaneous, group rituals in front of lines of police.[69] All three groups grounded their discussions of activism in the context of their religions. While activists of different religious affiliations did participate in separate planned actions, they also came together, both in the larger milieu of protests at the fence and in specific actions. For example, I spoke with members of all three groups who participated in the women's action and the rituals that it incorporated, such as web weaving and the spiral dance. When you also consider, for example, that the women in Jesse's dance troupe, who did the performance ripping the black cloth, were inspired by the Women in Black, Israeli peace activists,[70] then the spiral of influence swirls even wider.

However, there are also clear differences in their understandings of ritual in protest space. Many of the United Church women with whom I spoke do not understand themselves to have engaged in explicit ritualizing while at the Quebec City protest. The Catholic women which whom I spoke did refer to specific rituals in which they participated, but were less likely to describe the entire experience as ritualized. Pagan women, on the other hand, are more likely to describe the whole experience as ritualized; actions were purposefully planned around specific rituals or incorporated ritual elements, such as passing out water to other protestors with the blessing, "May you never thirst."[71] Stories of Pagans' Quebec City experiences also incorporate discussions of working to shift metaphysical energy.

Another difference between the three groups is concern about explicit ritualization within protest space. The Pagan women were very comfortable with creating and performing rituals in the midst of other protestors. As Lavender's comment about people appreciating inclusion indicates,[72] there is a sense that other protestors will welcome an opportunity to participate in Pagan ritual.

Catholic and United Church women, in contrast, expressed concern about engaging in explicit rituals in the midst of other protestors. As Angel said:

> Different Christians will pray or whatever and I don't really want to knock it, but, at the same time, it *is* alienating. It is an alienating thing to be doing on the street . . . . I mean, I don't want that to infringe on my ability to organize with a diversity of communities, so I wouldn't do that . . . . I think that when it comes out onto the street you have to be very careful, because Christianity is an incredibly privileged religion. It's not the same as if Muslims decide to pray on the street in North America. They're an underprivileged religion, so it's a very different thing to be doing. And I think Christians need to be careful, because they've pissed enough people off . . . . There's this feeling that it's just alienating people and making people angry. Also, the Christian Church has caused so much pain to so many people. It's only reminding people of that, so I think it's okay, I mean if a church identifies itself and marches in the PRIDE parade . . . but it does get sort of iffy when you're at an anti-globalization thing.[73]

Angel is very uneasy with overt Christian practice in public because of the social privilege that Christianity enjoys and the trauma it may cause to non-Christians. As uncomfortable with public, Christian ritualizing as Angel is, she can think of situations in which it would be appropriate to support causes traditionally condemned by churches, such as Gay Pride. Judy, a United Church member, expressed similar concerns: "Christianity has drowned out other spiritual traditions for so long . . . . And I didn't see a lot of other religious groups self-identifying at all in that time in Quebec."[74] Angel and Judy also maintain that public religious expression by traditions other than Christianity would be appropriate.

The very institutional power and privilege that makes them and their churches persuasive to government, police and media organizations is the same influence that these Christian activists desperately want to work against in North American culture more generally. They do not want to force their religious privilege on other activists or on non-Christians. The quandary becomes one of wielding the power of religious institutions against the state, but not, in the same blunt stroke, reinforcing the oppression of those not sharing the advantage of being Christian in a Christian-dominant culture.

Pagans may hope to establish their tradition as a serious and authoritive religion, thereby gaining the moral influence they see other religious groups as enjoying.[75] Because they do not understand themselves as a culturally dominant religious tradition, Pagans do not share Christians' concerns about oppressing others through public ritual. In fact, Pagans, are happy to pray and ritualize in public.

Conclusion

Feminist activists bring their spirituality with them into the public space of anti-globalization demonstrations. In Quebec City, Catholic, United Church and Pagan feminist activists used ritual to manage space, forge community, communicate their political messages and mitigate environments fraught with conflict, tension and confusion. Just as they turn to ritual within their religious groups to change themselves, their communities and the world, they turn to ritual in protest environments to express alternative visions to the industrial globalization and economic exploitation that international trade summits have come to represent.

However, for Christians, more so than for Pagans, finding a balance between rejecting religious institutions and using the social and legal power of these institutions towards just ends is a painful challenge. They do not want to exacerbate Christian dominance and, therefore, they may worry about unintended consequences of ritualizing in protest space. Because Pagans understand themselves to be outside culturally privileged religious structures, they do not face the same kinds of dilemmas in bringing their religion into civic spaces.

Feminist ritualizing in protest space engages a cultural dialogue about relatively new relationships between feminist spirituality and the politics of globalization. Further, such ritualization calls into question popular assumptions that mixing religion and politics yields necessarily conservative results. Engaging new movements in their religions, feminist activists incorporate their spiritual traditions into progressive political protest, hoping to literally change the world.

Notes

The author wishes to thank the following for their helpful readings of all or parts of this work: Pamela Klassen, Judy Taylor, Amira Mittermaier, Steven Flusty, Ron Grimes, Adrian Harris, Sarah King, Michael Ostling, David Perley, Arlene MacDonald, Chis Klassen, Tera Mallete, Carol Borden and David Ferris.

1. Steven Flusty, De-Coca-Colonization: Making the Globe from the Inside Out (New York: Routledge, 2004), José Corrêa Leite, The World Social Forum: Strategies of Resistance, translated by Traci Romine (Chicago: Haymarket Books, 2005); Boaventura De Sousa Santos, The Rise of the Global Left: The World Social Forum and Beyond (London: Zed Books, 2006); Starhawk, Webs of Power:Notes from the Global Uprising (Gabriola Island, BC: New Society Publishers, 2002); Amory Starr, Global Revolt: A Guide to the Movements against Globalization (London: Zed Books, 2005).

2. My structured fieldwork took place over a year, from April 2003 to April 2004.

3. Laurel Zwissler, "Spiritual, But Religious: 'Spirituality among Religiously Motivated Feminist Activists," Culture and Religion 8, no. 1 (March 2007): 51-69.

4. The Catholic Worker was founded by Dorothy Day and Peter Maurin in Chicago in 1933. Catholic Worker groups are residential communities based around ideas of Christian hospitality and service to the poor. For more on this and the following groups,

see Laurel Zwissler, "Demonstrations of Faith: Religious and Political Identity among Feminist Political Activists in North America" (PhD. dissertation University of Toronto, 2008).

5. The United Church of Canada formed in 1925 by uniting Presbyterian, Methodist, Congregational Union and the Western Council of Churches.

6. Reclaiming Witchcraft is a Pagan Witchcraft tradition founded in the San Francisco Bay area around 1980 by Starhawk among others, such as M. Macha Nightmare. See Jone Salmonsen, *Enchanted Feminism: Ritual, Gender and Divinity among the Reclaiming Witches of San Francisco* (New York: Routledge, 2002); Starhawk. *The Spiral Dance: A Rebirth of the Ancient Religion of the Great Goddess*, (San Francisco: HarperSanFrancisco, 1989 [1979]), *Truth or Dare: Encounters with Power, Authority, and Mystery* (San Francisco: Harper and Row, 1987), and *Webs of Power*; Starhawk and M. Macha Nightmare, *The Pagan Book of Living and Dying: Practical Rituals, Prayers, Blessings and Meditations on Crossing Over* (San Francisco: HarperSanFrancisco, 1997).

7. Susan Starr Sered, *Priestess, Mother, Sacred Sister: Religions Dominated by Women* (New York: Oxford University Press, 1994), 185.

8. On problems with definitions of "second wave" feminism, see Sherna Berger Gluck, et al. "Whose Feminism, Whose History? Reflections on Excavating the History of (the) US Women's Movement(s)," in *Community Activism and Feminist Politics: Organizing Across Race, Class and Gender,* edited by Nancy A. Naples (New York: Routledge, 1998), 31-56, and Becky Thompson, *A Promise and a Way of Life: White Anti-Racist Activism* (Minneapolis: University of Minnesota Press, 2001).

9. Carol Christ,. *The Laughter of Aphrodite: Reflections on a Journey to the Goddess* (San Francisco: Harper and Rowe, 1987).

10. Starhawk, *Spiral Dance.*

11. Ronald Hutton, *Triumph of the Moon: A History of Modern Pagan Witchcraft* (Oxford: Oxford University Press, 1999).

12. Expressed during the introductions to collective meetings (July 2, 2003 and September 29, 2003) and during interviews with founding members, some of whom include: River. June 26, 2003); Betty, July 14, 2003; Bea, January 22, 2004; Carrie, February 8, 2004; and Ashley, March 9, 2003.

13. Louise Leclair, "Carnivals Against Capital: Rooted in Resistance," in *Representing Resistance: Media, Civil Disobedience, and the Global Justice Movement,* edited by Andy Opel and Donnalyn Pompper (Westport, CT: Praeger Publishers, 2003), 3-15. For a broader discussion of the relationship of *carnival* to modernization, secularization, and capitalism, see also Charles Taylor, *Modern Social Imaginaries* (Durham, NC: Duke University Press, 2004).

14. Flusty, *De-Coca-Colonization*, 190-192.

15. Mikhail Mikhailovitch Bakhtin, *Rabelais and His World,* translated by Helene Iswolsky (Bloomington: University of Indiana Press, 1993).

16. Victor Turner, *Dramas, Fields, and Metaphors: Symbolic Action in Human Society* (Ithaca, NY: Cornell University Press, 1974).

17. Bakhtin, *Rabelais and His World.*

18. Catherine Bell, *Ritual: Perspectives and Dimensions,* (New York: Oxford University Press, 1997), 257.

19. Starhawk, *Webs of Power;* Leite, *The World Social Forum*; Flusty, *De-Coca-Colonization.*

20. Interviews: Lavender, Pagan July 18, 2003; Jenna, Catholic, July 10, 2003; Judy, United Church, Mar.16, 2004; Angel, Catholic, Apr. 2, 2003.

21. See Flusty, *De-Coca-Colonization,* 194; Starhawk, *Webs of Power,* 85-86.

22. Josipa Petrunic, "Activist Groups Demand Quebec City Inquiry," *Globe and Mail* (May 22, 2001). Also available at *Common Dreams* (http://www.common dreams.org/headlines01/0522-04.htm/ May 22, 2001, accessed Jan 16, 2007).

23. The People's Summit began on April 16, 2001. See "Building a Hemispheric Social Alliance in the Americas," in *Common Frontiers Website* (http://www.common frontiers.ca/Current_Activities/Hemispheric.html#1/ accessed January 19, 2007); Hector de la Cueva on behalf of the Hemispheric Social Alliance, *Declaration of the People's Summit* (http://www.copa.qc.ca/Anglais/Reunions_missionsa/Avril2001a/Dec_Peup_A. html/ April 19, 2001, accessed January 19, 2007).

24. Michel Chossudovsky, "The Quebec Wall," in *The Emperor's New Clothes* website (http://emperors-clothes.com/articles/choss/quebec.htm/ April 18, 2001, accessed January 19, 2007); "Thousands Converge on Quebec as 'People's Summit' Gets Underway" *CBC News* (http://www.cbc.ca/canada/story/2001/04/15/peoplesummit_010415. html/ April 16, 2001, accessed Jan 19, 2007); Gumisai Mutume, "Quebec Braces for Anti-Globalisation Protests" *Inter Press Service* available at *Common Dreams* (http://www.commondreams.org/headlines01/0419-02.htm/ April 19, 2001, accessed Jan 19, 2007).

25. Starhawk, *Webs of Power*, 86.

26. See Starr, *Global Revolt*, 127-138; Kevin Danaher and Jason Mark, *Insurrection: Citizen Challenges to Corporate Power* (New York: Routledge, 2003), 282-283; Flusty, *De-Coca-Colonization*, 189-190; Janet Conway, "Civil Resistance and the 'Diversity of Tactics' in the Anti-Globalization Movement: Problems of Violence, Silence, and Solidarity in Activist Politics," *Osgoode Law Journal* 41, no. 2&3 (2003): 516-518.

27. Alexander Panetta, "Violence Blamed on Black Bloc: Group Came to Prominence at Seattle Riots," *Toronto Star* (April 21, 2001), B2.

28. See page 10.

29. See Organizing Autonomous Telecoms, *OAT Website* (http://oat.tao.ca/ n.d, accessed Sept. 21, 2005).

30. See Food Not Bombs, *Food Not Bombs* website (http://www.foodnotbombs.net/ n.d, accessed January 19, 2007).

31. Interview: Angel, Catholic, April 4, 2003.

32. Interview: Judy, United Church, January 16, 2004.

33. See Allison Acker and Betty Brightwell, *Off Our Rockers and into Trouble: The Raging Grannies* (Victoria, BC: TouchWood Editions Ltd, 2004); Toronto Raging Grannies, *Toronto Raging Grannies Website* (http://torontoraginggrannies.nonprofitnet.ca/ n.d, accessed Jan. 19, 2007); and The Raging Grannies International, *The Raging Grannies Website*. (http://www.geocities.com/raginggrannies/ n.d, accessed January 19, 2007).

34. Interview: Lavender, Pagan, July 17, 2003.

35. Conway, "Civil Resistance and the 'Diversity of Tactics' in the Anti-Globalization Movement," 510.

36. Interview: Lavender, Pagan, July 17, 2003.

37. Starhawk, *Webs of Power*, 81. Also available from *Nettime Archive* (http://amsterdam.nettime.org/Lists-Archives/nettime-l-0103/msg00043.html/ March 10, 2001, accessed October 20, 2004).

38. *Nettime archive.*

39. The Mothers of the Plaza de Mayo came together starting in 1977 to protest the forced disappearances of their loved ones under the military junta in Argentina. See Marguerite Bouvard, *Revolutionizing Motherhood: The Mothers of the Plaza de Mayo* (Wilmington, DE: Rowman and Littlefield, 1994).

40. Interview: Lavender, Pagan, July 18, 2003.

41. Interview: Jesse, Catholic, March 17, 2004. See also Jo Roberts, "Dancing into the Revolution: Reflections on Quebec City and the Continuing Struggle Against Globalization," *The Mustard Seed: The Toronto Catholic Worker Community* 11, no. 1. (Winter 2002): 1.

42. Interview Jenna, Catholic, July 10, 2003.

43. Interview: Lavender, Pagan, July 18, 2003.

44. Interview Abby, Catholic, February 16, 2004. See also Roberts 2002 1.

45. Interview Abby, Catholic, February 16, 2004.

46. Citizens of Bolivia, Canada, United States, India, and Brazil, "The Cochabamba Declaration" (http://www.nadir.org/nadir/initiativ/agp/free/imf/bolivia/cochabamba.htm/ Dec. 8, 2000, accessed Aug. 29, 2006). This document is available on many activist websites and has become a focus for water-rights activism. Also available in Starhawk, *Webs of Power*, 83.

47. Interviews: Lavender, Pagan, July 18, 2003; River, Pagan, Jun. 26, 2003. See also Starhawk, *Webs of Power*, 90-91.

48. Interviews: Judy, United Church, Mar. 16, 2004; Regina, Catholic, August 1, 2003; Abby, Catholic, Feb. 16, 2004.

49. Interview: Jenna, Catholic, July 10, 2003.

50. Interviews: Jesse, Catholic, March 17, 2004; River, Pagan, Jun. 26, 2003; Sue, Pagan, July 17, 2003; Antonia, Pagan, July 21, 2003. See also Starhawk, *Webs of Power*, 87-88 and 90-91.

51. Interview: Angel, Catholic Apr. 2, 2003.

52. Interview: Sue, Pagan, July 16, 2003.

53. Interview: Sabina, Pagan, February 5, 2004.

54. For discussion of determining the efficacy of such ritualization, see page 18.

55. Interviews: Jenna, Catholic, July 10, 2003; Sabina, Pagan Feb. 5, 2004; Camille, Catholic, July 15, 2003.

56. Interviews: Judy, United Church, Mar. 16, 2004; Abby, Catholic, Feb 16, 2004; Sabina, Pagan, Feb. 5, 2004.

57. Sociologist Stephen Hart argues that activists often self-censor because they believe that the more generic the description of their aims and the less surprising their actions, the broader the appeal of their calls for change will be. Hart contrasts this "constrained discourse" with "expansive discourse" grounded in personal experience and passion about the cause. Stephen Hart, *Cultural Dilemmas of Progressive Politics: Styles of Engagement among Grassroots Activists* (Chicago: University of Chicago Press, 2001).

58. Interviews: Lavender, Pagan, July 18, 2003; Jesse, Catholic, Mar. 17, 2004.

59. Interviews: Lavender, Pagan, July 18, 2003; Abby, Catholic, Feb 16, 2004; Judy, United Church, Mar. 16, 2004.

60. Interview: Lavender, Pagan, July 17, 2003.

61. Ronald L. Grimes, "Infelicitous Performances and Ritual Criticism" in *Ritual Criticism: Case Studies in Its Practice, Essays on Its Theory* (Columbia, SC: University of South Carolina Press, 1990), 191-209.

62. Interviews: Lavender, Pagan, July 18, 2003; Jenna, Catholic, July 10, 2003.

63. Interview: Jenna, Catholic, July 10, 2003.

64. Interviews: Judy, United Church, Mar. 16, 2004; Angel, Catholic, Apr. 2, 2003.

65. Interview: Sabina, Pagan, Feb. 5, 2004.

66. Interviews: Angel, Catholic, Apr. 2, 2003; Abby, Catholic, Feb 16, 2004; Antonia, Pagan, July 21, 2003. Starhawk, *Webs of Power*, 90-91.

67. Interview: Abby, Catholic, Feb. 16, 2004.

68. Interviews: Judy, United Church, Mar. 16, 2004; Jenna, Catholic July 10, 2003; Abby, Catholic Feb. 16, 2004.

69. Interviews: Jenna, Catholic July 10, 2003; Abby, Catholic Feb. 16, 2004; Lavender, Pagan, July 18, 2003; River, Pagan, June 26, 2003; Sabina, Pagan, Feb 5, 2004.

70. Roberts "Dancing into the Revolution," 1; Women in Black, *Women in Black International Website* (http://www.womeninblack.net/mission/html/ n.d, accessed January 19, 2007). This site has since been discontinued. See *Women in Black: For Justice. Against War.* http://www.womeninblack.org/ n.d. (accessed July 22, 2008).

71. Interviews: Lavender, Pagan, July 18, 2003; River, Pagan, July 26, 2003.

72. See page 13.

73. Interview: Angel, Catholic, Apr. 2, 2003.

74. Interview: Judy, United Church, Mar. 16, 2004.

75. Thanks to Carol Borden for helping me articulate this point.

Bibliography

Acker, Allison and Betty Brightwell. *Off Our Rockers and into Trouble: The Raging Grannies.* Victoria, BC: TouchWood Editions Ltd, 2004.

Bakhtin, Mikhail Mikhailovitch. *Rabelais and His World.* Trans. Helene Iswolsky. Bloomington: University of Indiana Press, 1993.

Bell, Catherine. *Ritual: Perspectives and Dimensions.* New York: Oxford University Press, 1997.

Bouvard, Marguerite. *Revolutionizing Motherhood: The Mothers of the Plaza de Mayo.* Wilmington, DE: Rowman and Littlefield, 1994.

"Building a Hemispheric Social Alliance in the Americas." *Common Frontiers Website.* http://www.commonfrontiers.ca/Current_Activities/Hemispheric.html#1/ n.d. (accessed January 19, 2007).

Chossudovsky, Michel. "The Quebec Wall." *The Emperor's New Clothes* website. http://emperors-clothes.com/articles/choss/quebec.htm April 18, 2001. (accessed January 19, 2007).

Christ, Carol. *The Laughter of Aphrodite: Reflections on a Journey to the Goddess.* San Francisco: Harper and Rowe, 1987.

Citizens of Bolivia, Canada, United States, India, and Brazil. "The Cochabamba Declaration." http://www.nadir.org/nadir/initiativ/agp/free/imf/bolivia/cochabamba.htm Dec. 8, 2000. (accessed Aug. 29, 2006).

Common Dreams. *Common Dreams Website.* http://www.commondreams.org/ n.d. (accessed Jan 19, 2007).

Common Frontiers. *Common Frontiers Website.* http://www.commonfrontiers.ca/ n.d. (accessed January 19, 2007).

Conway, Janet. "Civil Resistance and the 'Diversity of Tactics' in the Anti-Globalization Movement: Problems of Violence, Silence, and Solidarity in Activist Politics." *Osgoode Law Journal.* 41, no. 2&3 (2003): 505-530.

Danaher, Kevin and Jason Mark. *Insurrection: Citizen Challenges to Corporate Power.* New York: Routledge, 2003.

de la Cueva, Hector, on behalf of the Hemispheric Social Alliance. *Declaration of the People's Summit.* http://www.copa.qc.ca/Anglais/Reunions_missionsa/Avril2001a/ Dec_Peup_A.html/ April 19, 2001. (accessed January 19, 2007).

Flusty, Steven. *De-Coca-Colonization: Making the Globe from the Inside Out.* New York: Routledge, 2004.

Food Not Bombs. *Food Not Bombs.* http://www.foodnotbombs.net/ n.d. (accessed January 19, 2007).

Gluck, Sherna Berger, et al. "Whose Feminism, Whose History? Reflections on Excavating the History of (the) US Women's Movement(s)." In *Community Activism and Feminist Politics: Organizing Across Race, Class and Gender,* edited by Nancy A. Naples. New York: Routledge, 1998. 31-56.

Grimes, Ronald L. "Infelicitous Performances and Ritual Criticism." In *Ritual Criticism: Case Studies in Its Practice, Essays on Its Theory.* Columbia, SC: University of South Carolina Press, 1990. 191-209.

Hart, Stephen. *Cultural Dilemmas of Progressive Politics: Styles of Engagement among Grassroots Activists.* Chicago: University of Chicago Press, 2001.

Hutton, Ronald. *Triumph of the Moon: A History of Modern Pagan Witchcraft.* Oxford: Oxford University Press, 1999.

Leclair, Louise. "Carnivals Against Capital: Rooted in Resistance." In *Representing Resistance: Media, Civil Disobedience, and the Global Justice Movement,* edited by Andy Opel and Donnalyn Pompper. Westport, CT: Praeger Publishers, 2003. 3-15.

Leite, José Corrêa. *The World Social Forum: Strategies of Resistance.* Translated by Traci Romine. Chicago: Haymarket Books, 2005.

Mutume, Gumisai. "Quebec Braces for Anti-Globalisation Protests." *Inter Press Service.* Available at *Common Dreams.* http://www.commondreams.org/headlines01/041902.htm/ April 19, 2001. (accessed Jan 19, 2007).

Nettime Archive. http://amsterdam.nettime.org/Lists-Archives/nettime-l-0103/msg00043.html/ March 10, 2001. (accessed October 20, 2004).

Organizing Autonomous Telecoms. *OAT Website.* http://oat.tao.ca/ n.d. (accessed Sept. 21, 2005).

Panetta, Alexander. "Violence Blamed on Black Bloc: Group Came to Prominence at Seattle Riots." *Toronto Star.* April 21, 2001. B2.

Petrunic, Josipa. "Activist Groups Demand Quebec City Inquiry." *Globe and Mail.* May 22, 2001. Also available at *Common Dreams* http://www.commondreams.org/headlines01/0522-04.htm/ May 22, 2001. (accessed Jan 16, 2007).

The Raging Grannies International. *The Raging Grannies Website.* http://www.geocities.com/raginggrannies/ n.d. (accessed January 19, 2007).

Roberts, Jo. "Dancing into the Revolution: Reflections on Quebec City and the Continuing Struggle Against Globalization." *The Mustard Seed: The Toronto Catholic Worker Community* 11, no. 1. (Winter 2002): 1.

Salmonsen, Jone. *Enchanted Feminism: Ritual, Gender and Divinity among the Reclaiming Witches of San Francisco.* New York: Routledge, 2002.

Santos, Boaventura De Sousa. *The Rise of the Global Left: The World Social Forum and Beyond.* London: Zed Books, 2006.

Sered, Susan Starr. *Priestess, Mother, Sacred Sister: Religions Dominated by Women.* New York: Oxford University Press, 1994.

Starhawk. *The Spiral Dance: A Rebirth of the Ancient Religion of the Great Goddess.* San Francisco: HarperSanFrancisco, 1989 [1979].

————. *Truth or Dare: Encounters with Power, Authority, and Mystery.* San Francisco: Harper and Row, 1987.

————. "Weaving a Web of Solidarity: A Feminist Action against Globalization." Nettime archive: http://amsterdam.nettime.org/Lists-Archives/nettime-l-0103/msg00043.html/March 10, 2001. accessed October 20, 2004.

————. *Webs of Power: Notes from the Global Uprising.* Gabriola Island, BC: New Society Publishers, 2002.

Starhawk and M. Macha Nightmare. *The Pagan Book of Living and Dying: Practical Rituals, Prayers, Blessings and Meditations on Crossing Over.* San Francisco: HarperSanFrancisco, 1997.

Starr, Amory. *Global Revolt: A Guide to the Movements against Globalization.* London: Zed Books, 2005.

Taylor, Charles. *Modern Social Imaginaries.* Durham, NC: Duke University Press, 2004.

Thompson, Becky. *A Promise and a Way of Life: White Anti-Racist Activism.* Minneapolis: University of Minnesota Press, 2001.

"Thousands Converge on Quebec as 'People's Summit' Gets Underway." CBC News. http://www.cbc.ca/canada/story/2001/04/15/peoplesummit_010415.html/ April 16, 2001. (accessed Jan 19, 2007).

Toronto Raging Grannies. http://torontoraginggrannies.nonprofitnet.ca/ n.d. (accessed Jan. 19, 2007).

Turner, Victor. *Dramas, Fields, and Metaphors: Symbolic Action in Human Society.* Ithaca, NY: Cornell University Press, 1974.

Women in Black. *Women in Black International Website.* http://www.womenin black.org/ n.d. (accessed January 19, 2007).

————. *Women in Black: For Justice. Against War.* http://www.womenin black.org/ n.d. (accessed July 22, 2008).

Zwissler, Laurel. "Demonstrations of Faith: Religious and Political Identity among Feminist Political Activists in North America." PhD. dissertation: University of Toronto, 2008

————. "Spiritual, But Religious: 'Spirituality among Religiously Motivated Feminist Activists." *Culture and Religion* 8, no. 1 (2007): 51-69.

Chapter Nine:
Across Generations: Women's Spiritualities, Literary Texts, and Third Wave Feminism

Dawn Llewellyn

Introduction

It is almost impossible to speak of feminist history without talking in 'waves',[1] such is the pervasiveness of the wave metaphor for depicting the progression of the first, second and third stages of the feminist movement.[2] Usually accompanying the emergence of each wave are generational sets of meanings, as the advent of each successive wave becomes tied to a younger age group of feminist women. While a familiar device used to capture the unfolding story feminism, this chapter draws attention to the possible shortcomings of uncritically assuming generational meanings of the wave and suggests that strong, age bound definitions of this trope can be limiting. Therefore, this chapter urges caution against unwarily characterizing feminist and women's spiritualities of the third wave as a phenomenon comprising mainly a particular generation of women when, it is suggested, aspects of third wave feminism cross aged-based parameters. After outlining how generational meanings have been attributed to the wave metaphor and highlighting some of the more troubling aspects associated with these meanings, this chapter then turns to interviews with women—who according to their birthdates would usually be defined as second wave—whose narratives reflect third wave themes within the interplay between non-sacred, literary texts and these women's spiritual lives. Specifically, this chapter focuses on two interconnected ways in which participants' reading experiences reflect values linked to the emergence of third wave feminism. First a concern for the highly individual nature of spirituality and second a departure from second wave gynocritical reading strategies. The very literary nature of feminist and women's spiritualities makes women's reflections on their reading (of non-sacred texts) and it's relationship to spirituality and religion an apposite site to find representations of the third wave that cross generational boundaries within contemporary religious feminisms.

'Aging the Wave': Generational Meanings of the Wave Metaphor

Since the wave metaphor came to prominence at the start of the second stage of feminism, it has been underscored by generational connotations as feminists began designating their burgeoning women's movement 'the second wave' while retrospectively naming the nineteenth century proto-feminist era as 'the first wave'.[3] For instance, Germaine Greer situates her iconic work, *The Female Eunuch* (first published in 1970), as "part of the second wave" and a "new feminism" which may be continuous with an earlier time, but replaces the suffragettes with a set of "younger women with a new and vital cast."[4] Greer draws on the wave to signify a bifurcation between an old and young form of feminism. The second wave may be following a previous movement, but as Astrid Henry has commented, for Greer: "'second' is tantamount to 'new' (and 'improved') making the first wave analogous with 'old.'"[5] In this trope, as a new wave emerges, it brings with it youth and relevance; meaning 'better' and more 'radical' ways of being and doing feminism. Even in the early history of the 'wave', the metaphor functions generationally and hierarchically, as the newest wave assumes a position of superiority compared to its predecessors.

The wave metaphor has continued to be given a generational understanding by the first set of publications announcing the third wave. These early volumes, edited and written by self-identified third wave feminists began to herald a new generation of activism, defiant against post-feminism and conservative speculation that 'feminism is dead'. Barbara Findlen's *Listen Up: Voices from the Next Feminist Generation,* Leslie Heywood and Jennifer Drake's *Third Wave Agenda,* and Jennifer Baumgardner and Amy Richard's *ManifestA,* were released from the mid-1990s and began to mark out third wave territory.[6] These texts often demarcated the third wave's origin as belonging to a specific generation of women and according to these volumes, teenagers and women in their 20s and early 30s are the wave's progenitors. For example, Heywood and Drake's collection contains essays by women born "between 1963 and 1974" and all contributors would have been in their 30s at the time their collection was printed.[7] The generational association remains in instances when the third wave is defined as comprising feminists who were raised in the wake of second wave victories. Baumgardner and Richards—as noted in the subtitle to *ManifestA: Young Women, Feminism and the Future*—are self-named young feminists of the third wave. They identify their fellow third wavers as being "in their late teens through their thirties;"[8] women who grew up in an era in which feminism is as present as "fluoride" in the water.[9] In a British context, Natasha Walter illustrates "feminism for a new generation" by collating statements from "young women—some in their teens, most in their twenties and early thirties" in *On the Move: Feminism for a New Generation*;[10] and Kristen Aune and Louise Livsey maintain that although they are "just past thirty" they consider themselves "young, third wave feminists."[11] While the exact boundaries of the third wave are often queried, and diversity and contradiction are often presented as its hallmarks[12] as Ednie Kaeh Garrison has also noted, "The only general consensus to have emerged is that it has become a name for young women who identify as feminists (but not feminists of the sixties and seventies)."[13]

Setting clear aged-based perimeters is an approach shared by third wave voices and a strategy motivated by an enthusiasm to establish the third wave as a different chapter in feminist development. Third wavers strongly assert their movement is in contradistinction to "False Feminist Death Syndrome," Jennifer L. Pozner's wry take on the "backlash" against feminism and media based aspersions claiming the end of feminism.[14] Part of the third wave agenda affirms the continuing need for feminism by highlighting existing gender-based discrepancies and presenting the third wave as a vibrant, socially energetic and culturally savvy movement. When associated with a youthful group, the third wave can out-date the backlash by presenting itself as more recent, and therefore more in-tune with and relevant to the lives of contemporary women. Aligning contemporary feminism with a fresh cohort attempts to set the third wave apart from previous forms of feminism, especially the second wave. Baumgardner and Richards, claim this impetus is innate, (in a similar way to Greer's differentiation from the suffragettes) occurring as each generation begins to negotiate their position in society: "The difference between the First, Second and Third waves is our cultural DNA . . . .Each generation has a drive to create something new."[15] Using this language of 'inheritance' admits the third wave debt to and continuity with earlier women's movements, while articulating a feminism that has been defined by the third wave, in their own terms, and expresses a feminism that engages with their immediate shifting societal contexts of third. The third wave attempts to create discourses that provide young women with "ideas befitting the current political, economic, global and technological climate"[16] and so speaks through zines, blogs, on-line forums, alternative music and other forms of popular culture.[17] The third wave asserts that the concerns facing today's feminists are different because they are living in different times[18] and so feminists of the third wave adapt feminism and apply them to third wave forms.[19]

Attaching the wave to a specific age range is an effective way of creating space for the experiences of secular and religious/spiritual of young/er feminists.[20] However, uncritically adopting the generational aspects of the wave, as a way of understanding the development of contemporary feminist spiritualities,

could replicate some difficult features of this metaphor. While not wanting to
negate third wave feminist experiences and their right to be heard and recognizing the importance of considering the religious and spiritual experiences of
younger women and younger feminists, inserting age brackets into the wave
seems arbitrary and exclusive, ruling out women born between the isolated
waves of feminist history. Rita Alfonso and Jo Trigilio, feminists caught between the waves, describe their uncertainty as to whether they belong to the second, or third stages of feminism: "I feel as if I am standing on the beach with my
surfboard, too late to catch the peak of the second wave and unwilling to con-
form to the rules of pack riding the third."[21] More recently, Jo Reger has la-
mented:

> . . . I feel feminist, but do not fit into the second (i.e. starting in the 1960s and
> 1970s and continuing into the backlash 1980s) or third wave (i.e argued by
> some as beginning in the 1990s) description. I am barely a baby boomer and
> too young for the second wave, and not quite a member of Generation X, mak-
> ing me too old for the third wave.[22]

Giving the wave metaphor such a specific generational association with particular aged boundaries, whether as specific as dates of birth or with the addition of
the prefix 'young' to 'feminist', creates cracks into which some feminists disappear. For instance, where are the feminists that campaigned between the first and
second waves?[23] Or as Aune and Livsey ask: "Where are . . . Christine de Pizan,
Aphra Behn, the women in World War Two?"[24] Further questions reveal flaws
in the generational depiction of feminism: What happens to women under 30
when they are no longer 'young' feminists? Do they relinquish the third wave
and pass it on? Do they hold on to it and wait for the fourth, fifth, sixth wavers
to arrive and establish their own set of feminist agendas for their political era?
Can women over 40 join London Third Wave or be a Riot Grrrl? Can women
born in second wave contribute to third wave feminism—or vice versa?[25] Presenting feminism as a linear meta-narrative of generational waves is an attempt
at specificity and discreteness, separating the feminist movement into organised
and intentional epochs. Designating the waves by age is a mechanism for seeking precision; however it conversely results in a lack of clarity.

The collusion of 'age' with 'wave' when portraying feminist history has
caused some hostility between feminists of different ages. When the second
wave began to demarcate a different agenda from the suffragettes, at least four
decades separated the two feminist eras, therefore limiting opportunities for intergenerational dialogue. However, there is much closer proximity between the
second and third waves which creates a greater capacity for interaction, but as
recent scholarship on generational understandings of the wave reports, the
closeness in age has been a source of conflict and misunderstanding.

These tensions are frequently vocalised through the "matraphor," Rebecca
Dakin Quinn's naming of the mother-daughter metaphor that has typified the

relationship between second and third wave feminists, establishing another facet to the wave's generational undertone.[26] The relationship between second and third wave feminists can easily be allegorised as a maternal-filial bond, especially when third wave feminists are literally the daughters of the second wave's founding figures.[27] Astrid Henry has paid significant attention to this trope, and the manner in which it is used to capture, and exacerbate, intergenerational affiliations. Second wavers are said to grieve for the apparent (feminist) political apathy of younger women; while younger women claim their feminism is not acknowledged and their voices not heard. Third wave attempts to claim a different feminism can be read as a premature and ungrateful calling of the end to second wave feminism—an "act of amputation"[28]—when many second wave feminists remain committed, and involved in feminist politics, teaching and activism.

The wave metaphor, when used generationally, is too simplistic. As a way of depicting the differences between the phases of feminism's evolution, it neatly divides feminist history into separate partitions. However, feminism has progressed through interdependence between the waves, characterised by the "networks of overlapping peoples and causes that have weaved a history of inter-relatedness."[29] A strong adherence to the wave metaphor overlooks the cross-generational conversations that have taken place in feminism's changing historical contexts. Rebecca Walker's *To Be Real* represents one of the first annunciations of the third wave and even in its attempt to signal a clear break from previous feminism includes pieces by Gloria Steinem, bell hooks and Angela Y. Davis—founders of second wave feminism. The third wave indebtedness to the second wave is most clearly reported by Heywood and Drake. They argue the "definitional moment" of third wave feminism came from the anti-essentialist voices, led by women of color, critiquing the preceding second wave white, middle class, Anglo-American feminism.[30] This recognizes that the third wave surfaces in response to the second wave gains and continuing objectives.

By segmenting feminism into separate generations, the wave fails to recognize interdependence and the important influence of one wave upon the previous or the following. As Lisa Hogeland rejoins, "generational thinking is always unspeakably generalizing"[31] and so misses instances where the second and third wave overlap. By focusing the story of feminism too readily on a generational trajectory, the wave can misdirect us away from other places—less bound by age—where the third wave is emerging.

I have tried to point to some of the problems inherent in the seemingly innocent use of the wave metaphor to mark differences between second and third wave feminists. The aged based parameters are often exclusive and capricious, and the familial mother-daughter trope troubles the relationship between younger and older feminists. While these criticisms circulate round much of feminist literature, and recent debate has seen some feminists recast and critique the wave metaphor,[32] the third wave is often presented as a marker of age.

This chapter is quietly defiant against unwarily slipping into generational understandings of the wave metaphor, and instead prefers to find places where second and third wave sentiments cross generational divides. I suggest that the relationship between literary texts and spirituality, within the context of women's religious and spiritual lives, is a site in dialogue with third wave feminism. Literature, specifically writing by women, has been foundational in the development of feminist spiritualities. Women's writing has resourced the deconstruction and reconstruction of Christian traditions where women have been customarily excluded. It has fuelled feminist theology by creatively reimagining the divine, incorporating women's experiences of the sacred, and has expressed women's theological reflections. In doing so it has challenged patriarchal structures of sacred texts, religious practices and church history and is therefore an apt site from which to view developments in religious feminism, as Heather Walton notes "it is impossible to fully comprehend the development of feminist theology without asking what women were reading."[33] While Walton theoretically charts the influence of women's writing on feminist theology, I turn to women's embodied reading experiences. Rather than a textual investigation, this chapter draws on interviews with women from a range of denominations and spiritual positions, having asked them to reflect on the literary texts they consider to have influenced their spiritual or religious lives. The women selected to 'take part' in this chapter are in their 50s to 80s and felt the feminist "click" at the height of the second wave.[34] For instance, Pat is very active in the Catholic Women's Network and became aware of "feminism within the church . . . in the early 70s." Maggie is a member of an ecumenical church and belongs to an inter-faith group. She maintains that "most of my, kind of struggles, over the years have been of course with, as you'd expect from a woman of my age [64], to do with feminism". Margot, a Roman Catholic describes her feminist activism: "I've been arrested, I've protested, I was at Greenham Common." This is an experience she independently has in common with Scarlet, born in 1953, who identifies as "Quaker/pagan/lesbian/feminist/pacifist." Anne belongs to Sea of Faith[35] and regularly attends Quaker meetings. She was born in 1931 and recalls finding "personal liberation" during the "great wave of 70s feminism...we wrote our own liturgies . . . we marched in the street and danced in the Cathedrals!" Focusing on this group of participants is purposive for this chapter. While these women have been and continue to be effective participants in the women's movement, they have not remained rooted to the second wave. Their self-identified feminism may not carry the third wave label explicitly, yet their narratives contain themes that are emblematic of an engagement with the ideological (rather than generational) shift from the second to third waves.[36] Women such as Pat, Maggie, Margot, Scarlet and Anne have moved their feminism beyond generational lines drawn by the wave metaphor.

Individual spiritualities in the third wave

I feel like I'm quite solitary in my particular spiritual configuration (Scarlet)

In contemporary women's spiritualities, the use of literary texts reflects two in-terrelated values associated with the emergence of third wave feminisms. First, a concern for the highly individual nature of the spiritual experience, the valida-tion of which relies on the second value, the disruption of gynocriticism—a branch of feminist literary criticism evinced by second wave explorations of women's writing and their contributions to literary culture.[37]

The emphasis on individuality is a visible impulse operating in the inter-view narratives and in third wave discourses.[38] There has been a call for "new subjectivities"[39] within third wave feminism, instigated by critiques from women of color and other local feminisms. While a means of diversifying a movement which has been up to this point predominantly white and hegemonic, the focus on differences has also been translated in practice into an emphasis on individuality and the personal "I" rather than a collective "we".[40] As Heywood and Drake note, despite knowing its dangers, "the ideology of individualism is still a motivating force in many third wave lives,"[41] overshadowing notions of sisterhood and solidarity that were arguably central to previous feminisms.[42] Drawing on the profits gained by the renovation of the second wave, third wave feminists are emphasising the particularity of gendered identities. For instance, Baumgardner and Richards, articulate the multiple possibilities of being women:

middle-class white women, rich black lesbians, and working-class straight Asian women, an organic intertwining with movements for racial and economic equality, as well as gay rights, is inherent in the feminist mandate [. . .] In real-ity, feminism wants you to be whoever you are—but with a political conscious-ness. And vice-versa: you want to be a feminist because you want to be exactly who you are.[43]

Here, 'women' carries different combinations of identity. The repetition of 'you' at the end of this paragraph is heavy, stressing that women's *personal* franchise is enabled via feminism in the third wave.

As third wave voices are partial to "doing things for themselves,"[44] partici-pants' accounts accent the importance of naming and defining the strictures of their subjective spiritualities. One of the most common tropes participants use to frame their spiritual trajectory is as "journey," with readers referring to influen-tial texts as "landmarks" (Nicola) shaping and representing their experiences. While a "spiritual journey" at first seems to position participants as passive ("I am on a spiritual journey"), it is used primarily to underline the individual tenor to their spiritual or religious trajectory. For instance, when arriving at Eileen's home,[45] I was slightly overwhelmed at the vast array of books she had sorted into piles. Each heap symbolized a shift in her spiritual life and was themed according to the contribution it had made to her spiritual development. In the pre-interview chatter, she gestured towards the table heavily laden with texts remarking: "If you want to understand my spiritual journey if you like, here it is." The textual aspect of the "spiritual journey" alludes to the potential that literary texts hold for enabling personal religious and or spiritual affirmation, as readers are moved by their reading experiences, they move forward on their spiritual journey.

Reading encounters encourage participants to accentuate the especial nature of their spirituality because it is a treasured activity, and ostensibly conceived as (but not restricted to) a solitary and private act.[46] Jane, a Quaker, comments that "[reading] is a personal thing . . . I can close off everything else" and Nicola points to the "interiority of reading." As Janice Radway's study of romance literature highlights, silent reading "connotes a free space" that allows the reader to "attend to their own requirements as independent individuals who require emotional sustenance and solicitude."[47] The close nature of reading creates a personal space that centers participants as the meaning makers in their spiritual lives, bringing their spiritual subjectivities sharply into focus so readers can "find what I need for myself" (Scarlet).

Gynocriticism and Reading for "Sameness"

The books we pick are the ones that there is something in us that we relate to or keys into something. It sounds a bit selfish in a way . . . but that's how it works. (Gillian)

Gynocriticism, as a predominantly second wave strategy for discovering unknown women writers, is a compelling device that widened the canon of western (primarily male authored) texts. As a method of uncovering women's narratives within literary cultures, it forms a suitable partnership with feminist theology as both seek to use women's experiences as a source for creating new (secular and sacred) traditions. Gynocriticism rests on two interlocking features that finds expression in religious feminism. First, female authorship (as opposed to male authorship) guarantees the representation of women's authentic spiritual experiences and second, this assurance is necessary for women readers to secure spiritual validation in their own spiritual lives. Carol Christ's pioneering *Diving Deep and Surfacing* is a notable example of the partnership between feminist theology and gynocriticism. Christ argues that women commonly embody four aspects in their "spiritual quest." These stages are *nothingness, awakening, insight* and *new naming*, junctures she finds represented in women's literature by Kate Chopin, Margaret Atwood, Doris Lessing, Adrienne Rich, and Ntozake Shange, directing her attention to these writers for motifs that distil women's authentic, archetypal spirituality. Christ's approach is not only a textual analysis of women's literature which uncovers empowering images that name women's journey to spiritual subjectivity; her claim is stronger. It is an assertion that women must read literature by women for their spiritual fulfilment: "One task facing women writers is to write stories in which the spiritual and social quest can be combined in the life of a living, realistic woman. And also, one task facing readers is not to be fully satisfied with women's literature until it does."[48] Christ's reliance upon a universal notion of women's spiritual quest and its expression in women's literature is a claim for the authority of 'women's experience' as an essential category from which feminist religious thinking must start, and a resource through which all women can find affirmation.[49]

Women's literature has had an invaluable impact upon women's concepts of the spiritual and religious, shaping and shaped by women's apprehensions of the sacred. Walton has recently illustrated this by documenting how the novels that "everyone was reading" are emblematic of the most recent developments in feminist theological thinking.[50] Walton takes novels by Doris Lessing's (*The Golden Notebook*), Alice Walker (*The Colour Purple*) and Toni Morrison (*Beloved*) to represent developments in feminist theology from 1970s, 80s and 90s respectively and as a device to chronicle the influence of women's writing on feminist theology. She recognises the diversity of strategies feminist theologians have employed in utilising this inspiring resource, first women's literature is taken as the voice of women's sacred experiences, second as a means to counter essentialism and finally as a challenge to monotheological discourse. However, while acknowledging the importance of women's writing, Walton also draws attention to feminist theology's "innocent" reliance on gynocritical values when feminist theology "reads" literature. Within the work of contemporary feminist theological debate, Walton identifies (and is critical of) a tendency to favour realist fiction written by women, as the most authentic vehicle for the representation of women's spiritual experiences and as the most fruitful source to enable reformation, rejection and re-writing of authoritative structures and the revision of Biblical narratives.[51] Walton questions the way religious feminism has naturalised women's writing (and realism in particular) as the obvious partner to feminist theology, and warns that this dependence has led to a textual closure and a curtailing of an open right to response as these literary products are being read as 'sacred texts.' To counter this narrowing of literature, Walton suggests a re-focus on language as the means through which readers can engage more radically and creatively with their sacred texts. Walton wants to retain 'our sacred texts' but wants to encourage a less inhibited list of what that might include.

Gynocriticism upholds that confirmation of women's spiritual experiences occurs through an encounter with sameness, proffered through women's authorship and realist fiction. The biographical eclipses the literary content of the literature as the author's "personal identity reassures readers that her writing can be treated as a valid source."[52] The woman author is read as having unique access to imagining the spiritual and religious experiences of women. Feminist religious readings focus on women's writing for 'realistic' representations of women's experience, looking for themes, characters and images that resonate with, and subsequently sanction, women's spiritual lives. The author must be 'woman' to guarantee the authenticity of the spiritual experiences presented in the text. As Annelies van Heijst argues feminist theologians are reading for identification, "because they wish to see their meanings (theological or feminist themes) endorsed in the literary text."[53] Religious feminists, looking for validation seek identification, preferring to leave the creation of alternative sacred textual traditions in the imaginative hands of women writing about women's spiritualities.

Overturning Gynocriticism and Reading for "Difference"

Participants in this study, although located by age in second wave feminism, overturn this gynocritical pattern of reading. As the third wave dislocates essentialist renderings of identity, it departs from strategies that rely on singular notions of 'woman'—such as gynocriticism's dependence on the woman author. Participants, within accounts of their reading, also depart from the link between women's authorship and women's experiences, negating it as necessary for spiritual validation. Gynocriticism starts with the female author, who in turn validates women's spiritual experiences; in contrast, participants foreground their spiritual validation in the reading experience, and the author starts to lose its former prominence. The mirroring of experiences in literary texts remains vital to the validation of their spirituality, and participants' key texts are those that offer nourishment through confirmation. However, this is not anchored to a particular gendered authorial voice nor attached to narrative themes exploring women's spiritualities. The textual search for affirmation is such a central tenant of participant's reading experiences that it surpasses the reliance on women's authorship and subsequently participants find validation outside of the gendered and genre-bound margins of gynocritical literature.[54]

For participants, their reading practices attend to their spiritual trajectory by providing an opening in which their individual experiences of the sacred are mirrored and thus validated. Texts that participants named as having significance in their religious and spiritual lives were those that "explicitly expressed what implicitly you have realised" (Pat); "affirming what I thought" (Carol) and "affirming . . . what I already know" (Linda). However, their individual experiences are emulated in places beyond women's writing. For instance, Lizzie identifies as a "spiritual searcher," and one of her key texts is by a Native American writer, Ed McGaa. His work, *Rainbow Tribe: Ordinary People Journeying on the Red Road*, is an application of Native American spirituality to contemporary society and for Lizzie, this text "validated her" because it mirrored a spiritual imagining—a vision of a snowbird—she had previously to this reading. As the episode in the book paralleled a specific happening, she "felt like I was on the right track in terms of exploring." The book confronted Lizzie's experience, thus securing it as authentic and legitimate. For Carol, the most significant texts are those that "speak to me," a common explanation of spiritual readings amongst participants. Carol has left Catholicism, finding the language, hierarchy and structures exclusive and authoritarian, so is "searching" spirituality through reading. Her critical position outside of the church often leaves her feeling uncertain about her own ideas, but the texts that are significant are those that support her thinking: "whereever there is truth that connects with my truth [. . .]". By reading *Doubts and Love: What is Left of Christianity?* by Richard Holloway, (the liberal former Bishop of Edinburgh and noted broadcaster and writer) Carol found her "spiritual home." Holloway's work could be classified as "popular theology" and for Carol was a text that "affirmed me in some of the ways I'd been thinking and developing." This reading matched her own intellectual ambivalence toward Christianity, and simultaneously provided encouragement to continue pursuing her own searching. Linda is an Anglican priest but identifies her position as "holistic Christianity," her term for the amalgamation of Christian, Celtic, Goddess, and Native American influences. Linda finds validation through identification with the male protagonist in Stephen Donaldson's series *The Chronicles of Thomas Covenant,* a book she was reading when she was considering leaving Anglicanism. The main character's quest for "hope and redemption," drew parallels with her own need for "self worth, hope, empowerment." These similarities led to a powerful recognition: "I had a choice to be who I wanted to be . . . it gave me the sense that I didn't need to be in the church to be a Christian . . . it also gave me the space to explore who I was." For Lizzie, Carol and Linda, their personal spirituality has been validated through male-authored Native American writings, contemporary theology, and speculative fiction. While McGaa and Holloway overtly consider broad religious and spiritual themes to which, it could be argued, participants are likely to turn when exploring religion and spirituality textually, it is literature that is unbeholden to the gynocritical partnership between women's writings and feminist theology that depicts the innermost experiences and feelings of these participants. It is validation through identification, but with gendered difference at the source.

For some participants, spiritual validation stays entrusted to women authors. Nicola, Gillian, and Maggie spoke of their need to hear women's voices in a tradition where women are not very prevalent. For example, Nicola reads (amongst others) Adrienne Rich, Elizabeth Jennings, Katharine Raine and Maya Angelou as a "way of keeping myself within a patriarchal tradition and . . . pushing on at the boundaries to keep widening that tradition." She connects to their work, and reading their poetry is affirming: "I could contact the plural, authentic, unique, individual women poet's voice which . . . tells me I have a voice that's . . . worthy of being nurtured." As women of the second wave, their introduction to feminism came through women's literature. For Nicola and Gillian it was studying at University, while Maggie recalls Marilyn French's *The*

Women's Room which "circulated with the group of women that I was mixing with." Their reliance on women authors is perhaps a legacy of their second wave roots, coming to feminism at a time when feminist theologians were supplementing and replacing patriarchal narratives with women's stories. However, while maintaining a strong connection to writing by women, their key texts include writing by men and genres from outside feminist theology's circumscribed set. Maggie claims that non-fiction such as John Berger's *Ways of Seeing* "politicised" her by introducing her to the notion of the male gaze; Oliver Sacks' *Awakenings* brought home that spirituality is also about "humanness" while the poem *The Border* by Edwin Muir is a poem that "feeds" her. Although Nicola, Maggie and Gillian prefer women's voices, they still venture further by crossing genres, illustrating an unguarded approach to discovering other sources of validation.

While validation can originate in a literary text that mirror experiences, it also emanates from the unfamiliar and the uncomfortable. Anne attends Quaker and Sea of Faith meetings, having once been a lay preacher. Within Anne's catalogue of spiritual texts, she spoke of readings that caused fissure and disconcertion. A "guiding light" in reaching her decision to leave Christianity was the feminist systematic theology of Daphne Hampson. It caused an intellectual "upset" as Anne apprehended a previously unknown, and disturbing realisation that "I thought the Christian myths go deep, I thought I could use them. It was Hampson's arguments against that that really upset me . . . I couldn't go on using this language [Christianity]." Anne's spiritual journey is entwined with feminism, and while her encounter with Hampson was decisive ("the crux") and ultimately "confirming" it first caused a deep rupture that ultimately led to Anne's rejection of the institutional church. It could be argued this experience is another example of reading for validation through a women's voice, however affirmation came via estrangement and fissure. Anne rarely reads theology now, finding affirmation in "the numinous and the ultimate" through reading poetry and fiction—although the reading "needn't be happy." For instance, Gerald Manley Hopkins' sonnets stir distressing emotions:

> It makes me feel what it's like to be in the pits of pathological depression, of manic depression . . . So in his manic phase you get these soaring poems of joy, and in his depressing phase you get the terrible silences, which are almost unbearable.

For Anne, it is the alterity of Hopkins' verse that encapsulates the "transcendent" and "nourishes." Like Heather Walton's notion of "poesis of trauma," literature that "speaks strangely to us, finds words for things that do not exist or have been previously unspoken"[55] can also confirm participants' spiritual experiences, highlighting that the reading experiences of participants can be validated through the destabilizing possibilities of literature.

Within the interview narratives, the texts that incur a sense of affirmation in the reader are those marked as significant. Before embarking on the fieldwork, I anticipated that as second wave feminists, participants would have been influenced by gynocriticism, and would adhere to an unofficial canon of feminist classics when cataloguing the texts that most influenced their spirituality. I expected writers such as Margaret Atwood, H.D., Marilyn French, Doris Lessing, Michèle Roberts, Sally Gearhart, Starhawk, Alice Walker, Virginia Woolf and Marion Zimmer Bradley to regularly appear; authors who are included on the reading lists for university courses that teach women's spiritualities and literature; authors who have received attention from literary critics and religious feminists for writing women's spiritualities; and authors noted for their influence on the development of feminism and its religious manifestations. However, the search for personal validation amongst participants is stronger than the dependence on particular authors or genres.

Participant's spiritual bookshelves house discrete collections of texts which are rarely replicated across interviewees, as Scarlet comments "I actually don't know very many people who would have that same lot of books." Such textual variety interrupts the connection between women authors and women's spiritual experiences, as the texts most influential upon their spiritual lives are written by men and women, representing divergent kinds of literature. While Heather Walton is looking forward to religious feminists reading beyond the partnership between women's authorship and women's experiences, participants in this study are reading texts from unpredicted places, demonstrating an openness and willingness to seek confirmation in writings that fall outside the circumscribed realm of women authors and the genre of realist fiction. Participants' catalogues include: David Almond, Thomas Berry, Neil Douglas Clotts, Stephen Donaldson, John Donne, T.S. Eliot, Matthew Fox, Mark Haddon, George Herbert, Richard Holloway, Gerald Manley Hopkins, C.S. Lewis, Gabriele Garcia Marquez, W. Somerset Maugham, Ian McEwan, Terry Pratchett, Phillip Pullman, Vikram Seth, William Shakespeare, George Bernard Shaw, Brian Swimme, and R.S. Thomas. Genres such as contemporary fiction, metaphysical poets, speculative fiction and fantasy, children's novels, writings of the mystics, Hindu and Buddhist religious writings, 'mind/body/spirit', ecology, poetry, romance, autobiography and biography, historical fiction and even the odd cookery book. To ensure spiritual validation, literary texts still reflect subjective experiences, but despite a second wave feminist history, participants are departing from reading approaches associated with this era and embracing themes in line with the gradual turn to the third wave.

Conclusion

This chapter explores an aspect of third wave women's spiritualities which traverse generational boundaries that typically characterise discussions of contemporary feminisms. It proposes that women's reflections of reading, within the context of their spiritual development, is emblematic of a dialogue with third wave feminism. In particular, readers in this study go beyond the lists of author and titles anticipated by feminist theology naming their own unique collections as significant to their spiritual or faith lives as those that emulate their subjective positioning. As this validates their spiritual experiences, it inverts second wave reading strategies in the process, disconnecting women's authorship from women's writing, and departing from women's literature as the sole source of insight for women and their spiritual identities. The emphasis on individuality and the reversing of gynocriticism are motifs embodied by women whose feminism began in the 1960s and 1970s, and yet they are themes given prominence in the third wave.

This chapter draws on this example as a way to gently entreat against the unreflexive adoption of generational meanings of the wave metaphor. The artificial age-based parameters of the wave narrow feminist history too readily, and stimulate a view of feminism's progression that can overlook generational crossings between and through different cohorts of women, or fail to notice where feminist currents coalesce, and second and third wave feminisms dialogue. For feminist work on women's experiences of the religious and spiritual to continue to strengthen, it needs to glimpse a wider portrait of its changing contexts by looking for expressions of contemporary third wave feminism in places other than those set aside for a particular generational cohort.

Notes

With particular thanks to Sarah Gibson, Bransby Macdonald-Williams, Katharine Moody, Deborah Sawyer and Marta Trezbiatsowka.

1. A point also noted by Astrid Henry, *Not My Mother's Sister: Generational Conflict and Third Wave Feminism* (Bloomington and Indianapolis: Indiana University Press, 2004), 58.

2. Although this is the dominant chronology, other versions of feminist history consider the rise of women's movements outside Anglo-America, contexts such as Chicana, Womanist, Asian and South Pacific feminisms. Furthermore, a different sequence is sometimes presented by feminist academic theology. See Mary C. Grey, "Feminist Theologies, European," in *A Dictionary of Feminist Theologies*, ed. Letty M. Russell and J. Shannon Clarkson (London: Westminster John Knox Press, 1996), 102-104; Margaret D. Kamitsuka, *Feminist Theology and the Challenge of Difference* (Oxford: Oxford University Press, 2007). Both suggest that feminist scholarship in religion began in the 60s and 70s, with the second wave emerging in the 80s.

3. Astrid Henry credits the term "second wave" to Marsha Weinman Lear's article 'The Second Feminist Wave' (*New York Times Magazine,* March 10, 1968, 24.) cited in Henry, *Not My Mother's Sister,* 58.

4. Germaine Greer, *The Female Eunuch,* (Flamingo, Harper Collins: London, 1993), 13-15.

5. Henry, *Not My Mother's Sister,* 59.

6. Jennifer Baumgardner and Amy Richards, *Manifesta: Young Women, Feminism, and the Future* (New York: Farrar, Straus and Giroux, 2000), Barbara Findlen, ed., *Listen Up: Voices from the Next Feminist Generation,* 2nd ed. (Emeryville: Seal Press, 2001), Leslie Heywood and Jennifer Drake, eds., *Third Wave Agenda: Being Feminist, Doing Feminism* (Minneapolis: University of Minnesota Press, 1997). As a testament to their influence, feminist third wave discussions are replete with references to these U.S based texts and others including Rory Dicker and Alison Piepmeier, eds., *Catching a Wave: Reclaiming Feminism for the 21st Century* (Boston: Northeastern University Press, 2003), Jo Reger, ed., *Different Wavelengths: Studies of the Contemporary Women's Movement* (New York and London: Routledge, 2005) and Rebecca Walker, ed., *To Be Real: Telling the Truth and Changing the Face of Feminism* (New York: Anchor Books, 1995). While Stacy Gillis, Gillian Howie, and Rebecca Munford, eds., *Third Wave Feminism: A Critical Exploration,* 2nd ed. (Basingstoke: Palgrave, 2007), Stacy Gillis and Rebecca Munford, eds., *Harvesting Our Strengths: Third Wave Feminism and Women's Studies,* vol. 4, *Journal of International Women's Studies* (2003) includes British based commentary upon the third wave.

7. Leslie Heywood and Jennifer Drake, "Introduction," in *Third Wave Agenda: Being Feminist, Doing Feminism* ed. Leslie Heywood and Jennifer Drake (Minneapolis: University of Minnesota Press, 1997), 4.

8. Baumgardner and Richards, *Manifesta,* 401.

9. Baumgardner and Richards, *Manifesta,* 17.

10. Natasha Walter, ed., *On the Move: Feminism for a New Generation* (London: Virago Press, 1999),1.

11. Kristen Aune and Louise Livsey, "Reclaiming the F-Word and Recovering Dialogue: Younger Feminists, Older Feminists and (Mis)Communication," (2007). Aune and Livsey are both members of London Third Wave (Aune co-founded this organisation in 2002). It identifies as a young feminist group with over 200 members that meets fortnightly to discuss, support and organise feminist activism (www.thefword.org.uk).

12. Heywood and Drake, "Introduction."

13. Ednie Kaeh Garrison, "Contests for the Meanings of Third Wave Feminism: Feminism and Popular Consciousness," in *Third Wave Feminism: A Critical Exploration,* ed. Stacy Gillis, Gillian Howie, and Rebecca Munford (Basingstoke: Palgrave, 2007), 185. Garrison is also critical of the way third wave praxis and ideology is too simply and superficially designated a particular generation of women, particularly through the media.

14. Jennifer L. Pozner, "The 'Big Lie': False Feminist Death Syndrome, Profit and the Media," in *Catching a Wave: Reclaiming Feminism for the 21st Century,* ed. Rory Dicker and Alison Piepmeier (Boston: Northeastern University Press, 2003), 31-56. "Backlash" is Susan Faludi's notable term encapsulating anti-feminist (and mainly media fuelled) discourses. Susan Faludi, *Backlash: The Undeclared War against Women* (London: Vintage, 1993).

15. Baumgardner and Richards, *ManifestA,* 129.

16. Amber E. Kinser, "Negotiating Spaces for/through Third-Wave Feminisms," *NWSA Journal* 16, no. 3 (2004), 131.

17. For examples of the third wave's engagement with various cultural forms, see Heywood and Drake, *Third Wave Agenda* and Reger, *Different Wavelengths.*

18. Aune and Livsey, "Reclaiming the F Word".

19. Melissa Klein, "Duality and Redefinition: Young Feminism and the Alternative Music Community," in *Third Wave Agenda: Being Feminist, Doing Feminism,* ed. Leslie Heywood and Jennifer Drake (Minneapolis: University of Minnesota Press, 1997), 207-225.

20. Third wave publications also acknowledge that young women may reject the label 'feminist' but concur with many aspects of feminism. For instance, Baumgardner and Richards dedicate *ManifestA* to "to those of our generation who say "I'm not a feminist but..." and others who say, "I am a feminist, but..." Baumgardner and Richards, *ManifestA..* Natasha Walter also explores the asymmetry between explicit feminist identification and holding feminist values in Natasha Walter, *The New Feminism* (London: Little Brown and Company, 1998).

21. Rita Alfonso and Jo Trigilio, "Surfing the Third Wave: A Dialogue between Two Third Wave Feminists," *Hypatia* 12, no. 3 (1997), 8.

22. Jo Reger, "Introduction," in *Different Wavelengths: Studies of the Contemporary Women's Movement* ed. Jo Reger (New York and London: Routledge, 2005), xvi.

23. Feminist history is being reassessed to challenge notions that organised feminism faded in the years between the waves. See Beverly Guy-Sheftall, "Response from a 'Second Waver' to Kimberly Springer's 'Third Wave Black Feminism?'" *Signs* 27, no. 4 (2002), Kinser, "Negotiating Spaces for/through Third-Wave Feminisms." 128-129.

24. Aune and Livsey, "Reclaiming the F-Word."

25. I do not mean to imply that third wave feminists condone the exclusion of older women, or that second wave feminists ignore the third wave; but to highlight the inconsistencies in the wave metaphor when used uncritically to imply generational difference.

26. Henry, *Not My Mother's Sister*, 2.

27. For instance, the third wave feminist Rebecca Walker has written about her relationship with her mother, Alice Walker. See Walker, *To Be Real* and Astrid Henry's analysis of the relationship between second wave mothers and their third wave daughters in *Not My Mother's Sister*.

28. Rory Dicker and Alison Piepmeier, "Introduction," in *Catching a Wave: Reclaiming Feminism for the 21st Century*, ed. Rory Dicker and Alison Piepmeier (Boston: Northeastern University Press, 2003), 14.

29. Aune and Livsey, "Reclaiming the F-Word."

30. Heywood and Drake, "Introduction.", 8.

31. Lisa Hogeland, "Against Generational Thinking, or, Some Things That "Third Wave" Feminism Isn't," *Women's Studies in Communication* 24, no. 1 (Spring 2001), 110.

32. Nancy Whittier and Ednie Kaeh Garrison have attempted to nuance the wave metaphor. Whittier's "political generations" are "a group of people (not necessarily of the same age) that experiences shared formative social conditions at approximately the same point in their lives." Although this distinguishes phases of feminist history, it relies on changing historical contexts rather than birthdates. Garrison suggests that the electromagnetic radio wave is more suited to capturing the complexities of feminist history, as radio waves exist simultaneously in different bandwidths "sometimes fading and dissolv-

ing, other times interrupted or appropriated or colonized, oftentimes overlooked because we can't hear or perceive a signal we haven't got an ear for." See Nancy Whittier, *Feminist Generations: The Persistence of the Radical Women's Movement* (Philadelphia: Temple University Press, 1999), 180 and Ednie Kaeh Garrison, "Are We on a Wavelength Yet? On Feminist Oceanography, Radios and Third Wave Feminism," in *Different Wavelengths:Studies of the Contemporary Women's Movement* ed. Jo Reger (New York and London: Routledge, 2005) 244.

33. Heather Walton, *Imagining Theology: Women, Writing and God* (London: T & T Clark, 2007), 2.

34. 'The click', attributed to Jane O'Reilly, is the moment when a woman first becomes aware that her life is inflected with the gender oppression. Cited in Kinser, "Negotiating Spaces for/through Third-Wave Feminisms," 137.

35. Sea of Faith Network is a British based organization, active since the 1980s. Inspired by Don Cupit's BBC television series and book of the same name, it self identifies as postmodernist, religious, nonrealist and humanist group that recognizes the decline in traditional religion, and the constructed and plural nature of religious meanings and practices: "The Network explores the implications for spiritual, social and ecological issues that arise from embracing the provisional nature of religious insight." Membership is eclectic and the group regularly organizes a range of workshops and meetings, regionally and nationally. See www.sofn.org.uk for further information.

36. Jo Reger has pointed to some of the complexities in finding women who openly take on a third wave label. See Reger, "Introduction." and Susan Beechey, "When Feminism Is Your Job: Age and Power in Women's Policy Organizations," in *Different Wavelengths: Studies in the Contemporary Women's Movement* ed. Jo Reger (New York and London: Routledge, 2005).

37. The term was coined by Elaine Showalter, "Toward a Feminist Poetics," in *The New Feminist Criticism: Essays of Women, Literature and Theory*, ed. Elaine Showalter (London: Virago, 1986), 125-143. and Elaine Showalter, *A Literature of Their Own: British Women Novelists from Brontë to Lessing* (London: Virago, 1978).

38. To some extent, the use of semi-structured interviews as the preferred research method encouraged participants to focus on their subjective experiences of reading. This was purposive as semi-structured interviews were the most appropriate choice for investigating readers' individual reading habits.

39. Catherine Orr, "Charting the Currents of the Third Wave," *Hypatia* 12, no. 3 (1997), 37.

40. Henry, *Not My Mother's Sister*, 40-45.

41. Heywood and Drake, "Introduction.", 11.

42. This is not to suggest that the third wave is self-interested (see Tyler's discussion of the negative cultural representation of second wave feminism as "selfish" in Imogen Tyler, "The Selfish Feminist: Public Images of Women's Liberation," *Australian Feminist Studies* 22, no. 53 (2007). Rather, I want to highlight that the second movement was a diverse faction, but its politics manifested in the Women's Liberation Movement and so appears united through an emphasis on collective social transformation. The third wave, in contrast, is usually portrayed as comprising localized, individual acts of feminism. While this seems to suggest a dichotomy between the personal and collective, the third wave also attempts to bridge individuality and community. See Astrid Henry, "Solitary Sisterhood: Individualism Meets Collectivity in Feminism's Third Wave," ed. Jo Reger (New York and London: Routledge, 2005), Dawn Llewellyn, "Forming Community in

the Third Wave: Literary Texts and Women's Spiritualities," in *Reading Spiritualities: Constructing and Representing the Sacred* ed. Dawn Llewellyn and Deborah F. Sawyer (Aldershot: Ashgate, Forthcoming).

43. Baumgardner and Richards, *Manifesta,* 56-57.

44. Aune and Livsey, "Reclaiming the F-Word and Recovering Dialogue."

45. Eileen also came to feminism during the 1970s and for many years has been a freelance writer and consultant on "holistic values, corporate spirituality, business ethics and community relationships." She is a member of a liberal church community.

46. Despite being an individual activity, reading is also a means by which participants form communities in support of their spiritual and religious lives. See Llewellyn, "Forming Community in the Third Wave".

47. Janice Radway, *Reading the Romance: Women, Patriarchy and Popular Literature* (Chapel Hill and London: The University of North Carolina Press, 1984), 91-93:93.

48. Carol P. Christ, *Diving Deep and Surfacing: Women Writers on Spiritual Quest,* 3rd ed. (Boston: Beacon, 1995), 39-40.

49. Christ later addressed this essentialism. See Judith Plaskow and Carol P. Christ, "Introduction," in *Weaving the Visions: New Patterns in Feminist Spirituality,* ed. Judith Plaskow and Carol P. Christ (San Francisco: HarperSanFrancisco, 1989).

50. Walton, *Imagining Theology.*

51. Walton, *Imagining Theology.*

52. Heather Walton, "Our Sacred Texts: Literature, Theology and Feminism," ed. Dawn Llewellyn and Deborah F. Sawyer (Aldershot: Ashgate, Forthcoming).

53. Annelies van Heijst, *Longing for the Fall,* trans. Henry Jansen (Kampen: Kok Pharos, 1995), 26.

54. In connection to 'death of the author' discourses (as Walton has observed) feminist theology has largely been averse to venturing into poststructuralist literary theory as an engagement suggests that women's authorship no longer holds special status as a source for women's experiences. For participants, while they invert gynocritical methods to secure personal spiritual validation, the author function is ambivalent. While there is disconnection, there can be great personal attachment between participant and author, once a text has been marked as significant. See Roland Barthes, "The Death of the Author," in *Authorship: From Plato to the Postmodern,* ed. Seán Burke (Edinburgh: Edinburgh University Press, 1977), Michel Foucault, "What Is an Author?" in *Language, Counter-Memory Practice: Selected Essays and Interviews by Michel Foucault* (Ithaca: Cornell University Press, 1977), Heather Walton, *Literature, Theology and Feminism* (Manchester: Manchester University Press, 2007).

55. Walton, *Imagining Theology*; Walton, *Literature, Theology and Feminism* and Walton, "Our Sacred Texts: Literature, Theology and Feminism."

Bibliography

Alfonso, Rita, and Jo Trigilio. "Surfing the Third Wave: A Dialogue between Two Third Wave Feminists." *Hypatia* 12, no. 3 (1997): 7-16.

Aune, Kristen, and Louise Livsey. "Reclaiming the F-Word and Recovering Dialogue: Younger Feminists, Older Feminists and (Mis)Communication." 2007.

Barthes, Roland. "The Death of the Author." In *Authorship: From Plato to the Postmodern,* edited by Seán Burke, 125-30. Edinburgh: Edinburgh University Press, 1977.

Baumgardner, Jennifer, and Amy Richards. *Manifesta: Young Women, Feminism, and the Future*. New York: Farrar, Straus and Giroux, 2000.

Beechey, Susan. "When Feminism Is Your Job: Age and Power in Women's Policy Organizations." In *Different Wavelengths: Studies of the Contemporary Women's Movement*, edited by Jo Reger, 117-36. New York and London: Routledge, 2005.

Christ, Carol P. *Diving Deep and Surfacing: Women Writers on Spiritual Quest*. 3rd ed. Boston: Beacon, 1995.

Dicker, Rory, and Alison Piepmeier. "Introduction." In *Catching a Wave: Reclaiming Feminism for the 21st Century*, edited by Rory Dicker and Alison Piepmeier, 3-28. Boston: Northeastern University Press, 2003.

———. eds. *Catching a Wave: Reclaiming Feminism for the 21st Century*. Boston: Northeastern University Press, 2003.

Faludi, Susan. *Backlash: The Undeclared War against Women*. London: Vintage, 1993.

Findlen, Barbara, ed. *Listen Up: Voices from the Next Feminist Generation*. 2nd ed. Emeryville: Seal Press, 2001.

Foucault, Michel. "What Is an Author?" in *Language, Counter-Memory Practice: Selected Essays and Interviews by Michel Foucault*, 113-38. Ithaca: Cornell University Press, 1977.

Garrison, Ednie Kaeh. "Are We on a Wavelength Yet? On Feminist Oceanography, Radios and Third Wave Feminism." in *Different Wavelengths: Studies of the Contemporary Women's Movement*, edited by Jo Reger, 237-56. New York and London: Routledge, 2005.

———. "Contests for the Meanings of Third Wave Feminism: Feminism and Popular Consciousness." In *Third Wave Feminism: A Critical Exploration*, edited by Stacy Gillis, Gillian Howie and Rebecca Munford, 185-97. Basingstoke: Palgrave, 2007.

Gillis, Stacy, Gillian Howie, and Rebecca Munford, eds. *Third Wave Feminism: A Critical Exploration*. 2nd ed. Basingstoke: Palgrave, 2007.

Gillis, Stacy, and Rebecca Munford, eds. *Harvesting Our Strengths: Third Wave Feminism and Women's Studies*. Vol. 4, *Journal of International Women's Studies*, 2003.

Grey, Mary C. "Feminist Theologies, European." In *A Dictionary of Feminist Theologies*, edited by Letty M. Russell and J. Shannon Clarkson, 102-104. London: Westminster John Knox Press, 1996.

Guy-Sheftall, Beverly. "Response from a "Second Waver" to Kimberly Springer's "Third Wave Black Feminism?"" *Signs* 27, no. 4 (2002): 1091-94.

Heijst, Annelies van. *Longing for the Fall*. Translated by Henry Jansen. Kampen: Kok Pharos, 1995.

Henry, Astrid. *Not My Mother's Sister: Generational Conflict and Third Wave Feminism*. Bloomington and Indianapolis: Indiana University Press, 2004.

———. "Solitary Sisterhood: Individualism Meets Collectivity in Feminism's Third Wave." In *Different Wavelengths: Studies of the Contemporary Women's Movement*, edited by Jo Reger, 81-96. New York and London: Routledge, 2005.

Heywood, Leslie, and Jennifer Drake. "Introduction." In *Third Wave Agenda: Being Feminist, Doing Feminism*, edited by Leslie Heywood and Jennifer Drake, 1-20. Minneapolis: University of Minnesota Press, 1997.

———, eds. *Third Wave Agenda: Being Feminist, Doing Feminism*. Minneapolis: University of Minnesota Press, 1997.

Hogeland, Lisa. "Against Generational Thinking, or, Some Things That "Third Wave" Feminism Isn't." *Women's Studies in Communication* 24, no. 1 (Spring 2001): 107-21.

Kamitsuka, Margaret D. *Feminist Theology and the Challenge of Difference*. Oxford: Oxford University Press, 2007.

Kinser, Amber E. "Negotiating Spaces for/through Third-Wave Feminisms." *NWSA Journal* 16, no. 3 (2004): 124 - 153.

Klein, Melissa. "Duality and Redefinition: Young Feminism and the Alternative Music Community." In *Third Wave Agenda: Being Feminist, Doing Feminism*, edited by Leslie Heywood and Jennifer Drake, 207-225. Minneapolis: University of Minnesota Press, 1997.

Llewellyn, Dawn. "Forming Community in the Third Wave: Literary Texts and Women's Spiritualities." In *Reading Spiritualities: Constructing and Representing the Sacred*, edited by Dawn Llewellyn and Deborah F. Sawyer. Aldershot: Ashgate, Forthcoming.

Orr, Catherine. "Charting the Currents of the Third Wave." *Hypatia* 12, no. 3 (1997): 29-45.

Plaskow, Judith, and Carol P. Christ. "Introduction." In *Weaving the Visions: New Patterns in Feminist Spirituality*, edited by Judith Plaskow and Carol P. Christ, 1-13. San Francisco: HarperSanFrancisco, 1989.

Pozner, Jennifer L. "The 'Big Lie': False Feminist Death Syndrome, Profit and the Media." In *Catching a Wave: Reclaiming Feminism for the 21st Century*, edited by Rory Dicker and Alison Piepmeier, 31-56. Boston: Northeastern University Press, 2003.

Radway, Janice. *Reading the Romance: Women, Patriarchy and Popular Literature*. Chapel Hill and London: The University of North Carolina Press, 1984.

Reger, Jo. "Introduction." In *Different Wavelengths: Studies of the Contemporary Women's Movement*, edited by Jo Reger, xv-xxx. New York and London: Routledge, 2005.

———, ed. *Different Wavelengths: Studies of the Contemporary Women's Movement*. New York and London: Routledge, 2005.

Showalter, Elaine. *A Literature of Their Own: British Women Novelists from Brontë to Lessing*. London: Virago, 1978.

———. "Toward a Feminist Poetics." In *The New Feminist Criticism: Essays of Women, Literature and Theory*, edited by Elaine Showalter, 125-43. London: Virago, 1986.

Tyler, Imogen. "The Selfish Feminist: Public Images of Women's Liberation." *Australian Feminist Studies* 22, no. 53 (2007): 173-90.

Walker, Rebecca, ed. *To Be Real: Telling the Truth and Changing the Face of Feminism*. New York: Anchor Books, 1995.

Walter, Natasha. *The New Feminism*. London: Little Brown and Company, 1998.

———, ed. *On the Move: Feminism for a New Generation*. London: Virago Press, 1999.

Walton, Heather. *Imagining Theology: Women, Writing and God*. London: T & T Clark, 2007.

———. *Literature, Theology and Feminism*. Manchester: Manchester University Press, 2007.

———. "Our Sacred Texts: Literature, Theology and Feminism." In *Reading Spiritualities: Constructing and Representing the Sacred*, edited by Dawn Llewellyn and Deborah F. Sawyer. Aldershot: Ashgate, Forthcoming.

Whittier, Nancy. *Feminist Generations: The Persistence of the Radical Women's Movement*. Philadelphia: Temple University Press, 1999.

Contributors

Glenda Lynna Anne Tibe Bonifacio is an Assistant Professor in Women's Studies at the University of Lethbridge. Her research interests centre on the intersections of gender, religion, and citizenship in the context of migration, development and globalization. Some of her works have been published in the *Asian and Pacific Migration Journal, Asian Women,* and *Review of Women's Studies*

Sarah Marie Gallant is a doctoral candidate studying under Dr. Morny Joy at the University of Calgary. During her undergraduate studies, Sarah focused on the medieval heretical group known as the Cathars and the attempt to portray them as proto-feminists. Her current research examines medieval hagiographical texts and the ideal female figures presented therein, with a specific interest in the underlying theory of imagination that informs the overall construction of these texts. The comparison of medieval hagiography with the writing of contemporary spiritual feminists was the subject of her Masters thesis.

Chris Klassen teaches in the Religion and Culture department at Wilfrid Laurier University. Her book, *Storied Selves: Shaping Identity in Feminist Witchcraft* was published in 2008 by Lexington Books. She is currently studying the concept of nature and technology in contemporary Canadian Pagan discourse.

Dawn Llewellyn is a doctoral candidate in the Department of Religious Studies, Lancaster University, UK. Having completed an undergraduate degree in Philosophy and Theology followed by an MA in Women's Studies, her current research explores the role of reading literary texts within the development of women's spiritual identities and its relationship to third wave feminism. Dawn is also co-editor (with Deborah F. Sawyer) and contributor to *Reading Spiritualities: Constructing and Representing the Sacred* (Ashgate, forthcoming).

Kate McCarthy is Professor of Religious Studies at California State University, Chico, where she also coordinates the Women's Studies program. She is the author of *Interfaith Encounters in America* (Rutgers University Press 2007) and co-editor of *God in the Details: American Religion in Popular Culture* (Routledge, 2001).

Gena Meldazy holds a Bachelor of Honours Degree in Fine Arts Cultural Studies from York University, 2008. She currently resides in Toronto, co-hosting on two radio programs and editing for various magazines. Her future research interests include heteronormative identities in media, ethnomusicology, and international music communities and their political economy.

Anna Mercedes teaches Theology and Gender at the College of Saint Benedict and Saint John's University in central Minnesota. She focuses her work on feminist theology, particularly Christology. She is a graduate of the Lutheran Theological Seminary at Philadelphia, and is completing her doctorate in Theological and Religious Studies at Drew University. She also enjoys cooking from scratch, good conversations, and walking hand-in-hand with her toddler.

Catherine Telford-Keogh has a BA in Fine Arts, specializing in sculpture, with an option in Women Studies, from the University of Waterloo. She became interested in feminist Witchcraft in her early 20s after reading Starhawk's work, *The Spiral Dance*. Catherine's practice as an eclectic Witch is informed by postmodern feminism as well as her practice as an artist. She is aspiring to complete an MFA in Visual Arts followed by a PhD in Women's Studies.

Jennifer Thweatt-Bates is a doctoral candidate in the area of Christian Theology and Science at Princeton Theological Seminary. Her dissertation topic focuses on theological anthropology and the posthuman, exploring the ways that current notions of hybridity and near-future technological possibilities affect the way we construct notions of the human, and the human-divine relationship. When not dissertating, she knits, cooks, does yoga and hangs out with her 2-year-old.

Giselle Vincett completed a doctorate in sociology of religion at Lancaster University (UK) in the autumn of 2007. Her thesis was a comparative study of feminist Christian women, Goddess Feminists, and women who fuse the two traditions, in the UK. She has co-edited a forthcoming book on how women challenge secularisation theory (one of the key tenets of sociology of religion) and has a paper on Quaker Paganism included in a forthcoming book on the sociology of British Quakerism. She is currently a research fellow at the University of Edinburgh, where she is doing research with young Scottish Christians on the changing nature of contemporary religion.

Laurel Zwissler holds a PhD from the Centre for the Study of Religion and the Collaborative Program in Women and Gender Studies at the University of Toronto. She has previously published "Spiritual, But Religious: 'Spirituality' among Religiously Motivated Feminist Activists" in *Culture and Religion*, March 2007 and "Jesus Christ, Action Hero: Christianity Battles Evil in Canadian Horror Film *Jesus Christ, Vampire Hunter*" available at odessafilmworks.com. Her research interests include anthropology of religion, secularization theory and other models of religion in the public sphere, feminist movements in religion, and religious implications of globalization. She also makes zines, reads comics, and drinks too much coffee.

Index